FRANK O'CONNOR

Critical Essays

5/12/07 .

To Brian,

With lots of
admiration &
love,
Hilary xx

FRANK O'CONNOR
Critical Essays

Hilary Lennon

EDITOR

FOUR COURTS PRESS

Set in 10.5 on 14 point AGaramond for
FOUR COURTS PRESS LTD
7 Malpas Street, Dublin 8, Ireland
e-mail: info@fourcourtspress.ie
http://www.fourcourtspress.ie
and in North America for
FOUR COURTS PRESS
c/o ISBS, 920 N.E. 58th Avenue, Suite 300, Portland, OR 97213.

A catalogue record for this title
is available from the British Library.

ISBN 978-1-84682-012-0

Printed in England
by MPG Books, Bodmin, Cornwall.

Contents

Acknowledgments

This book would not have been possible without the financial support of the TCD Association and Trust, the school of English, Trinity College, Dublin and the Irish Research Council in the Humanities and Social Sciences. The editor would like to express her deep gratitude to each of these bodies.

The collection is mainly the result of papers presented at the Frank O'Connor Centenary Conference, Trinity College, Dublin, 12–14 September 2003. The rest of the essays in the publication are by scholars whose work has helpfully contributed towards filling some of the gaps in the conference programme. Many thanks to my colleagues in the school of English, TCD, for their help and support with the conference and the putting together of this collection. I am most grateful to Nicholas Grene and Stephen Matterson; thanks also to Terence Brown, Gerald Dawe, Edwina Keown, Eiléan Ní Chuilleanáin, Diane Sadler and Carol Taaffe. A special word of thanks is owed to Paul Delaney for all of his good advice and support.

I wish to thank those who assisted with the staging of the conference: Brenda Brooks, Joseph Cleary, Gerard Donovan, Charles Fanning, Charles Foley, Sarah Hill, Josh Johnston, Micheal Johnston, Darryl Jones, Éilis Ní Dhuibhne, Geraldine Meaney, Conor McCarthy, Kasandra O'Connell, Sunniva O'Flynn, Louis de Paor, Noel Phelan, Antoinette Quinn, Julie Anne Stevens, Jonathan Williams, the staff of TCD, and especially the Michael O'Donovan family.

Many thanks to Conall Ó Murchadha for his advice on technical matters. Sincere thanks to all the contributors in this collection for making my job as editor such an enjoyable one. I wish to thank everyone at Four Courts Press; including Martin Healy and Anthony Tierney, and particular thanks to Michael Adams and Martin Fanning for guiding this project to publication. My special gratitude to Frank and Bridget Lennon for their support during the work on this collection.

For permission to quote from material published and unpublished, and for making available the cover photograph, I am very grateful to Harriet O'Donovan Sheehy and the Frank O'Connor Estate; I also wish to thank Robert Evans for permission to reprint Alan Titley's essay from *Frank O'Connor: new perspectives* (1998), and Brendan Kennelly for permission to reprint his poem 'Light dying' (1966).

Contributors

NICHOLAS ALLEN is author of *George Russell (Æ) and the new Ireland, 1905–30* (2003), and editor, with Aaron Kelly, of *The cities of Belfast* (2003). His current project is *The republic of modernism,* a study of Irish culture after 1922. Allen is assistant professor in the English department, University of North Carolina at Chapel Hill.

TERENCE BROWN is a professor of Anglo-Irish literature in Trinity College, Dublin where he is a senior fellow of the college. He is also a member of the Royal Irish Academy and of the Academia Europaea. He has published widely on Irish literature and on Irish cultural history and has lectured on those subjects in many parts of the world. Among his recent works are: *The life of W.B. Yeats: a critical biography* (1999, 2001) and *Ireland: a social and cultural history, 1922–2002* (2004, a revised and augmented version of a book first published in 1981).

PAUL DELANEY is a lecturer in English at Trinity College, Dublin. He is the author of a number of articles and reviews on different aspects of Irish culture, and he is also the editor of Daniel Corkery's short fiction (2003). He is currently completing a study of representations of Travellers in Irish writing.

PHILIP EDWARDS was professor of English literature at Trinity College, Dublin from 1960 until 1966. He has now retired, as emeritus professor of English of the University of Liverpool. He has written many books and articles on Shakespeare and the drama of his time, on voyage literature, and on Irish writers.

ROBERT C. EVANS is professor of English at Auburn University Montgomery. With Richard Harp, he co-edited *Frank O'Connor: new perspectives* (1998); in 2003 he edited and contributed to *Frank O'Connor's 'Ghosts': a pluralist approach.* Most recently he is the author of 'Frank O'Connor and the Irish holocaust' in George Cusack and Sarah Goss (eds), *Hungry words: images of famine in the Irish canon* (Dublin, 2006).

MAURICE HARMON, now retired from University College Dublin where he worked as a professor of Irish literature, has had a particular interest in the Frank O'Connor generation of writers. He has written critical introductions to the work of Seán O'Faoláin and Austin Clarke and a biography of O'Faoláin. His most recent book, *Selected essays* (2006), contains articles on Mary Lavin, Patrick Kavanagh, Benedict Kiely and others.

BRENDAN KENNELLY is professor emeritus of Trinity College, Dublin, and has published over twenty books of poetry, including *My dark fathers* (1964), *Cromwell* (1983), *The man made of rain* (1998) and *Familiar strangers: new and selected poems, 1960–2004* (2004). His most recent publications are *Now* (Northumberland, 2006), and *When then is now: three Greek tragedies* (Northumberland, 2006).

JOHN KENNY is a lecturer in English, National University of Ireland, Galway. His specialist areas are twentieth-century fiction, especially of the contemporary period, and the history, theory and practice of literary journalism and book-reviewing. He regularly reviews for the *Irish Times* and is presently preparing two books on the work of John Banville.

DECLAN KIBERD is professor of Anglo-Irish literature at University College Dublin. He is the author of numerous articles and books on Irish literature, including *Idir dhá chultúr* (1993), *Inventing Ireland: the literature of the modern nation* (1995), *Irish classics* (2000) and *The Irish writer and the world* (2005).

HILARY LENNON currently teaches in the school of English, Trinity College, Dublin and is also completing her doctoral thesis. Her research focuses on the works of Frank O'Connor in the 1930s and '40s.

HARRIET O'DONOVAN SHEEHY married Michael O'Donovan (Frank O'Connor) in 1953. For over forty years she has written and spoken about Frank O'Connor. She has also worked extensively on her private collection of O'Connor's papers, and has overseen several posthumous publications of O'Connor's writings, and has recently generously donated a substantial part of her collection to Boole Library, University College Cork.

EMILIE PINE is a lecturer in Irish and British theatre at the University of York. She has published several articles on Irish film and theatre of the 1930s and is currently working on *The politics of nostalgia: a study of Irish culture in the 1990s*.

RUTH SHERRY is professor of English literature in the Norwegian University of Science and Technology. She has published numerous articles on Frank O'Connor; she has also edited, introduced and published the texts of two of his plays, *The invincibles* (1980) and *Moses' rock* (1983), and edited and introduced the play *Rodney's glory* (1992).

MICHAEL STEINMAN is professor of English at Nassau Community College, New York. He is the author of *Frank O'Connor at work* (1990), and is the editor of *A Frank O'Connor reader* (1994) and *The happiness of getting it down right: letters of Frank O'Connor and William Maxwell* (1996), as well as a special issue of *Twentieth Century Literature* devoted to O'Connor (Fall 1990).

CAROL TAAFFE is an IRCHSS Government of Ireland post-doctoral fellow in the school of English, Trinity College, Dublin. She is currently completing a book on Flann O'Brien and Irish cultural debate in the post-independence years.

ALAN TITLEY is a professor of Modern Irish at University College Cork and has published several articles and books on Irish literature and culture, including *An tÚrscéal Gaeilge* (1991) and *A pocket history of Gaelic culture* (2000). He is also the author of several short story collections, novels and plays, including *Tagann Godot* (1991), *An fear dána* (1993) and *Amach: úrscéal gairid* (2003), as well as being a regular media contributor in Ireland on issues in arts and politics.

Light dying

(In Memoriam Frank O'Connor [Michael O'Donovan])

BRENDAN KENNELLY

Climbing the last steps to your house, I knew
That I would find you in your chair,
Watching the light die along the canal,
Recalling the glad creators, all
Who'd played a part in the miracle;
A silver-haired remembering king, superb there
In dying light, all ghosts being at your beck and call,
You made them speak as only you could do

Of generosity or loneliness or love
Because, you said, all men are voices, heard
In the pure air of the imagination.
I hear you now, your rich voice deep and kind,
Rescuing a poem from time, bringing to mind
Lost centuries with a summoning word.
Lavishing on us who need much more of
What you gave, glimpses of heroic vision.

So you were angry at the pulling down
Of what recalled a finer age; you tried
To show how certain things destroyed, ignored,
Neglected was a crime against the past,
Impoverished the present. Some midland town
Attracted you, you stood in the waste
Places of an old church and, profoundly stirred,
Pondered how you could save what time had sorely tried,

Or else you cried in rage against the force
That would reduce to barren silence all
Who would articulate dark Ireland's soul;
You knew the evil of the pious curse,
The hearts that make God pitifully small
Until He seems the God of little fear
And not the God that you desired at all;
And yet you had the heart to do and dare.

I see you standing at your window,
Lifting a glass, watching the dying light
Along the quiet canal bank come and go
Until the time has come to say goodnight;
You see me to the door; you lift a hand
Half-shyly, awkwardly, while I remark
Your soul's fine courtesy, my friend, and
Walk outside, alone, suddenly in the dark.

But in the dark or no, I realise
Your life's transcendent dignity,
A thing more wonderful than April skies
Emerging in compelling majesty,
Leaving mad March behind and making bloom
Each flower outstripping every weed and thorn;
Life rises from the crowded clay of doom,
Light dying promises the light re-born.

Introduction

It is rare to encounter a general twentieth-century short-story anthology, and rarer still an Irish short-story anthology, without the inclusion of a Frank O'Connor entry. The American writer, Richard Ford, makes several references to O'Connor's literary influence on the genre in his introduction to the *Granta book of the American short story* (London, 1992). Yet, until the appearance of a collection of articles in America, edited by Robert Evans and Richard Harp and whose primary motivation in publishing the book was 'inspired by a desire to create and re-new interest' in O'Connor,[1] the most comprehensive book-length criticism of his *œuvre* was over twenty-five years ago with William Tomory's monograph, *Frank O'Connor* (Boston, 1980). A cursory survey of the rest of the secondary material available is revealing. A number of articles and edited publications of his writings appeared in recent years, including the ongoing work by O'Connor critics and contributors to this collection, Michael Steinman and Ruth Sherry. Two periodical issues on O'Connor were published; in 1990 a monograph of close textual criticism on variant drafts of seven O'Connor stories was also published.[2] Robert Evans and Richard Harp's collection helpfully contained a more up-to-date selected bibliography, situated contiguously in tandem to the still informative bibliography (also selected) that was first published.[3] The only other monograph on O'Connor to date is Maurice Wohlgelernter's *Frank O'Connor: an introduction* (New York, 1977), an uneven analysis that contextualizes aspects of O'Connor's work within a socio-political account of the time.

It would appear that the vast majority of scholarly work on O'Connor was published between the late 60s and early 80s and was chiefly under American authorship. Cork writer and actor, James McKeon, published a popular biography but it is the American scholar, James Matthews, who published the only critical biography to date, a biography that interpreted most of O'Connor's activities in a

---

1 Robert C. Evans & Richard Harp (eds), Introduction, *Frank O'Connor: new perspectives* (West Cornwall, CT, 1998), xv. **2** Michael Steinman, *Frank O'Connor at work* (Syracuse, NY, 1990). The two journal publications were: Michael Steinman (ed.), *Twentieth Century Literature*, 36:3 (Fall 1990), and James Alexander (ed.), *Journal of Irish Literature*, 4:1 (Jan. 1975). Steinman's issue contained some useful articles and interviews with and about O'Connor; Alexander's issue published a selection of O'Connor's generic writings. **3** Maurice Sheehy (ed.), *Michael/Frank: studies on Frank O'Connor with a bibliography of his writing* (Dublin, 1969). This book was edited by one of O'Connor's good friends and mainly consisted of discerning, elegiac contributions by friends and colleagues of the writer.

somewhat harsh light.[4] Nonetheless, it would seem that it is mainly because of American interest (which includes nearly all of the unpublished postgraduate theses on him) that O'Connor's work has managed to survive into the new century of scholarly criticism. This collection of essays attempts to redress this imbalance. The majority of the essays in this publication were first presented as papers at the Frank O'Connor Centenary Conference, held in September 2003 at Trinity College, Dublin. The remaining essays are by scholars whose work has contributed towards filling some of the gaps in the conference programme.

A brief consideration of O'Connor's life and work will help situate his significance in twentieth-century Irish literature and cultural debate. Michael O'Donovan was born in Cork in 1903. He began using a pseudonym, composed of his own middle name and his mother's maiden name, soon after the controversy that took place over the publication of Lennox Robinson's short story in *To-Morrow*, 'The Madonna of Slieve Dun' (August 1924). Robinson was accused of blasphemy (the country girl in the story claimed she had been 'visited' in the same way as Mary) and he was forced to resign his position as secretary and treasurer of the Advisory Committee to the Carnegie Trust in Ireland. O'Connor later claimed that as a trainee public librarian he was worried that his own job might also be at risk because of his writing.[5] The first appearance of the pseudonym was in the *Irish Statesman* on 14 March 1925 when he published a verse translation of 'Suibhne geilt speaks'.[6] Michael O'Donovan went on to become an extremely prolific writer as Frank O'Connor. In a literary career that spanned forty-one years he managed to produce eleven collections of short stories. He also published two novels, one book of original poetry, seven books of translated Irish poetry, one biography, an autobiography, three travelogues on Ireland, eight plays, two selected anthologies of Irish writing, five books of literary criticism, and over two hundred and fifty articles and reviews on cultural, social and political issues. O'Connor additionally gave his attention to a great deal of radio work which included talks, dramatic productions, and broadcasts of his short stories; he was

4 James McKeon, *Frank O'Connor: a life* (Edinburgh, 1998); James Matthews, *Voices: a life of Frank O'Connor* (Dublin, 1983). McKeon's publication also contained a selected bibliography that productively included new listings.   5 'Frank O'Connor', interview by A. Whittier, intro. and ed. by Malcolm Crowley, *Writers at work: the Paris Review interviews* (New York, 1958), 63.   6 Michael O'Donovan had already published poetry under 'M. O D' and 'M. O Donnabhain' in the short-lived republican periodical *An Long* (May–June 1922). While changing his name was perhaps in part actuated by a contemporary literary trend (Æ, Brinsley McNamara and Seán O'Faoláin had already changed their names, for example), O'Connor's eventual choice of pseudonym might have been influenced by the fact that he thought the Irish and English versions of his names too similar and therefore too risky, considering the erotic undertones of 'Suibhne geilt speaks'.

also actively involved in a myriad of letter debates in Irish newspapers from the 1920s to the 1940s. Within two years of his death in 1966, the second volume of his autobiography, an eighth book of translated Irish poetry and a sixth book of literary criticism appeared. Fifteen more collections of his short stories were published posthumously. While some of these publications were selected editions of previously collected stories, many of them also contained unpublished material or uncollected magazine/literary periodical stories, or new drafts of previously published stories (O'Connor constantly revised his stories, even those already published, due to his never-ending striving for perfectionism in the form). Moreover, he left behind a lifetime of almost daily-written correspondence to family, friends and colleagues, and an extensive collection of papers. O'Connor was a driven, determined and prodigious writer.

The seeds of this considerable intellectual and artistic endeavour were first planted during an upbringing that witnessed major political revolution in Ireland. He came to consciousness at a time when the country was undergoing its protracted and bloody transition from a colonial state to a constitutional, independent modern nation; it had a profound effect on the formation of the fledgling writer. While it was his national schoolteacher, Daniel Corkery, who turned him away from reading English public-schoolboy stories and stimulated a curiosity in European literature and in all-things Irish, in particular the Irish language, it was the events of the 1916 Rising that sparked his interest in Irish nationalism. Joining the Gaelic League, discovering Corkery's first collection of short stories soon after this, *A Munster twilight* (1916), seeking Corkery out and eventually becoming part of his small intellectual group, the Twenty Club, cemented O'Connor's pre-independence nationalism. O'Connor joined up as a Volunteer in the War of Independence but, due to his relative youth, saw little military action. He played mainly a propaganda role for the anti-Treaty side during the Civil War. In February 1923 O'Connor was captured by Free State soldiers and was held in Gormanstown Internment Camp just outside Dublin until his release in December of that year. O'Connor never went to university but he later considered this period in his life as rich an education as anything a college could have offered him, as he became acquainted with men like Frank Gallagher, Seán MacEntee, and Seán T. O'Kelly.[7] But by the time he left prison, O'Connor's attitude had transformed. One result of this transformation was a shift in his atti-

---

7 Gallagher became editor of the *Irish Press* and went on to write an account of the Civil War in *The four glorious years* (1953) and Partition in *The indivisible Island* (1957). Seán MacEntee became minister of Finance in Éamon de Valera's government in 1932 and Seán T. O'Kelly became president of Ireland in 1945.

tude towards organized religion and governmental politics: 'what we [both sides of the Civil War] were bringing about was a new Establishment of Church and State in which imagination would play no part'[8]; he began to view the Catholic church and the Free State government as adversely dominating forces at work in Irish society and this too had a deep affect on the emerging young writer.

Along with O'Connor's witnessing of atrocities committed during the Civil War, a hunger strike organized by the anti-Treaty prisoners in Gormanstown in November 1923 influenced his new line of thinking. The purpose of the hunger strike was to embarrass the Free State government into releasing the prisoners or, at the very least, initiate a politically expedient situation that would break the stalemate that had been caused by Éamon de Valera's ceasefire order (the prisoners were left in a temporary political vacuum with the anti-Treaty side's refusal to officially surrender). O'Connor, along with just two other republican prisoners, bravely voted against the thousand men who were for the strike. He thought it an absurd idea and doomed to failure. The strike was eventually called off and O'Connor witnessed the debasement of his fellow prisoners as they clambered on top of each other in the rush for food. It left a lasting impression. The experience intensified O'Connor's disaffection with idealized politics, provoked a strong sense of estrangement from his current convictions and consequently increased his belief in the importance of maintaining his individual liberty at all costs. Years later, he recalled in his autobiography that 'we knew we should never again find ourselves with so many men we respected and we felt their humiliation as though it were our own. In the years to come, traveling through the country, I would meet with the survivors of the period ... the death-in-life of the Nationalist Catholic establishment'.[9] In 1952 O'Connor would write his memory of the hunger strike, albeit with artistic changes, into a short story that was pointedly entitled 'Freedom'. In terms of maintaining his intellectual and artistic freedom, it is well known at this stage that O'Connor, along with other writers in the decades after independence – including Sean O'Casey, Liam O'Flaherty, Seán O'Faoláin, Flann O'Brien, Mary Lavin and Patrick Kavanagh – were the principle means by which counter-Revival aesthetics were launched; it is also a near critical commonplace that these writers played a dominant role in the development of an oppositional perspective on church and state discourse throughout this period. O'Connor's lifelong struggle with the role of the state and Catholicism in Irish life, and his conflicting relationship with the country and the people, had its roots in his Civil War experiences. It was this tension of contraries that became central to his writing.

8 O'Connor, *An only child* (London, 1961), 210.   **9** Ibid., 271.

The war experiences delineated the beginning of O'Connor's passage from a romantic adolescent to a more independent realistic adult, but he was an adult who also developed a mixed attitude towards his country. He was a young man who became disillusioned with, and frequently and bitterly fought against, Free State government and church policies; he was also a young man who retained a deep love for the country, its people, its culture and traditions. His impulse to circumvent what he saw as the limitations of Irish life was coupled with a desire for a reconciliation of his aspirations for Ireland with the country's socio-political reality. This confliction also extended to his ambivalent nationalistic beliefs. O'Connor maintained a sympathetic attitude towards what he considered 'heroic' pre-independence nationalism but displayed vacillating, at times unequivocally harsh, opinions on post-independence nationalism – a nationalism which he generally associated with the Catholic bourgeoisie that was now presiding over Irish society. Despite O'Connor's frequent and often public criticism of Catholic bourgeois nationalism, he also regularly spoke about what he saw as the 'tragedy of Partition', nowhere more evident than in one of his *Sunday Independent* 'Ben Mayo' articles in 1944: 'The people are bewildered because they are divided and they have been divided ever since the split and the civil war. We shall not see the end of Partition until they are reunited. *It has been proved over and over again that the united strength of Irish nationalism is immense* ... Before anything more can be done to unite all Ireland, Irish nationalism must become once more a united force'.[10] Despite this seemingly pro-nationalistic stance, his ambivalent opinion of post-independence church and state policy resulted in him ultimately believing that it was the overly pietistic and conservative Free State that was the main obstacle to achieving a united country.[11]

His contrary attitude also extended to his creative writings. He generally wrote from the perspective of an insider, one who based his fiction on an intimate knowledge of the people, yet O'Connor was also a writer that depicted his characters with an outsider's detachment. His writings focused on Irish life as it affected 'ordinary' Irish people – the stories had mainly domesticated heroes and 'adventures' drawn from the everyday. In O'Connor's depiction of Irish relationships, gentleness, amiable humour, compassion or (especially later in life) sentimentality for his characters was displayed. He was particularly sympathetic towards his

10 O'Connor, 'Partition – the people are bewildered says Ben Mayo', *Sunday Independent* (7 May 1944); repr. in *The Journal of Irish Literature*, 4:1 (Jan. 1975), 128 [O'Connor's emphasis]. O'Connor served up this opinion behind the 'mask' of Ben Mayo, but he would also reiterate this stance on several occasions in later years – for examples, see Matthews, *Voices*, 340. **11** Matthews, *Voices*, 350.

younger characters. But the writings also displayed anger, disappointment, flippancy or comic mockery towards those aspects of Irish life he considered hypocritical, authoritarian, falsely pious, or mediocre.[12] O'Connor produced a sensitive examination of the social forces that pertain to the Irish middle-class small-town way of life ('The Luceys' and 'The Mad Lomasneys', for example); moreover, his work generally revealed little interest in the Ascendancy class, a sympathy for the Irish poor ('The patriarch' and *The saint and Mary Kate*, for example) and a pointed critique of the *arriviste petit bourgeois* ('The late Henry Conran' and *Time's pocket*, for example). Yet, his writings strongly focused on the place of the individual within society and reserved condemnation for those forces that hampered individual desires ('The procession of life' and 'The custom of the country', for example). O'Connor aspired to social 'freedom' for people to express their individuality, but paradoxically he also desired the comfort of a traditional sense of community. His stories represented 'submerged population groups' – his oft-cited term for those he considered marginalized, lonely or alienated in society and who, he believed, formed the kernel of short-story material. He once said that 'the short story remains by its very nature remote from the community – romantic, individualistic',[13] nonetheless his stories were often less about individualism than of problematic relationships and characters who also seemed to belong to, fitted into, or symbolized Irish communities ('In the train' and 'Peasants', for example). His created individual characters often served as mediums to entire 'communities' for the reader.

O'Connor's conflicted attitude was comprised in part from his exploration of the Irish past and traditions present in modern Ireland. One such area was in his critical and creative exploration of the tradition of religious belief and practice in Irish society. His examination of Irish religious practices continually questioned what he perceived as the overly-controlling role of the Catholic church in Irish social affairs. Despite this judgement, O'Connor also wrote some of the most discriminatory portraits of priests and bishops available in the canon of twentieth-century Irish literature.[14] While O'Connor mocked a passive deference

12 For the former see, for example, 'After fourteen years', 'Michael's wife', 'Uprooted', 'There is a lone house', 'The bridal night', 'Fish for Friday', 'Androcles and the army', 'Ghosts', 'Old age pensioners'; on childhood see, for example, 'First confession', 'My Da', 'The stepmother', 'The man of the house', and the collection *Larry Delaney: lonesome genius*, intro. Patrick Cotter (Cork, 1996). For the latter see, for example, 'Grandeur', 'The babes in the wood', 'Baptismal', 'The miser', 'The holy door', 'A thing of nothing', *The lost legion* and *Dutch interior*. **13** O'Connor, *The lonely voice* (London, 1963), 20–1. **14** See 'The conversion', 'Lost fatherlands', 'Vanity', as well as the collection *The collar: stories of Irish priests*, selec. & intro. by Harriet O'Donovan Sheehy (Belfast, 1993). His

for tradition, his stories also delicately explored people's loyalty or attraction to the past ('The majesty of the law' and 'The long road to Ummera', for example). In turn, his work also communicated the belief that outmoded beliefs and customs could possibly lead to social stagnation and sexual sterility ('A bachelor's story' and 'A thing of nothing', for example). His creative work also featured attempts to symbolically lament the dying out of traditional Gaelic culture or represent the surviving fragmented consciousness of a traumatized history that was present in contemporary social discourse (*The lost legion* and *The statue's daughter*, for example); alternatively, O'Connor utilized the past as a perceived relevant yardstick with which to gauge post-independence cultural development and change (*The invincibles*, *Moses' rock* and *Rodney's glory*, for example). Despite his creative observations on the dying out of Gaelic culture and his tendency to use the past for comparative contemporary analysis, O'Connor's critical work strongly displays his own deep interest in Irish cultural history and his relentless campaign to encourage a public reading of the Irish past as capable of providing the post-independence nation with a rich, internationally respected, cultural heritage if properly preserved. This is evidenced, for example, in his recording of traditional Irish beliefs (*A book of Ireland*), his travelogue descriptions of Ireland's national monuments (*Irish miles* and *Leinster, Munster, and Connaught*), his critical assessment of Ireland's literary history (*The backward look*), and his translating what amounted to, as previously mentioned, his eight books of mainly early medieval to nineteenth-century Irish-language poetry.

His pervasive antinomy also extended to his theories of readership and his engagement with the material conditions of reception in the post-independence decades. O'Connor firmly argued that artists represent 'nothing' in their work but he also strongly argued for instrumentalism in art – which would result in a literature that somehow could embody a type of non-referential creative writing that could also inspire social change. Here was a writer that continually bespoke the primacy of technique in writing considerations but paradoxically was someone who also viewed the writer as a social 'reformer'.[15] He was a writer who wrote for 'the lonely reader down the country' but who also aimed at reaching a 'community' of such like-minded readers, those imagined members of the reading public who, like O'Connor, felt estranged from post-independence society. O'Connor saw the writer in the role of medium for readers; in a Yeatsian vein one who could

depiction of nuns was not as discerning as his portraits of the priesthood – see for example: 'The ugly duckling', 'A case of conscience' and 'The miracle' (a different story to 'The miracle' in *The collar* collection); this was perhaps due to the fact that O'Connor remained close friends with a number of priests throughout his lifetime. **15** Whittier, *Paris Review interview*, 63.

access the shadowy world of what is hidden in the readers' unconscious: 'All that
the artist knows is that he is a sort of transformer station for them; that his place is
in the doorway between the two rooms with the lights of consciousness partly
dimmed … He is half medium, half critic'.[16] His writing of the material conditions of reception pointed always to an Irish setting. O'Connor engaged with his
perception of Irish church and state hegemonic control over the reading audience,
and his conjectures on author-reader relationships tried to undermine an institu-
tionalizing of the contemporary reader. He linked the private act of reading with
the broader socio-political context, and an important part of his oppositional act
to a hegemonic control of reading was located in his theory of the short-story
form. According to O'Connor, the genre itself could embody social opposition as
it functioned as 'a private art intended to satisfy the standards of the individual,
solitary, critical reader … [who will] see into the shadows' of the story.[17] V.S.
Pritchett described this process as one of 'seeing through', whereby presentation of
character and incident in the short story allowed the reader to see other planes of
meaning beyond the surface. The reader completed the disclosure of what lies
behind the surface of the story. Contrary to his advocacy at times that art was primarily concerned with aesthetics, the gaps and omissions inherent in the short
story form, he also believed, would leave a far greater onus on the reader to complete the picture proffered in the story; it created space for the reader's 'moral
imagination' and 'moral judgment' to dilate into social considerations.[18] For
O'Connor, the short story did not depend on any identification process between
the reader and the characters, and instead involved a direct relationship between
the writer and reader in specific historical conditions. The 'superior' reader, particularly at a local homologous level, could recognize and critique the characters and
way of life presented in these realist or naturalist stories (O'Connor inhabited
both styles at varying times); his stories were so much of their time and place that
they might, he idealistically hoped, stimulate readers' critical engagement with life
in mid-century Ireland. This in turn might subvert church and state hegemony,
not in any radical socially transformative sense but more in terms of the development of organic intellectuals in the country who could actively debate the social
and political issues of the day and provide domestic dissent to the official position.

O'Connor carried his conflicted attitude towards Ireland into his personal
life, his work as a librarian, his time spent as a director of the Abbey Theatre in the
mid-late 1930s, his working for the Ministry of Information and the BBC during

16 O'Connor, 'Charles Dickens', *Irish Times* (8 Sept. 1945).   **17** O'Connor, *The lonely voice*, 14, 25.
18 Ibid., 25. In similar terms, O'Faoláin described the short story as a 'pointing finger' in his study of
the genre – *The short story* (Old Greenwich, CT, 1951), 32.

World War II, his regular contributions to the *New Yorker* from the 1940s to the 1960s, his teaching at Trinity College, Dublin, and Harvard, Northwestern, Stanford and Berkeley American universities (most of his books of literary criticism were produced out of his lectures), and his already-mentioned *engagé* publishing output. Over the course of these decades, the works of O'Connor comprised a cultural history of mid-century Ireland as they were implicated directly in the processes of social and political friction or accord that engulfed Irish life.

Why he suffered from relative critical neglect on this side of the Atlantic could pertain to any number of reasons. His most successful creative efforts were in the short-story genre, a genre that seemed to have attracted substantially less critical attention in Irish Studies than any other form of creative writing. Internationally, introductions to and stylistic theorizing about the twentieth-century modern short story has produced several book publications. These publications contain for the most part, if one removes Joyce from the equation, either no mention at all or just passing reference to the Irish practitioners.[19] Irish short-story writers produced their own theories of the genre, including O'Connor's influential study, *The lonely voice* (1962). These writers had also begun to receive more critical attention with the appearance of such publications as Patrick Rafroidi and Terence Brown's (eds), *The Irish short story* (Gerrards Cross, Bucks., 1979) and James F. Kilroy's (ed.), *The Irish short story: a critical history* (Boston, 1980). Yet, the long shadows cast by the 'giants' of twentieth-century Irish literature, Yeats, Joyce and Beckett, seemed to have focused most of the attention away from the genre (Joyce's *Dubliners* and Beckett's *More pricks than kicks* were largely ignored in the early days of Joycean and Beckettian critical perusals) and from more 'minor' writers like O'Connor. Scholarship gaps on nineteenth and mid-twentieth century Irish short-story writers appear to be closing of late. The tales and short stories by such Irish writers as William Carleton, Oscar Wilde, Somerville & Ross, Daniel Corkery, Liam O'Flaherty, Elizabeth Bowen, Seán O'Faoláin, Mary Lavin and Maeve Brennan, for example, have received increased academic examination in recent years. In the case of O'Connor, scholarly attention in the past might have been affected by his reputation.

From very early on in his career O'Connor was critically established as an old-fashioned realist. He had always loudly proclaimed his admiration for naturalist and realist nineteenth-century writers such as, among others, Gogol, Flaubert,

---

19 Some of the few exceptions to this treatment of Irish short-story writers and of O'Connor in particular are: H.E. Bates, *The modern short story: a critical survey* (London, 1941), Walter Allen, *The short story in English* (Oxford, 1981) and Clare Hanson, *Short stories and short fictions, 1880–1980* (New York, 1985); all three books contain some critical commentary on his work.

Maupassant, Trollope, Chekhov and Babel; he especially professed the influence of Ivan Turgenev on his writing. Old-fashioned realist was a term that, while not always meant derogatorily by critics in their reviews of O'Connor's work, did facilitate the gradual building of his lasting reputation of being a dated and perspicuous writer, who wrote simple, funny, popular stories (or 'coloured balloons' as Patrick Kavanagh once termed them). The consensus seems to have been that his work did not merit academic explication. All of O'Connor's fictional and dramatic writings, except for the few stories set in England and which were mostly based on the Irish diaspora experience, were deliberately placed in a local Irish setting (he once said that he knew to a syllable how everything in Ireland can be said). Despite his committed belief to the subversive potential of place in the Irish short story, ironically it was this strong presence of place and time that ultimately led to a labeling of him as dated. Moreover, he was well known for his sometimes visceral criticisms of Irish life throughout his career. This did not endear him to the social and political establishment. Several of his books were banned over the years; he also endured an unofficial 'blacklisting' by the state authorities during World War II. The pressures of enlisting nationwide support and perpetuating a neutral consensus during the war years ensured the disappearance of O'Connor's lucrative radio work; O'Connor and his family subsequently endured financial hardship throughout the 1940s. At one stage, he was publicly denounced as an 'anti-Irish Irishman' in an editorial of the *Irish Press* (15 December 1949) for an article he had just published which revealed some of the true social conditions in Ireland ('Ireland' in *Holiday*, 6 December 1949). O'Connor eventually went into exile in America for most of the 1950s where his career flourished (and which would explain some of the lasting American interest in his work). When he returned to Ireland in September 1961, he gradually began receiving recognition and was awarded an honorary doctorate by Trinity College, Dublin, in July 1962. It was all too brief as he died on 10 March 1966. By the end of the twentieth century most of Frank O'Connor's books were out of print.

More recent events in Ireland and Britain would indicate a growing upsurge of interest in O'Connor's work and reputation. The popular as well as critical upsurge includes the setting up of the perpetual Frank O'Connor International Short Story Festival in 2000 by the Cork-based Munster Literature Centre. The largest international monetary prize for a short-story collection is currently the Frank O'Connor International Short Story Award, also organized by the Munster Literature Centre and in association with the *Irish Times* since 2006. In terms of state and popular recognition of the writer, while it was not organized on any grand scale, it was in evidence during O'Connor's centenary on 17 September 2003.[20] Renewed attention was also given to his writings with the republication of *The lonely voice* (Cork, 2003). Penguin Classics republished his two autobiographies as one volume and this publication was introduced by Declan Kiberd, who stated that the 'volumes are justly counted among the classics of Irish writing'.[21] A new collection of his short stories was selected by British writer Julian Barnes (*My Oedipus complex and other stories* [Penguin Classics, 2005]). Barnes' introduction to the collection was prominently placed in an edition of Britain's *Guardian* 'Review' literary supplement, alongside a large picture of O'Connor on its cover with the subtitle of 'the restless genius of Frank O'Connor' (2 July 2005). Why O'Connor has re-emerged in popular and critical circles on these islands after a long hiatus is an interesting question; whether this interest will sustain itself is another question. This collection of critical essays is perhaps then timely. O'Connor's writings, his reputation, his relevance to the issues and readership of today, and his place in Irish literature, are some of the aspects examined in these articles.

Nicholas Allen's article returns O'Connor to the decade following the Civil War and contextualizes him within the cultural debates of the 1920s. Allen focuses in particular on O'Connor's critical stances in the literary periodicals of the period and in turn examines how this mindset manifested itself in his early short stories. Terence Brown gives a complete overview of O'Connor's life and work, and charts his progression as a writer through each succeeding decade until his death in 1966. He also addresses O'Connor's relative critical neglect and examines his relevance to a twenty-first-century readership. Paul Delaney engages with the infamous rift between O'Connor and his former mentor, Daniel Corkery. He critically examines their personal and literary relationship and assesses the instances of public disputes between the two (along with Seán O'Faoláin when he entered the fray). Robert C. Evans provides a detailed archival investigation into O'Connor's critical reception in his first decade of publishing in America, and analyzes the reputation bestowed on O'Connor by 1930s America literary critics. Maurice Harmon's

20 Cork City Council purchased the birthplace of O'Connor and it was officially opened on 22 September by the minister for Arts, John O'Donoghue, as the new home for the Munster Literature Centre. RTÉ (Raidió Telefís Éireann), Ireland's state-owned radio and television service, broadcasted several selections of O'Connor's radio work, and RTÉ television screened a new documentary about O'Connor on 30 Dec. 2003. In addition to state recognition, short stories were republished daily in Cork city newspaper – the *Evening Echo*, lengthy articles appeared in the *Sunday Independent* (18 Aug.) and the *Irish Examiner* (21 Aug.) and short publicity pieces were published in the *Irish Times* (6, 15, 23 Sept.). **21** Declan Kiberd, 'Introduction' in O'Connor, *An only child and my father's son* (London, 2005), xiii.

article presents a close textual reading of several of O'Connor's short stories and assesses the formation and ability of O'Connor as a writer. John Kenny contextualizes O'Connor within theoretical formulations of the short-story genre. He focuses in particular on assessing theories tendered by the Irish practitioners and also proffers his own critical evaluation of the form. Declan Kiberd also contextualizes O'Connor, this time within the context of the lasting literary and political influence, as well as the several translations (including O'Connor's), of Brian Merriman's eighteenth-century *Cúirt an mheán oíche* (*The midnight court*). Kiberd also engages with the issue of male literary personification of women, as evinced in *Cúirt* and the poem's male translators. The politics of O'Connor's theatrical theories, as well as his work and achievements as a director in the Abbey Theatre, are examined by Hilary Lennon. She also critically assesses his staged Abbey plays. Emilie Pine's essay considers the role of film-making in mid-century Ireland and assesses the similarities and divergences between O'Connor's 'Guests of the nation' and Denis Johnston's film adaptation, gauged within the context of their respective attitudes towards the War of Independence and post-independence nationalism. Autobiography as a genre is inspected by Ruth Sherry as she performs a textual criticism of O'Connor's own autobiographical writings, and reappraises his stories of childhood in light of this scrutiny. Michael Steinman engages with the literary reputation allotted to O'Connor, and contrasts this reputation with his close reading of one of the more neglected short stories, 'The lonely rock'. Carol Taaffe's article assesses O'Connor's attitude towards literary modernism, in particular as it is evinced in his criticisms of the works of Joyce; she in turn explores the criticisms of O'Connor by Flann O'Brien and Patrick Kavanagh. O'Connor's views of literature in the Irish language are critically appraised by Alan Titley; he also examines O'Connor's choices and assesses his ability as a translator of Irish language poetry. Two essays in this collection produce a more personal portrait of the man. Philip Edwards recalls his memories of O'Connor's skills as a teacher and describes his pioneering attempt to set up an 'Irish Studies' degree programme in Trinity College, Dublin. The widow of O'Connor, Harriet O'Donovan Sheehy, remembers many snippets of meaningful moments that they shared in their life together. Finally, Brendan Kennelly's conference recital of his memorial poem to O'Connor, 'Light dying', is reproduced at the beginning of this book.

Overall, the purpose of this collection was not to present a single elucidation of Frank O'Connor but instead aimed to advance a platform whereby a multiplicity of critical opinion on his life and works might emerge.

Frank O'Connor and critical memory

NICHOLAS ALLEN

Frank O'Connor finished the Civil War in disappointment. Committed to the losing side, he faced a future without prospects or preferment, the civil service, that avenue for Irish ambition, closed to him as a republican.[1] His continuing thought was to become a writer. What kind of writing O'Connor might pursue was still unknown, as any account of his work during the 1920s shows – Irish translations, poetry, criticism and short stories all first steps in his fledgling career. The variety of O'Connor's writing suggests the flexibility that makes his later prose so engaging, O'Connor's careful manipulations of speech and scene the building blocks of an art that seems artless, the artifice of realism near invisible. In the 1920s when O'Connor began to practise his trade publicly, a sense of seamless fiction must have seemed impossible, the writer's world a daunting mix of aesthetics and politics. The literary revival still carried force, Yeats parading Dublin as Nobel Laureate and senator, George Russell supporting the new regime in the pages of the *Irish Statesman*. In politics, a hostile press caricatured the republican opposition, the Free State pursuing a vigorous campaign of harassment and enforcement, freedom a mirage that flickered in the heat of censorship and reaction.

O'Connor's contemporary Liam O'Flaherty fought these problems with a tenacity born from his own experience of the First World War and the revolution to follow. Three years after he occupied Dublin's Rotunda Buildings in the hope of beginning a socialist putsch with the unemployed as his army (he was in the end rescued by the IRA from stone-throwing locals who laid siege to his small force),[2] O'Flaherty wrote to the *Irish Statesman*, which he dismissed as concerned 'almost entirely with parish politics, and rambling discourses on things that might appeal to well-fed middlemen who like to appear broad-minded, interested mildly in

---

1 'At the age of twenty I was released from an internment camp without money or job. The Civil War had just ended, and since I had taken the loser's side I found that ex-gaolbirds like myself did not get whatever positions were available under the new government'. Frank O'Connor, *My father's son* (London, 1968), 11. 2 One journalist found the revolutionaries singing 'The red flag' and 'The soldier's song' as local residents laid siege to their position before 'the IRA took control outside'. *Freeman's Journal* (21 Jan. 1922), 3.

ideas that have been carefully pre-digested before being offered to your bourgeois palates',[3] the attack pointed since Russell spent the previous quarter-century fighting the middle-man in his battle for rural co-operation. O'Flaherty saw independence as continuation of old problems, Ireland even now 'submerged beneath the rotting mound of British traditions'.[4] The question of Ireland's sovereignty had prompted Civil War in June 1922, the Anglo-Irish Treaty painted as necessary compromise or deadly surrender, depending on one's position. The binary created promised a paralysis more lasting than the crisis post-Parnell. Clothed in invective, O'Flaherty offered an alternative:

> The younger generation is tired of bravado and politicians and mountebanks. The younger generation alone can decide whether in twenty years' time we will be still a nation of bigoted or intolerant people or whether we are going to build up a civilisation distinctly our own, a civilisation and culture that will make us a force in Europe.[5]

Europe, the United States of America, the international in any figuration, become the spaces in which new writing is imagined. The attraction to elsewhere can be read as escape, literature following the path of emigration as did so many others. I want to follow a different entry to Frank O'Connor's writing here, arguing that his art patrols the borders of Irish articulacy, the 'outside' a category that allows his work maintain dialogue with a state from which he remained distant, the international a place that allowed for aesthetics, yes – but also context, the sense of the world looking in a fundamental strand of Irish writing since Synge went to Aran after Paris. Following from this, I want to read from O'Connor's short stories in journals like the *Irish Statesman*, the *Irish Tribune*, the *Dublin Magazine* and *Atlantic Monthly* to register how these 'outsides' work.

It took some courage in the first place for O'Connor to publish in the *Irish Statesman*. George Russell, the journal's editor, was public in his radical sympathies from the 1913 Lock Out. He had also written of that icon of nationalist resistance, Terence MacSwiney, lord mayor of Cork and Volunteer, who died on hunger strike in protest at his arrest in Brixton Prison.[6] The Civil War changed his

---

3 Liam O'Flaherty, 'A view of Irish culture', *Irish Statesman* (20 June 1925), 461.   4 Ibid.   5 Ibid.
6 Russell wrote before MacSwiney's death 'There is that within us can triumph over pain, / And go to death alone, slowly and unafraid. / The candles of God are already burning row on row, / Farewell, Lightbringer, fly to thy heaven again', *The Times* (2 Sept. 1920), 11.

perspective on revolutionary activity, Russell editing the *Irish Statesman* for seven years from September 1923 as a weekly buttress to the government. This did not mean he agreed with all their policies, Russell's greatest disappointment the institution of a literary censorship in 1929 that betrayed, as he felt, the implicit understanding that culture had its own, inviolate, guardians. Republicans did not observe these distinctions and wrote regularly to Russell, complaining of his bias. Mary MacSwiney, for one, complained that:

> A Republican is always at a disadvantage in writing to THE IRISH STATESMAN because of necessity he has either to impugn either the sincerity or the intelligence of the Editor and so disturb the assured sense of superiority in both these qualities which flows so placidly through the columns of the Imperial journal.[7]

The claim to sincerity is bound to the sentiment of authenticity, first entry to any post-Treaty controversy (a later complaint of a symposium in the Gate Theatre was that 'the subject 'Should the Theatre be International?' was gradually fined down to the burning questions: 'Where were you in 1916?' or 'What did you do in 1922?').[8] O'Connor began his approach to a new writing in an early explanation of his critical method in the *Irish Statesman* of 12 June 1926. His sense of self-exposure is fraught and evident, given that letters to the journal were more concerned with the conditions in which prisoners were kept in Free State jails. O'Connor's contemplation of the quotidian, his attempt 'to interest the ordinary reader in Irish literature', grew 'not from the sentimental or the patriotic or the historical point of view, but from the point of view of contemporary criticism'.[9] The foundations of that criticism are not exposed, though we know O'Connor read the *Times Literary Supplement*, the *New Statesman*, *The Spectator* and *The Studio*. What this criticism does, whatever its provenance, is encode a developing Ireland of individual liberation; 'I believe too much', he wrote, 'in those O'Higgins and Hacketts of ours to think that their language will end up in the hothouse of sentiment'.[10] O'Connor's choice of F. R. Higgins (a misprint, presumably, for O'Higgins) and Frances Hackett is significant. Both wrote poetry and prose that was erotic and violent, and both were banned when censorship was enforced. Both exposed a social world

---

7 Mary MacSwiney, 'Imperialism', *Irish Statesman* (6 Dec. 1924), 397. **8** 'The symposium', *Motley* (Dec. 1932), 5. **9** Frank O'Connor, 'An Irish anthology', *Irish Statesman* (12 June 1926), 379. **10** Ibid., 380.

of complex interaction, Higgins drawing a western Ireland whose rawness found its way to the nightclubs of Dublin, Hackett later writing *The green lion*, a replay in part of the scandal that accompanied Parnell's adultery. Liam O'Flaherty, Lennox Robinson and William Butler Yeats all used sexual violence as motif of Irish culture post-independence. O'Connor's promotion of Higgins and Hackett is guerrilla criticism, the planting of small explosions in art that breach set ideas of expression. This, perhaps, betrays O'Connor's experience in the republican movement, anti-Treaty propaganda subtle in its manipulation of any argument against its enemies. O'Connor's strategy of argument and appeal bears its genesis in the reading of political pamphlets, posters and handbills, even if expressed in the measured tones of the critic. Read, as example, his review of Erlande's *Life of John Keats*, which exposes:

> a fault in Keats which most critics overlook, if they perceive it at all (Matthew Arnold perhaps excepted). Keats was intellectually limited; the society in which he lived (and every time one studies his life the fact becomes clearer) was a provincial society; his ideas were provincial, and his life lacked general interests. *Endymion* suffered from it; so did *Hyperion*, both first and second drafts.[11]

The obsession with textuality, the drafting of documents, proceeds from a culture determined through the 1920s and after by the response to precise formulations of loyalty and possession. Without ascribing any continuing sympathy to one cause or another in O'Connor's mind, the sense remains of a *mentalité* motivated by these surrounding disputes. O'Connor continues that Keats:

> is essentially a national instead of an international poet – as Milton is, and Wordsworth, and as so many other of the English poets are – as great as any, beyond denial, but not I think what he would have wished himself to be. For as often as I read his letters I feel that Keats if he had lived would have been among the European and not the English poets; that he had the power which Heine speaks of, the power to project *Gestalten* – figures – whether they be dramatic creations or dramatized ideas; as Heine himself had, and Dante and Goethe and, in lessening degree, Shelley and Byron.[12]

---

11 Frank O'Connor, 'Review', *Irish Statesman* (17 Aug. 1929), 477.   12 Frank O'Connor, *Irish Statesman* (17 Aug. 1929), 478.

To which O'Connor might have added Collins and de Valera. The power to project these figures lay in the hands of a new generation of writers who busied themselves in the commission of biographies of the revolutionary past, O'Connor writing of Collins, O'Faoláin going back further to O'Connell.[13] The power to project might be read as O'Connor's critical definition of success.

Confronted in the last issue of the *Irish Statesman* with a compilation of critical essays, *Our exagmination round his factification for incamination of work in progress*, all addressed to Joyce's expanding project in *transition*, and containing essays by Samuel Beckett and Thomas MacGreevy, O'Connor admitted that he admired Joyce's previous work only in its 'sensitiveness to form and style'.[14] Much of *Work in progress* was 'outside my interests'[15], a comment to suggest modernism as a branch of science, much like entomology. O'Connor did like

> the Anna Livia episode with its haunting four-dimensional pattern; the two washerwomen calling to one another across the river; the river itself flowing on, imagining all the rivers of earth and heaven and hell; then as night draws on the changing of the two women into a stone and a tree while their voices, become faint as echoes, fade out above the darkness of the river.[16]

Joyce's *Work in progress* was the most controversial modernist text of the 1920s, critics unsure how to generate meaning from its shards of recognition. O'Connor's focus on this section from *Anna Livia Plurabelle* suggests the parameters of his own aesthetic. The female form, rivers and judgment are all present in his early short stories, as is the sense of a fading world, each text set in the past, action determined by the memory of things done. We can read the ghostliness of this into a culture so unsettled by Civil War, the destruction of any idea of consensus a contributor to the past's present persistence. Even here, there are hints of new growth, O'Connor's translations of the Sweeney myth in the pages of the *Irish Statesman* the creation of a space for madness and eroticism, the cursed king of ancient Ireland the roving equivalent of the censored text, moving from community to community, reader to reader, spreading unsettling sensations. 'Suibhne geilt speaks' is a good example.

---

13 O'Connor published his life of Michael Collins, *The big fellow*, in 1937, Seán O'Faoláin publishing his life of Daniel O'Connell, *King of the beggars*, the next year, in 1938.   14 Frank O'Connor, 'Joyce – the third period', *Irish Statesman* (12 Apr. 1930), 114.   15 Ibid., 115.   16 Ibid.

I love to run
And scale the mountains like a storm,
Waving my arms to scare the birds,
And screaming with them in their fright:
I love to frighten men and herds,
And I do hide in some high gully
Above their homes, and when the sun
Climbs on the ridge of a mountain fully,
Or when the great, round harvest moon
Is there, I leap across the light,
And stretch my coat tails to the sky,
And plunge the valley into night,
And make men bless themselves for fright,
And make the little children cry.[17]

Locating this wildness in the Gaelic tradition pitted O'Connor against what he perceived to be the new, unreal, orthodoxy of native traditions whereby the Irish language was a constriction of national sincerity. His determination to promote Irish as a contemporary language of contemporary problems led him to fierce controversy with members of the Gaelic Players, whose work he reviewed at the Peacock Theatre. Writing of Seamus Wilmot's *Casadh an rotha*, O'Connor remembered:

> I once judged some Gaelic dramatic competitions in an Irish country town, and among them was a juvenile performance of *The Babes in the Wood*. But the babes, whose version of the story differed from mine, died chanting I'll Sing a Hymn to Mary, and their restless little corpses were covered not by birds, but by a child playing the part of the Blessed Virgin, who appeared followed by a little boy with an electric torch, which he focussed with more or less consistency on the back of her head.[18]

There is, for all O'Connor's wit, an element of the present in this past production, the electric torch forerunner of the wider electrification soon to follow. The religiosity of the scene is what galls, and again the contemporary pressure of church on state subsists in O'Connor's refusal to surrender the Irish language to a particular belief. This position is, in a basic sense, republican, O'Connor setting limits

---

17 Frank O'Connor, 'Suibhne geilt speaks', *Irish Statesman* (14 Mar. 1925), 11.   **18** Frank O'Connor, 'At the Peacock', *Irish Statesman* (26 Oct. 1929), 154.

between art and religion. After an angry reply from Wilmot in a later issue of the *Irish Statesman* ('As far as Gaelic plays are in question, F. O'C., methinks, should have remained with his 'Babes in the Wood in any Irish Country Town'),[19] O'Connor relented, finding Wilmot's play 'no worse than the rest of the nonsense'.[20] His concern was that without some increase in criticism, a future generation would equate Irish with ignorance and English with culture:

> It may be an ungenerous thing to say, but I feel it a disgrace that thousands of pounds of public money should be wasted on the literary efforts of Mr Wilmot and his kind while the capital city of Ireland is without a subsidised orchestra, much less a State-supported opera. These are things that Irish people do not think of, but they, and not the work foisted on us by the Government Publications Committee and the Gaelic Players, that make or damn Ireland in the eyes of world.[21]

The opera is a particular type of state-sponsored project. It stages music, creating narrative from visual and aural elements, the orchestra, sets and singers all a sensorium that involves elements of carnival and pageantry. The melodrama of a Puccini, the epic pomp of a Wagner, seem far from official Ireland of the 1920s. O'Connor's vision does however draw its energy from the Free State's vernacular culture. Cabaret was a popular form throughout the 1920s, in private clubs and public theatres, pantomime, vaudeville and the silent cinema with its accompanying orchestra further forms of popular entertainment.[22] The submerged vitality of public culture in early independence Dublin is rarely acknowledged, but it is the beginning that allows O'Connor to call for a state opera. It is the constituency that O'Connor continued to address in his translations from Irish, particularly in poems like 'Celibacy (*Father Geoffrey Keating sang this*)'.

> Take your mouth from mine,
> Kissing's bitterer still;
> Flesh from flesh must part
> Lest of warmth come will.

---

19 Seamus Wilmot, 'Gaelic drama', *Irish Statesman* (9 Nov. 1929), 190. **20** Frank O'Connor, 'Author and reviewer', *Irish Statesman* (16 Nov. 1929), 212. **21** Ibid., 212. **22** 'For one example of cabaret, see the performance "of the Athos beauties in wonderful girls", and Leon Lewisoff and Izna Rossell in an exciting acrobatic waltz, a song by Bobby Macauley, entitled "Me and the boy Friend; a dance, Shake your feet", by Hazel Shelley, and a delightful dance by Mlle. Terpsichore, entitled "An eastern idol"', *Irish Independent* (26 June 1925), 10.

Your twined, branching hair,
Your grey eye, dew-bright,
Your rich, rounded breast
Turn to lust the sight.

All but sleep with you,
Yield my flesh as thrall,
Woman full of while,
You are free of all![23]

That exclamation mark often lets O'Connor down in his poetry (and he was a bad poet), the blatant appeal to heightened emotion an unnecessary trickery. Introducing temptation to the priesthood, bringing sex to the celibate, admitting the body to literature as a site of desire and pleasure, places O'Connor among the modernists, O'Flaherty, Yeats and others all playing in their various ways with sexual images in the post-Civil War period. O'Connor located these desires in a landscape of frustration, quietly catching those moments of disjunction between what is and what is wanted. He tried to bridge the distance between real and ideal in irony, a step into the distance that allowed for some movement beyond the defined terms of association that were maintained as a means to continue the cultural Civil War. Writing in the *Irish Tribune*, O'Connor promised himself not 'so foolish as to imagine that we can have a nation without the national tradition, that is to say, without the sum of what we have learned, but neither am I foolish enough to think that without our national tradition we cannot have a "bus service"'.[24]

This pragmatism feeds into 'Sion', published a month later, and which details the narrator's meeting a girl in the cinema queue in London, realizing after conversation starts that each knew the other from Cork, where Sylvia Beaumont's father worked the coal boats between Ireland and England. From this, O'Connor draws a Cork at odds with its rebel image, a city in sympathy with its possessors. Sylvia's mother would visit the narrator's family when her husband was at sea, 'she and my father … always talking of England … and between them they used to praise all England and all Englishmen'.[25] Her presence was a prompt to his father's service in

---

23 Frank O'Connor, 'Celibacy (Father Geoffrey Keating sang this)', *Irish Statesman* (6 Feb. 1926), 681–2.   24 Frank O'Connor, 'The heart has reasons', *Irish Tribune* (25 June 1926), 18.   25 Frank O'Connor, 'Sion', *Irish Tribune* (6 Aug. 1926), 9.

the colonies, Cork connected outward to a memory of places far beyond its shores. This gender interaction allows the narrator's father speak from memory, enabling access through empire to the wide world. The reverse happens when Sylvia and the narrator speak in whispers before the cinema's flickering screen.

> Her father, she told me, was dead, and I could only say 'O'. He had been drowned some nine years before.
>
> She crept up closer to me and caught my hand which was about her waist. We talked again of home and how beautiful it was there, and she told me that she dreamt of it often. She felt that she could never be happy outside Ireland.
>
> Neither could I, and I told her so, but it was not often that I found it so difficult to bring enthusiasm for home into my voice. I was embarrassed and I was glad that in the darkness she could not see my embarrassment.[26]

The narrator's embarrassment is multiple, the creeping hand and sad nostalgia combining to displace the exile's proper reply that yes, there is no happiness outside Ireland. That O'Connor disfigures this fundamental motif of the Irish abroad in a cinema, that site of temptation and object of the Free State's first censorship laws, suggests his quiet, conscious, motivation of modernity and its displacements against any settled sense of home.

The idea recurs in O'Connor's stories of the period, figures of modern experience, the cinema, the train, the factory, all pitched in with the established signifiers of belonging, the countryside, the convent, the inner city with its near rural familiarity. 'After fourteen years', published in the *Dublin Magazine*, at that time a quarterly edited by Seumas O'Sullivan, maintains this uncertain world in its portrait of Nicholas Coleman's return to the countryside from the town where he works, to visit a woman he knew in childhood, now a nun. Their conversation is stilted as each skirts the subjects they cannot discuss, bound as they are by the constraints of later lives. Their parting is telling as each tries to find a way to speak to the other, pacing silently, near separately, she 'trying desperately, with anguish, to formulate his name and speak it without emotion, even as he was trying to formulate hers'.[27] They leave each other.

---

26 Frank O'Connor, 'Sion', *Irish Tribune* (6 Aug. 1926), 10.   **27** Frank O'Connor, 'After fourteen years', *Dublin Magazine* (Apr.–June 1929), 46.

The farmers coming from the fair, shouting to one another forward and behind from their lumbering carts, brought to his mind his dreams of yesterday, and he grieved that God had created men without the innocence of natural things, had created them subtle and capricious, with memories in which the past existed like a statue, perfect and unapproachable.[28]

The non-negotiable past is a rock in Coleman's memory, a trauma that allows no approach. O'Connor's appreciation of Joyce can be read in this, the projection of a definite image working against the easier resolutions of expressive communication. In denial of the happy ending, O'Connor maintains a place for desire, desire which disturbs the familiar landscape.

And as the train carried him back to the city the clangour of its iron wheels that said 'ruthutta ruthutta ruthutta' dissolved into a bright mist of conversation in which he could distinctly hear a woman's voice, but the voice said nothing; it was like memory, perfect and unapproachable; and his mind was weighed down by an infinite melancholy that merged with the melancholy of the dark countryside through which he passed – a countryside of lonely steelbright pools that were islanded among the silhouettes of hills and trees.

And the train took him ever farther and farther away, and said with its metallic voice:-

'Ruthutta ruthutta ruthutta!'[29]

The boom of E. M. Forster's Marabar Caves finds its passage from India to Ireland in O'Connor's story, the train's engine the only speaking voice, its repetitive motions removing Coleman further from the site of his anxiety. This is a further stage in the short story after Joyce, the singing Michael Furey outside the window replaced by a shade whose presence is visible, wordless. The end to speech is significant of an art that works from a culture in which words are weighted with political failure, definite commitment a definite problem. This emerges repeatedly in O'Connor's stories of the Civil War, which surface consistently in the period of his apprenticeship. 'September dawn' is in four parts, and represents O'Connor's attempt at new complexity. It follows two republican officers, Hickey and Keown, as they are chased by Free State soldiers. Disbanding their troop in the hope of

28 Ibid., 46–7. **29** Ibid., 47.

escape, the two career through the countryside before seeking shelter in the house of Keown's aunt. Two framed images on the wall combine sex and the republic, Parnell and Emmet two portraits of failed freedom. Within this setting, Keown, the brutal, violent of the two, drinks himself to sleep with whiskey, waking terrified in the middle of the night as he imagines soldiers outside, hunting for him. Hickey has a different awakening as he meets the household's serving girl in the morning's early hours.

> They scarcely spoke. She knelt beside the fireplace and turned the little wheel of the bellows. The seed of fire upon the hearth took light and scattered red lights about his feet. He watched her bent above it, the long golden plait hanging from her left shoulder, the young pointed face taking light from the new-born flame, and when she rose he took her in his arms and kissed her. And in that melancholy kiss an aching of longing was kindled, and he buried his face in the warm flesh of her throat as the kitchen filled with the acrid smell of turf, and the blue smoke drifting through the narrow doorway was caught and swirled away across the grey fields and the dark masses of the trees upon which the sun was rising.[30]

This taboo collage includes images of youth, sex and rural Ireland, all elements that the new state so strongly desired to control. Allowing a republican on the run to play with these forms suggests how the defeated of the Civil War still persisted in the literature of independence as emblems of adversity. The language of these moments is melancholy, regret the mode by which memory is acknowledged as a continuing agent in the public sphere. The morning tryst forms a writing that has left the parlour, no longer peering through the rafters as Synge did at the women below.[31] The actual moment of consummation is still obscure, floating off in O'Connor's story with the turf smoke. But the planned accident of meeting before the house wakes shows that desire can outwit restriction, imagination outplay repression.

This momentary hope is crushed in O'Connor's subsequent short story, 'Guests of the nation', which accounts for the imprisonment and execution of two

---

30 Frank O'Connor, 'September dawn', *Dublin Magazine* (July–Sept. 1929), 20.   **31** 'When I was writing *The shadow of the glen*, some years ago, I got more aid than any learning could have given me, from a chink in the floor of the old Wicklow house where I was staying, that let me hear what was being said by the serving girls in the kitchen'. J.M. Synge, 'Preface', *The playboy of the western world and other plays* (Oxford, 1995), 96.

British soldiers by the IRA during the War of Independence. First published in the *Atlantic Monthly*, with its wide international circulation, the story is set pre-Civil War; going back meant a step forward as 'Guests of the nation' is one of O'Connor's best. The story works in symmetry, the two British captives, Hawkins (known throughout as 'Awkins') and Belcher, held by Noble and the narrator, who goes by the name of Napoleon. In this it is possible to read the influence of Joyce, *Work in progress* suggesting the impact of colonial history through tangential allusion to the wars of the French republic ('This is the triplewon hat of Lipoleum. Tip. Lipoleumhat. This is the Willingdone on his same white harse, the Cokenhape'[32]). O'Connor's building collage includes one further IRA man who visits the house where the men stay, Jeremiah Donovan a part reincarnation of Jeremiah O'Donovan Rossa, the nineteenth-century Fenian. 'Guests of the nation' is in this sense part of the new fiction that masquerades as realism in the post-independence period, the identifiable elements of speech and setting contributing to a historical imagination that will not let pasts lie. This imagination can be read in disaffection with that revolutionary history. The argument alternatively might be that a commitment to stand against continues in this writing, futility recast as persistence. For if this story suggests anything it suggests that the new state, as republicans argued, was built on deadly compromise. Hints of this unease register early on. During the early period of Belcher and Hawkins' captivity,

> It seemed, as they explained it, that the Second used to have little evenings of their own, and some of the girls of the neighbourhood would turn in, and, seeing they were such decent fellows, our lads couldn't well ignore the two Englishmen, but invited them in and were hail fellow well met with them. 'Awkins told me he learned to dance 'The Walls of Limerick' and 'The Siege of Ennis' and 'The Waves of Tory' in a night or two, though naturally he could not return the compliment, because our lads at that time did not dance foreign dances on principle.[33]

This is barely fiction. As O'Connor wrote his short story, Ernie O'Malley, IRA commander and republican, was drafting his own memoir of the troubles, *On another man's wound*, the notes of which remain in handwritten notebooks. One section remembers social activity after the Easter Rising, when the Volunteers held

---

32 James Joyce, 'Opening pages of a work in progress', *transition*, 1 (Apr. 1927), 13–14. **33** Frank O'Connor, 'Guests of the nation', *Atlantic Monthly* (Jan. 1931), 80.

ceilidhs at which 'Only purely Irish dances were allowed, no sets or Continental dances'.[34] The favourites were:

> Round dances, the Eight Hand, Sixteen hand and fair Reels, the High Call Cap: moving in circles, reversing, side-stepping, crossing, dancing back to back. Line dances, The Siege of Ennis, The Bridge of Athlone, Rince Fada, The Waves of Tory: advancing and retreating, entering the breach, bending under a hand arch or moving as the tide.[35]

These dances continued post-1922, providing a regular meeting place for dissidents of all persuasions. O'Connor's invitation of the British soldiers to these events is an invitation to hybrid history, 'Guests of the nation' a careful uncovering of the complex roots of his contemporary society. He does this by his narrator's patrol of the margins. There is a certain comedy in Hawkins' debate on the afterlife, and his claim to be an anarchist, both of which direct his listeners to difficult questions of loyalty and judgment. When the message comes from the intelligence officer, Feeney (a play again on Fenian), the two soldiers are taken outside the safety of the house of their keeping. They move 'down towards the fatal bog',[36] this feature of the landscape becoming the recurrent, negative, motif for hidden memory. In the remaining pages the bog becomes the silent figure, like the voiceless woman who haunted Nicholas Coleman's train journey in 'After fourteen years'. In 'Guests of the nation', Hawkins answers the quiet with disbelief that his end is near.

> By this time I began to perceive in the dusk the desolate edges of the bog that was to be their last earthly bed, and so great a sadness overtook my spirit that I could not answer him. We walked along the edge of it in the black darkness, and every now and again 'Awkins would call a halt and tirelessly begin again about us being chums, and I was in despair that nothing but the cold and open grave made ready for his presence would convince him that we meant it at all.[37]

That cold continues in the word's association with Donovan, who works himself to anger before clumsily shooting Hawkins, who is finished by a second shot from

---

34 Ernest O'Malley, University College Dublin, MS p17b/147. **35** Ibid. **36** Frank O'Connor, 'Guests of the nation', 84. **37** Ibid., 85.

the narrator, bringing the reader to the point of the gun, before Belcher is killed. The dead men disappear in the ground.

> I don't remember much about the burying but that it was worse than all the rest, because we had to carry the warm corpses a few yards before we sunk them in the windy bog. It was all mad, lonely, and desolate, with only a bit of lantern between ourselves and the pitch-blackness, and birds hooting and screeching all round disturbed by the guns. Noble had to search 'Awkins first to get the letter from his mother. Then, having smoothed all signs of the grave away, Noble and I collected our tools, said good-bye to the others, and went back along the desolate edge of the treacherous bog without a word.[38]

The burial of memory coincides with the failure of language. 'Guests of the nation' is a careful attempt to replay the moment of this breakdown in all its fragility, a maintenance of the revolutionary past in the present, the bodies not yet recovered, the bog still holding its secrets. O'Connor's story works from a culture still in violent transition at the time of its writing. 'Guests of the nation' is, in the end, about more than the disillusion of revolutionary violence. The burial scene may be an end to the affair, but the narrator's silent farewell underlines the treachery of a place, the bog, which keeps its secrets intact for possible recovery. The narrator's disquiet over the bog is disquiet over language, Hawkins, that fountain of talk, dried up. The condition of silence is the story's tragedy and its subject, the condition O'Connor fights against in his manipulations of dialect, speech and narration. In this, O'Connor retains a commitment to a literature whose politics persist in memory, his art the complex staging of the frictions that make for freedom, working against the execution that threatens to silence its participants forever.

> Noble told me afterwards he felt he saw everything ten times as big, perceiving nothing round him but the little patch of black bog with the two Englishmen stiffening into it, but with me it was the way everything was small, as though the patch of bog where the two Englishmen lay was a thousand miles from me, and even Noble mumbling just behind me and the old woman and the birds and the bloody stars were all very far away, and myself too small and insignificant to say a prayer.[39]

38 Ibid., 87. **39** Ibid., 88.

Frank O'Connor and a vanishing Ireland

TERENCE BROWN

In 1969 the Irish-American critic and subsequent novelist Thomas Flanagan wrote of Frank O'Connor:

> He wrote close to a hundred short stories of which a full score at least –
> including 'Guests of the Nation', 'In the Train', 'Uprooted', 'The Luceys',
> 'The Mad Lomasneys', 'The Stepmother', 'The Holy Door', 'The
> Masculine Principle' – seem to me as fine as any in our literature. But in
> Ireland it will be a while before his work is properly appreciated, and ... as
> with Yeats, precisely because the personality was vivid and strong as the
> work is distinguished. The singular adventures, spiritual and public, out
> of which the literature of modern Ireland issued, made of its greatest
> writers exemplary figures, arguing within their art and outside it the
> meaning of Irish experience. But now Ireland has joined our common
> world, and hopes to join its common market, and there may no longer be
> room or need for a writer like Frank O'Connor.[1]

Flanagan points here to O'Connor's central achievement which was as a short-story writer. And I will be dealing mainly with that aspect of his *œuvre* in this essay, since it is there that I believe his claim on us as an artist most fully rests. But he does so in a way which raises doubts as to whether O'Connor, already somewhat neglected in Ireland at his death in 1966, would get his due in the new Ireland coming into being, the fruit of five decades of the Irish independence O'Connor had fought for and then found so great a disappointment. For Flanagan hinted in 1969 that as the significance of O'Connor's life in pre- and post-revolutionary Ireland ceased to be a matter of contention or admiration and faded into the historical frame, his work could lose its purchase on Irish sensibilities and cease to seem necessary to us.

The life certainly had striking, compelling significance as it was lived. Born on

---

1 Thomas Flanagan, 'The Irish writer' in Maurice Sheehy (ed.), *Michael/Frank: studies on Frank O'Connor with a bibliography of his writings* (Dublin, 1969), 150.

17 September in 1903 in a poor district of Cork city in an unhappy home, from the start literature offered Michael O'Donovan, a sensitive mother's boy, an escape from the grimness of circumstance that would mark him for life as a romantic for whom reality was often a painful intrusion. Formal schooling ended when he was twelve but not before he had encountered in the schoolteacher Daniel Corkery, later professor in University College Cork, the first of those older men who would serve as substitute fathers for the emotionally volatile creature he was (they would include both Æ and W.B. Yeats, when Corkery's influence had waned). It was Corkery who introduced him to the romance of the Gael and of the Irish language, replacing the idealism of the imperial dream he had relished in English school and adventure yarns in his boyhood with a more immediate glamour. For the reliques of ancient Gaeldom lay to hand in rural Cork (his own grandmother knew the language) and the pursuit of linguistic proficiency was accordingly vested with a nationalistic fervour which made it more attractive than the imperialism in whose service his own father had enlisted as a Munster Fusilier. By the time British forces were trying to suppress a war of independence in Ireland O'Connor's schooling in that nursery of freedom fighters, the Gaelic League, had brought the British soldier's son to membership of the volunteer force which fought the War of Independence and to a minor role in the legion of the rearguard after the Treaty. O'Connor was interned as a republican during the civil war. From the age of about thirteen, therefore, until his twentieth year he had been carried on a tidal wave of romantic feeling which then cast his generation on the shores of a disillusionment from which many of them never really recovered. The fact that so many of the revolutionaries *were* so youthful may in part account for the disillusionment numbers of them felt as they tried to make their way in life in the first decade of independence. The revolution had been their university (the prison camp in which O'Connor was interned had its literary men and savants who contributed to his education) and to read their memoirs is to be reminded of that unhappy breed of people who regret their undergraduate days for the rest of their lives, for whom it can never be glad confident morning again.

O'Connor in the 1920s was in his own terms a 'strayed reveller' from the Irish Literary Revival and it was in the receding tide of that cultural enthusiasm that had accompanied the political upheaval of period, that the young man first made his mark as a writer. It was as one of Æ's acolytes, while working as a librarian in Wicklow, that he began to see his work in print in the *Irish Statesman*. He published verse translations from the Gaelic, poems and critical prose. A short story 'War' published by AE in the *Irish Statesman* in 1926 (only republished posthumously) gave a sign of what was to be the matter and tenor of his first published collection of stories: a compassionate, disappointed, comic treatment of the War of Independence and its fratricidal aftermath. An almost studied indifference in *Guests of the nation* (1931), his first collection of short stories, about the ideological differences between Free Staters and republicans (one tale recounts how an opportunistic shop-keeper is ready to sell a British machine gun to either side), makes this work from the pen of an ex-republican prisoner, a work of forsaken enthusiasms. As such it registered the alienation of those in O'Connor's generation and the next, who as he himself famously put it 'would emigrate to the ends of the earth, not because the country was poor but because it was mediocre' in flight from a 'new Establishment of Church and State'.[2] The principal impression this collection leaves is of a scattered military campaign set against wild and inhospitable landscape in which grotesquely comic incident, even the absurd, vie with a compassionate revulsion from actual violence (as in the title story) and with an awakening eroticism. In much of O'Connor mature work the sexuality is treated with pragmatic realism and sometimes with a factitious man-of-the-world knowingness which can be tiresome (as in the cynicism dramatized in 'Don Juan's temptation' for example), but in *Guests of the nation* one senses the quick of almost Laurentian experience. In 'September dawn' a young volunteer on the run with a companion takes shelter overnight in an aunt's farmhouse. Hickey, the protagonist of the tale is already tiring of the futile, dangerous skirmishes of their retreat and encounters in a servant girl in his aunt's house intimations of the life he is missing (the conflict of love and country is made explicit in the story in the aunt's isolated veneration of the fallen Parnell). As a dawn breaks after a stormy night the power of sexual attraction is set in apposition with the violence and fear of guerrilla action in a charged symbolic conclusion:

> She asked if he had been disturbed by the wind and nodded, smiling. Then she knelt beside the fireplace and turned the little wheels of the bellows. The seed of the fire upon the hearth took light and scattered red sparks about his stockinged feet where he stood, leaning against the mantelpiece. He watched her bent above it, the long golden plait hanging across her left shoulder, the young pointed face taking light from the new-born flame, and as she rose he took her in his arms and kissed her. She leaned against his shoulder in her queer silent way, with no shyness. And

2 Frank O'Connor, *An only child* (1961), cited in Flanagan, 'The Irish writer', 153.

for him in that melancholy kiss an ache of longing was kindled, and he buried his face in the warm flesh of her throat, as the kitchen filled with the acrid smell of turf; while the blue smoke drifting through the narrow doorway was caught and whirled headlong through grey fields and dark masses of trees upon which an autumn sun was rising.[3]

Guests of the nation identified O'Connor as a promising new writer, whose early life had been lived as if the coming to adulthood of the writer himself had found its stirring expression in the invention of a nation. As Declan Kiberd has remarked, 'To read the autobiographies of Yeats, George Moore or Frank O'Connor is an experience akin to the study of Whitman's 'Song of Myself': it is to be constantly impressed and unnerved by the casual ease with which they substitute themselves as a shorthand for their country.'[4] So when O'Connor published *Guests of the nation* in 1931 with its subversive indifference to ideology, that action made his an oppositional voice in the new republican Ireland. Éamon de Valera would take power in 1932. Though the book (excepting the title story) was largely, prentice work it had an immediate relevance to post-independence Ireland that we can no longer experience. That a Michael O'Donovan/Frank O'Connor could produce such a book was a signal that the oppositional energies that the young had formerly directed against imperial power would now find a target in the forms of nationalism that were shaping the new state.

Had O'Connor in the 1930s and 40s chosen to explore how the erotic principle in life disturbs the public sphere, which 'September dawn' expressed in lyrical form, his opposition would have contributed to what Conor Cruise O'Brien writing as Donat O'Donnel characterized as 'literary Parnellism'.[5] He found this at work, indeed, in the writings of O'Connor's fellow Corkonian, Seán O'Faoláin, especially in his novel *Bird alone* (1936). Instead, O'Connor largely ignored overt sexuality as a theme in the short stories of 1930s (though his novel *Dutch interior* of 1940 was banned by the censorship probably because one its characters apparently has an abortion) and registered his alienation from the Free State predominantly in socio-cultural terms. His voice was raised in protest against the narrow provincialism of the new order. As a former irregular of civil war days, his choosing to write a celebratory, fierce biography of Michael Collins

---

3 Frank O'Connor, *Guests of the nation* (Dublin, 1979), 73. **4** Declan Kiberd, *Inventing Ireland* (London, 1995), 119. **5** See Donat O'Donnel, *Maria Cross: imaginative patterns in a group of modern Catholic writers* (London, 1953).

(*The big fellow* was published in 1937) was like a personal declaration of intellectual independence. Summarizing this aspect of his career one of his biographers concludes that in the first two decades of independence he established himself as

> Ireland's most abrasive voice of conscience. He believed he was standing alone, fighting a sort of guerrilla war against the forces of stupidity and vested interest. To clarify the image of Collins [which he did in a vigorously individual biography in 1937], to support the novels of his friends, to decry the pillorying of a public figure on the stage of the national theatre, to defend an old storyteller and his wife against hoodlum priests, were all simply moral obligations of the artist in a provincial country.[6]

At the same time he developed his technique as a short-story writer, simultaneously engaged and ironic in tone, to allow him to become an acute observer of the ways in which a narrow society deformed the lives of an Irish lower middle-class whose young people in particular (and O'Connor is very good on adolescence) bore the burden of a stultifying provincialism of mind and heart. Some of the best of the stories in his best single collection, *Crab apple jelly* (1944), explore this theme. I am thinking especially of 'The Luceys' and of 'The mad Lomasneys'. The former, which O'Connor for years considered his favourite among his tales, is a tragedy of small-town caution, while the second is an unsettling tale of missed marital opportunity, where any assertion of female independence in a constricted social environment is reckoned so unusual as to seem deranged. Rita, the individualistic girl of the story, is forced into a kind of madness in a maddening world as she selects a husband on a whim.

It was in Frank O'Connor's own private life that a form of Parnellism had real effect. For in the personal sphere, at the kind of professional cost which is unimaginable today, he refused to be governed by the mores of a puritanical time and the conventions of a society that had refined hypocrisy to an art form. If the new nation sought to define itself as a zone of sexual purity, where contraception and divorce were banned and where men and women were forced to endure loveless marriages, then he would not serve, and he would take the consequences of living as he saw fit, however difficult and painful.

Yet in registering protest in cultural terms, only coming close to direct denunciation of contemporary Irish sexual mores in his brilliant realization of Brian

---

6 James Matthews, *Voices: a life of Frank O'Connor* (Dublin, 1983), 221.

Merriman's sexually exuberant poem *The midnight court* (published in 1945 and banned in 1946), where the female sexual appetite that works frankly serves as rebuke to a censorious society, O'Connor was also taking real risks. It was an article of 1942 on specifically cultural issues, published in the English periodical *Horizon* that made him a marked man in Ireland. In an Irish issue of Cyril Connolly's periodical, which instantly met the censor's interdiction (probably because it included a sexually explicit section of Kavanagh's *The great hunger*), he opined in brutally direct terms about the current condition of Ireland in 'The future of Irish literature'. 'I am bewildered' he told an English readership, already inclined to view Ireland with disfavour as a cowardly neutral in a war to the death with Fascism,

> by the complete lack of a relationship between Irish literature and any form of life, within or without Ireland. Blandly, sentimentally, maundering to itself, Irish literature sails off on one tack, while off on another go hand in hand Mr de Valera and the Church, the murder gangs and the Catholic secret societies. It may be argued that they are the business of publicists, not of artists, but there are no publicists, there is no public opinion, and if the artists do not fight, who will? And if we don't fight, and new circumstances don't settle Mr de Valera's hash for us, what is to become of Ireland or Irish literature.[7]

It is certainly the case that O'Connor in *Horizon* was only expressing, if a bit more brutally, the kind of things that Seán O'Faoláin was reiterating in his *Bell* editorials in the 1940s about what Benedict Kiely was later to dub 'the grocers' republic'. But O'Connor had been washing dirty linen before an English audience, which made his sin a mortal one as far as 'official Ireland' was concerned. The outspoken critic had gone too far and became *persona non grata*. He was banned from the national airwaves. It was a bitter blow that gravely affected his capacity to make a living in his own country, a country that he loved with such a passion that his enraged indignation was aroused whenever he felt she let herself down. This is a note of large-hearted love and exasperation that sounds in his warmly engaging travel book of 1947, *Irish miles* (one of his best books I dare to suggest, certainly the one in which the reader feels closest to the emotionally mercurial, opinionated, passionate being so many who knew him well testify he was). In its pages an

7 Cited in Matthews, *Voices*, 188.

ancient vital civilisation is honoured in the midst of contemporary dilapidation and indifference. Architectural dereliction in the book is a measure of a people's current narrowness of vision. Anger mixes with comic invention and high-spirited exuberance as in the following passage. The narrator and his travelling companion Célimène are in Callan, County Meath, where there is one 'really charming church' and little else:

> After one good look at the church and the main street, Célimène put on an important air and exclaimed 'Sewing machine needles!'. There is a certain stage of dereliction in Irish country towns which tells her exactly what commodities vanished from the rest of the country are likely to found in it. In Virginia it was pot-scourers, and clothes pegs in Gurtnahoo. When she gets like that aesthetics are lost on her, and while she was colloguing inside the shop, I stood sadly at the door looking up at the ivy-covered tower till it seemed as the tower was looking down on me. It struck me with great force as I looked up and down the street that it and I were the only civilized things in it – I fear my head had been turned by the beauty of the Jerpoint tomb.
>
> 'What the hell brought us to this hole?' I asked aloud.
>
> 'It's all very well for you' the tower replied, unexpectedly. 'You can get out of it in the morning, But I have to stay on here'.[8]

Irish miles was in some ways a valedictory work. For by the late 40s and throughout the 1950s Frank O'Connor's life and career, which had involved a trajectory that had taken the youthful revolutionary to the role of disillusioned social critic, which had been so imbricated with the history of his country, took on representative quality in a new way. He became an exile, like so many of the post-independence Irish intelligentsia, first in England and then in the United States, as personal and professional necessity made Ireland impossible for him except as a visitor. The North American academy and the *New Yorker* gave him the kind of personal space and economic security in which he flourished in career terms as short-story writer and author of critical books in a way he would scarcely have been able to do in 1950s Ireland. When in the 1960s, in a liberalizing climate, he returned to live in his native country, and taught for a year and a little more at Trinity College, Dublin, it was as a widely renowned man of letters – short-story

---

8 Frank O'Connor, *Irish miles* (London, 1988), 48.

writer, his collected stories had appeared in two volumes in 1952 and 1954 (the second volume would become the basis of *Collection two* in 1964), translator (his translations from the Irish appeared as *Kings, lords and commons* in 1959), critic (with books to his name on the novel and on Shakespeare as well as that boldly-argued reflection on his own art form, *The lonely voice*, which was published in 1962), autobiographer (*An only child* with its vivid, intimate account of coming of age as a romantic sensitive plant in the rough soil of a Cork childhood and youth, appeared in 1962). As such he would, had he lived, have brought a much-needed internationalism of outlook and experience as well as vast, intimate knowledge of local Irish lore and tradition to Irish academe which in that decade was beginning to direct a more focussed attention to the field of Anglo-Irish literature than it hitherto had done. O'Connor's pioneering contribution to the field of Irish Studies, *The backward look* (published as *A short history of Irish literature* in the United States) appeared posthumously in 1967, helping to define a developing field while giving its Irish readers knowledge of what a resource had been taken from them by its author's untimely death on 10 March 1966.

So there we have the shape of O'Connor's career in its time and place, considered as one of the period's 'exemplary figures' – as Thomas Flanagan has it – as one of the country's writers 'arguing within their art and outside the meaning of Irish experience'. As that time and place have receded in memory since O'Connor's death (and Flanagan was right to detect a new period in the wings in 1969), it has been increasingly difficult for O'Connor to get his due as a writer in the new Ireland that has come into existence since Ireland joined the EEC in 1973, and since the Celtic Tiger roared in the 1990s, that knows little of the high romance which inspired a revolutionary generation, nor of the disillusionment and frustration of the first four decades of Irish independence. His tales it is true can be sure of representation in any collection of twentieth-century Irish short stories, but beyond that his work has, I fear, been significantly neglected. The critical literature on him remains small with only three monograph-length works published to date (the most recent appeared in 1998). And it is perhaps telling that two of the most widely-read recent general books on Irish literature, Declan Kiberd's *Inventing Ireland* and his *Irish classics* make only passing reference to O'Connor.

In part, of course, this neglect may be due simply to the trough in reputation which often follows an author's death and may also to a degree be because the short story as a form is often reckoned by critics to have less significance than the novel (Joyce's *Dubliners* only got the critical attention it deserved in the academic world when the genius of *Ulysses* had been indisputably established); but there is I think more to it than that. Ireland, I think, has changed in the last twenty or so years in ways that have made the kind of man Frank O'Connor was and the kind of Ireland about which he wrote so distinctively and knowledgeably seem almost wholly remote, scarcely comprehensible to many younger readers. And in this new climate with its different sensibility there are things that can seem unfashionably archaic about what O'Connor was and what he produced. It is not of course that the archaism itself is a barrier to acquiring a readership; Victorian writers like Trollope (whom, incidentally O'Connor admired) can, for example can command today a wide readership although many of their concerns and values can seem foreign to us. Yet it perhaps takes time for a writer like O'Connor who was so much of his time and place to be appreciated by succeeding generations. And we must remember that the Victorians seemed to a generation who read Lytton Strachey's *Eminent Victorians* in 1918, when that iconoclastic book appeared in the last year of a terrible, epoch changing war, the epitome of all that was hypocritical. For a readership becoming attuned to modernist experiment, a Trollope with his weighty three-deckers or indeed a Tennyson with his leather bound presentation copies could be denigrated with the single word 'Victorian' (in fact it has only been in recent years that Tennyson has begun to be appreciated again for the great poet he is).

O'Connor I sense was the chronicler of an almost vanished Ireland, and in fact was one of what is now, in this period of very rapid change, becoming a vanishing type. I mean by this notion of a 'vanishing type' those Irish inheritors of the nineteenth-century English role of man of letters, who in twentieth-century Ireland managed to combine a deep appreciation and knowledge of the native inheritance of legend, lore and tradition (often derived from oral sources) with literary production of real excellence in a variety of genres and who contributed too to critical debate. They wrote (and Benedict Kiely may be one of the very last of them) with secure knowledge of a provincial Ireland, now almost disappeared, which had certainly adapted to modernity but had not yet been swamped by the flood of mass-media versions of reality that currently determine the globalized zeitgeist. They were in touch too with a living tradition of oral and popular literature and song, and with that intersection in Irish life between history, mythology and local, familial lore which in the past bound the generations together. Their way of writing and talking actually reflected and reflects a way of being in the world which no longer seems in accord with the lived rhythms of our actual life. It is often a matter of tone in their writing, so close in fact to the tone of talk, a tone that can seem of a vanished age. For many years it was a normative tone in Irish literature as Thomas Kilroy advised us thirty years ago, just before our new age, if we take EEC entry as a watershed date:

> At the centre of Irish fiction is the anecdote. The distinctive characteristic of our 'first novel', *Castle Rackrent,* that which makes it what it is, is not so much its ideal, revolutionary as that may be, but its imitation of a speaking voice engaged in the telling of a tale. The model will be exemplary for the reader who has read widely in Irish fiction: it a voice heard over and over again, whatever its accent, a voice with a supreme confidence in its own histrionics, one that assumes with its audience a shared ownership of the told tale and all that it implies: a taste for anecdote, an unshakeable belief in the value of human actions, a belief that life may be adequately encapsulated into stories that require no reference, no qualification, beyond their own selves.[9]

We can hear that voice over and over again in Frank O'Connor's writings, with its confident opinionation, vigorous editorializing (even in the short stories), its assumption of an audience intimate with a shared social world. Here for example is a paragraph or two of a revised version of 'The custom of the country' from *The common chord* (1947; the original was more laconic). The story opens with the familiarity of man beginning a conversation in a pub:

> It is remarkable the difference that even one foreigner can make in a community when he is not yet accustomed to its ways, the way he can isolate its customs and hold them up for your inspection. Things that had been as natural to you as bread suddenly need to be explained, and the really maddening thing is that you can't explain them. After a while you begin to wonder if they're real at all. Sometimes you doubt if you're real yourself.[10]

An Englishman arrives in town and both 'fits' in and does not. The narrator, clearly a member of what now would now be called in our multi-cultural times, the host community, continues:

9 Thomas Kilroy, 'Tellers of tales', *Times Literary Supplement* (17 March 1972), 301–2. **10** Frank O'Connor, 'The custom of the country', *The mad Lomasneys and other stories* (London, 1970), 71.

Take for instance, the time when he started walking out with Anna Martin. Anna was a really nice girl even if she was a bit innocent. That is never much harm in a girl you care for. Anna's innocence showed even in her face, plump, dark, childish, and all in smooth curves from the bulging boyish forehead to the big dimpled chin, with features nesting in the hollows as if only waiting for a patch of sunlight to emerge.

Her mother, a widow woman of good family who had had the misfortune to marry one Willie Martin, a man of no class, kept a tiny huckster shop at a corner of the Cross. She was a nice well-preserved, well-spoken, little roly-poly of a woman with bad feet which gave her a waddle, and piles, which made her sit on a high hard chair, and she sat for the greater part of the day in the kitchen behind the shop with her hands joined in her lap and an air of regret for putting the world to the trouble, of knowing her, though all the time she was thinking complacently of the past glories of her family, the Henebry-Hayeses of Coolnaleama.[11]

That tone now seems – in its assured confidence, its apprehension of a culture as a whole way of life that can almost unconsciously take itself for granted until disturbed by the arrival of a stranger – truly of the past. To attempt to represent current Ireland in such terms would be to commit an obvious anachronism and it is telling that one of the most successful novels of the 1990s was Patrick McCabe's *The butcher boy*, which fed in blackly parodic fashion on the vision of small-town and provincial Irish life which had sustained fiction like that of Frank O'Connor, in stories like 'The custom of the country'.

If change, as I have been suggesting, has made O'Connor seem somehow superseded in our Ireland of post-modern ironies, fabrications, parodic takes on form and genre, filmic texts, where passionate commitments and vital opinions can only be indulged when proffered between quotation marks, it crucial to point that O'Connor was in the best of his stories remarkably attuned to the precise ramifications of change in his own day and explored them with a subtlety that could be an object lesson in artistic integrity to any young writer seeking to respond to the experience of cultural transformation in our own time. In this regard at the very least he makes his claim on us (and we must also remember that in the story 'Guests of the nation' he wrote the classic heart-stoppingly memorable account of the effects on its perpetrators of murder in a proclaimedly virtuous

11 Ibid., 71–2.

cause; for a century that saw countless acts of violence committed in the belief that the end would justify the means, 'Guests of the nation' was a grimly salutary text). I am thinking of stories such as 'The majesty of the law' and the remarkable 'In the train' which attend to moments when a modernising Ireland, with its central government and legal system, clash with immemorial custom. But I wish to conclude by invoking 'Uprooted' as an example of O'Connor at his best. This is an atmospheric masterpiece of displaced consciousness, of restlessness, of return to a natal place which can no longer be home, a study of ineluctable psychological change in the midst of social change. It is as apposite in our Ireland of immigration from developing countries as it was when migration involved leaving a distant parish and an island tradition for the capital city. The final movement of this five-part tale, when in the family home the teacher/narrator and his priest brother awake to the realization that their familial past can never be recovered, combines romantic longing with the cold realism of a new day in an unforgettable representation of the brute reality of displacement. It is essential O'Connor, depending on his acute ear for dialogue, his emotional sensitivity to the loneliness of the human person and, beneath his tendency to court sentiment for sentiment's sake – which can sometimes undermine his achievements – on his awareness of the implacable in human existence that gives life a tragic dimension.

'Fierce passions for middle-aged men': Frank O'Connor and Daniel Corkery

PAUL DELANEY

At an early age Frank O'Connor came under the influence of the writer and teacher Daniel Corkery. This influence was profound and fed into O'Connor's decision to write as a young man. Corkery also imparted an interest in the Irish language to his young charge, and later played a part in O'Connor's decision to take the republican side during the Civil War. The ensuing rift between the two writers is one of the more famous, bad-tempered episodes in Irish literary history. It would appear that from the moment the two men began to fall out, a few months after O'Connor's release from Gormanstown internment camp, in December 1923, many of their subsequent exchanges were marked by mistrust and misunderstanding. O'Connor seems to have stretched out a hand of friendship to his former mentor several times thereafter, but each of these gestures was met with a studied and perhaps wilful silence. The gift of a signed copy of *Guests of the nation* in 1931, for instance, went unanswered and this not surprisingly upset the younger writer. 'Catch me do it again', he is reported to have written to his sweetheart Nancy McCarthy.[1] For his part, Corkery seems to have grown reticent to engage in any kind of communication with O'Connor after the publication of this volume of short stories. It has even been alleged that Corkery refused to allow any mention of O'Connor – or his other great protégé Seán O'Faoláin – in his presence in his later years. James McKeon has summed up the relationship between the two writers by stating, quite simply, that the two men 'drifted apart when the pupil outgrew the master'.[2]

McKeon is not alone in advancing this thesis. Maurice Harmon has similarly asserted that O'Faoláin and O'Connor both 'outgr[e]w their dependence on Corkery' in the years after the Civil War.[3] Although this thesis is refreshingly brief, it nonetheless runs the risk of simplifying a complex – and, for O'Connor, at least, an enduring – association into something straightforward and patronizing. McKeon's thesis, of course, is supported by the popular charge that Corkery was a

1 James Matthews, *Voices: a life of Frank O'Connor* (Dublin, 1983), 78. 2 James McKeon, *Frank O'Connor: a life* (Edinburgh, 1998), 25. 3 Maurice Harmon, *Seán O'Faoláin: a life* (London, 1994), 66.

bigoted doctrinaire whose work became trapped in the narrow philosophies of the Irish Ireland movement. This charge has been advanced by scholars and critics over the years, and is borne out in some of Corkery's more infamous intellectual fantasies – such as his dismissal of the entire tradition of Anglo-Irish literature in *Synge and Anglo-Irish literature* (1931), and his belief that unless writers are absorbed in the forces of Nationalism, Religion (by which he meant Catholicism) and Land, their work should not be considered Irish.[4] Within this context, it is hardly surprising that Corkery's work has often been read as an exclusivist argument which set the limits for cultural expression in the fledgling Free State. Indeed, Corkery's name has been regularly invoked to signify an intolerant and insular mode of defining ideas of Ireland and 'Irishness'.[5]

While this is the principal way in which Corkery has come to be remembered, several commentators have suggested that his legacy is more complex and significant than this. Declan Kiberd, for example, has cautioned against an all-too-easy positioning of Corkery as 'the whipping-boy of all right-on-pluralists' and has argued that in many respects Corkery might be considered Ireland's first postcolonial critic.[6] Seán Ó Tuama has also lamented the fact that in his opinion this writer has become 'a casualty of ideological warfare' in recent times.[7] In the only full-length biography of Corkery which has been published to date, *'Life that is exile': Daniel Corkery and the search for Irish Ireland* (1993), Patrick Maume also argued in favour of a cautious reappraisal of this polemical figure.[8] In Maume's study Corkery emerges as a more complicated and less assured individual whose interests mutated – and narrowed – in the early decades of the twentieth century. In effect, Maume's story is that of a sensitive intellectual who became an increasingly exclusionary critical figure. According to the logic of this argument, it is not that O'Connor – or, indeed, O'Faoláin – simply 'outgrew' Corkery, but rather that each of the writers chose different paths and allowed their work to follow different directions in the post-independence period.

---

4 Daniel Corkery, *Synge and Anglo-Irish literature* (Cork, 1931).   **5** For a particularly virulent instance see George Brandon Saul, *Daniel Corkery* (Lewisburg, 1973).   **6** Declan Kiberd, 'W.B. Yeats: endings and beginnings: a review essay', *Éire-Ireland*, 32:2&3 (Summer & Fall 1997), 87; Declan Kiberd, *Inventing Ireland: the literature of the modern nation* (London, 1995), 558.   **7** Seán Ó Tuama, 'Daniel Corkery, cultural philosopher, literary critic: a memoir' in *Repossessions: selected essays on the Irish literary heritage* (Cork, 1995), 247.   **8** Patrick Maume, *'Life that is exile': Daniel Corkery and the search for Irish Ireland* (Belfast, 1993).

It is significant that O'Connor anticipated aspects of this thinking in the first volume of his autobiography, *An only child* (1961). Looking back to the period of the Troubles, and his involvement in republican activities at this time, O'Connor, like many other young men of his age, recalled that experience as being formative. 'I was changing', he remarked, and growing up too, the reader might add, 'but though I did not realize it till much later, Corkery was changing too … and the man I loved was turning into someone I should not even be able to understand'.[9] O'Connor suggested several reasons for this change and in particular drew attention to two incidents which had a profound effect on determining the scope of Corkery's subsequent interests as a writer and critic – the brutal murder of Tomás MacCurtain and the hunger strike of Terence MacSwiney. MacCurtain and MacSwiney were successive Lord Mayors of Cork and MacSwiney, especially, was a close friend of Corkery's. In *An only child*, O'Connor argued that Corkery was so disturbed by the deaths of both men that they left a lasting impression on the way that Corkery interpreted ideas like nationalism, self-sacrifice and the responsibilities of literature. According to O'Connor, a direct consequence of both episodes was a commitment – a life-long commitment – on Corkery's part, to the ideals that both men espoused and died for. This commitment was remarkably unlike O'Connor's response to the experience of the Civil War, which led to a loss of faith in politics and a turning away from what he termed 'the death-in-life of the Nationalist Catholic establishment'.[10] 'I was sick to death of the worship of martyrdom', O'Connor was to later recall, 'the only martyr I had come close to was a poor boy from the lanes like myself, and he hadn't wanted to die any more than I did.'[11] By contrast, O'Connor imagined that the deaths of MacCurtain and MacSwiney helped to turn Corkery into a prescriptive critic blinded by history and abstract principles.

This is the primary reason which is put forward in *An only child* to account for Corkery's narrowing of interest. However, it is also suggested that Corkery's fate was that of the cultural introvert who, in the words of Seán O'Faoláin, was stifled by 'the soft smother of the provincial featherbed'.[12] O'Connor and O'Faoláin both commented on the attractions and dangers of provincialism in their autobiographies, *An only child* and *Vive moi!* Both associated provincialism with regional pride and love of locality, for instance, but both writers also aligned it with frustration, narrow-mindedness and cultural dependency. What is more, both suggested

9 Frank O'Connor, *An only child* (London, 1961), 142. **10** O'Connor, *An only child*, 189. **11** Ibid., 177. **12** Seán O'Faoláin, *Vive moi!: an autobiography* (London, 1965), 135.

that Corkery was aware of its double-edged appeal. Some of the risks associated with provincialism are implicit in the epigraph which Corkery chose (via the American writer Henry David Thoreau) for his only novel, *The threshold of quiet* (1917) – 'the mass of men lead lives of quiet desperation'. These risks form a vital part of the fabric of that novel which details the disappointments and limitations of life in turn-of-the-century Cork. Not only did O'Connor and O'Faoláin both argue that their former mentor was conscious of the ambivalent lure of provincialism, however, they also imagined that Corkery – like many of the characters in *The threshold of quiet* – had fallen prey to it. This is why O'Connor supposed that his one-time mentor 'had a good deal of the harshness and puritanism of the provincial intellectual'.[13] It is also why O'Faoláin suggested that Corkery's 'circumstances and environment exhausted him' to the point where he became socially and intellectually 'dehydrated'.[14]

O'Connor and O'Faoláin both provided sensitive portraits of Corkery in their autobiographical works. Both drew an image of a kind, hospitable man who warmly encouraged their first efforts at writing. What is more, both paid special attention to various personal characteristics which they considered key to Corkery's being, such as self-control, intellectual curiosity, basic humanity and generosity of spirit. In many respects, their portraits of 'that gentle little man' (to quote O'Connor) are at odds with the more familiar image of Corkery as the *bête noir* or 'effective laureate' of de Valera's Ireland.[15] Although their portraits are strikingly similar, however, there is nonetheless a crucial difference in the textual space which each writer apportioned Corkery in their life stories. Whereas O'Faoláin's representation of Corkery is cut to two and a half pages (a decision which reduces Corkery's role in the subsequent development of O'Faoláin as a writer, and reinforces the apparent intention that the author of *Vive moi!* was in some ways self-fashioned), O'Connor's engagement with his elder mentor runs to several chapters and provides a crucial part of the celebrated fourth section of his autobiography, which deals with the Troubles and the fall-out from the Civil War.

O'Connor's prolonged engagement with Corkery was perhaps best explained by Sean Hendrick – another past pupil of Corkery's and for a time a friend of O'Connor's and a fellow IRA Volunteer. 'Whatever [O'Connor came to] think of Corkery the philosopher', Hendrick shrewdly remarked, 'he retained to the end an immense affection for Corkery the man.'[16] Certainly, the subtlety and detail in

---

13 O'Connor, *An only child*, 133.   **14** O'Faoláin, *Vive moi!*, 133–4.   **15** O'Connor, *An only child*, 171; David Cairns and Shaun Richards, *Writing Ireland: colonialism, nationalism and culture* (Manchester, 1988), 124.   **16** Sean Hendrick, 'Michael O'Donovan's wild son' in Maurice Sheehy

O'Connor's portrait suggests a considerable degree of affection and indicates a debt – critical, emotional, artistic and pedagogic – which O'Connor continued to feel towards the older writer. 'I never loved anyone without imitating him', O'Connor joked in *An only child*, 'and having a quite satisfactory mother, I was not particularly attracted to women or girls, but in the absence of a father who answered my needs, I developed fierce passions for middle-aged men.' Corkery, O'Connor continues, 'was my first and greatest love'.[17]

The quasi-Oedipal connotations which are invested in such a remark are reflected in many of O'Connor's short stories which engage with father-son or parent-child relationships. 'My Oedipus complex', 'The study of history', 'The babes in the wood' and 'The procession of life' are but a few examples. However, it is worth noting that such remarks also bear witness to the depth of Corkery's influence, and insofar as this is the case one could argue that they bespeak the limitations of any subsequent claim that the younger writer simply 'outgrew' his former mentor. Indeed, one might rather suggest that O'Connor continued to grapple with an enduring and sometimes difficult legacy – it was his 'first and greatest love', after all – long after he had set out on a creative path of his own. The difficulty for biographers, scholars and readers, however, is that there are only a few occasions when O'Connor recorded the extent of that influence in print.

Aside from the portrait which was later included in *An only child*, there are only a handful of articles which O'Connor ever penned about Corkery. A lecture on Synge to the Abbey Theatre Festival in 1938 was perhaps the fullest of these pieces, and provided as much a delayed response to Corkery's controversial study *Synge and Anglo-Irish Literature* as it gave an analysis of Synge's plays. O'Connor's lecture undermined the triumvirate of Nationalism, Religion and Land which Corkery had earlier identified as the bedrock of Irish writing, and chastised the older writer for demanding that literature should be 'a purely representative thing' which exploited 'a sort of knowingness'.[18] O'Connor also used the occasion to argue that Corkery had sold out to middle-class pieties and concerns which he considered detrimental to 'true' artistic expression, such as a preoccupation with classification and 'that middle class censoriousness which Synge abominated'.[19] As incisive as the critique was, though, it is significant that it ended with the rider that O'Connor still considered Corkery 'the greatest artist of his generation'.[20]

(ed.), *Michael/Frank: studies on Frank O'Connor* (Dublin, 1969), 13. **17** O'Connor, *An only child*, 103. **18** Frank O'Connor, 'Synge' in Lennox Robinson (ed.), *The Irish theatre: lectures delivered during the Abbey Theatre festival held in Dublin in August 1938* (London, 1939), 32, 52. **19** O'Connor, 'Synge', 46. **20** Ibid., 52.

O'Connor used this formulation on a few other occasions, most notably in a review of Corkery's third collection of short stories – the justly acclaimed *The stormy hills* – for the *Irish Statesman* in 1929. By the time this review was published, O'Connor had fallen out with Corkery. Even still, O'Connor used the occasion to record his belief that 'since Corkery is our best story-teller, I think his work will be the model for the next generation of Irish writers'. O'Connor was part of that generation, so it is worth identifying some of the characteristics which he thought worth celebrating in the older writer's work. In the course of his review, O'Connor singled out Corkery's 'intensity of observation' for special praise and also paid tribute to his former mentor's 'passionate love … for the people of Ireland, their religion, their manners and their speech'. According to O'Connor, Corkery's stories were inspired by a 'passionate love for the poor and noble people that are his folk and mine' – a people who had been 'anonymous' or hitherto unrepresented in the literary tradition, but who had been written into that tradition with such effect that his best stories could be considered 'the literature of an outlawed people'.[21] O'Connor's comments shed a revealing light on some of the more attractive aspects of Corkery's understated short fiction. They are also suggestive for what they reveal about O'Connor himself and what O'Connor inherited from his one-time mentor.

The commitment to realist techniques and a regionalist framework for writing, for instance, are crucial aspects of both writers' works and provide an obvious point of correspondence across the generations. At the same time, the commitment to realism was tempered for both writers with a residual romanticism and a celebration of the outcast figure – both writers wrote about lonely figures from an occasionally sentimental or nostalgic viewpoint. Both writers were also keenly interested in the sound of spoken language and attempted to capture the customs, idioms and forms of address of everyday characters in their stories. Indeed, O'Connor's famous observation late in his career that all of his work could be interpreted as a sustained attempt to record 'the tone of a man's voice, speaking', finds resonance in this early review, in the stress which is put on Corkery's attempts at translating the sound of a poor people's 'speech' into print. O'Connor's comments are of further interest, however, insofar as they anticipate some of the more celebrated aspects of his later theory of the short story form. The reference to anonymous, unrepresented or outlawed lives, for instance, finds an echo in the idea of 'submerged population groups' which O'Connor later developed in his seminal study of the short story form *The lonely voice* (1963).

21 Frank O'Connor, review, the *Irish Statesman* (26 Oct. 1929), 158.

In the latter study, O'Connor famously argued that the emergence of short stories marked the 'appearance in fiction of the Little Man' or 'submerged population groups'.[22] One such group is the fictional community of peasants who are memorably described by O'Connor in such stories as 'In the train', 'The majesty of the law' and 'Uprooted'. Describing the appearance of the characters in 'In the train' (1936), for instance, the narrator informs the reader that they were:

> Not such as one sees in the environs of a capital but in the mountains and along the coasts. Gnarled, wild, with turbulent faces, their ill-cut clothes full of character, the women in pale brown shawls, the men wearing black sombreros and carrying big sticks ... And, so much part of their natural environment were they, that for a moment they seemed to create about themselves rocks and bushes, tarns, turf-ricks and sea.[23]

These characters are quite unlike the more refined peasants one encounters in many Anglo-Irish texts (Synge's plays are the obvious exception). However, they bear a striking resemblance to many of the characters in Corkery's rural-based short fiction – 'Carrig-an-Afrinn', 'The stones' and 'The priest', which are all included in *The stormy hills*, all contain similarly wild, 'anonymous' characters. O'Connor's reference to outlawed lives also betrays the guiding influence of the Russian writer Ivan Turgenev, and in particular Turgenev's radical short-story collection *A sportsman's sketches*, which brought into print another anonymous people (the serfs) and experimented with ways of writing about that people from the perspective of an outsider. According to O'Connor's biographer, James Matthews, it was Corkery who first introduced *A sportsman's sketches* to O'Connor, and this volume provided O'Connor with a blueprint for the organisation of his stories in *Guests of the nation*.[24] It is significant that Corkery and O'Connor both continued to champion Turgenev as a model for short-story writers long after they had begun to disagree about so much else.

For all of its suggestiveness, though, O'Connor's review of *The stormy hills* for the *Irish Statesman* was only one of a small number of pieces which the younger writer ever wrote about his former mentor, and this lack of documentary or textual material makes it difficult for commentators to assess the full extent of

---

22 Frank O'Connor, *The lonely voice: a study of the short story* (London, 1963), 15, 18.   **23** Frank O'Connor, *Bones of contention and other stories* (London, 1936), 62.   **24** Matthews, *Voices*, 20, 68. Matthews notes that Turgenev was also the subject of O'Connor's first essay, which was written in Irish and awarded a prize by the Gaelic League. Matthews, *Voices*, 392, fn. 3.

Corkery's influence. This difficulty is compounded by the fact that Corkery seldom engaged with the presence of O'Connor in his writing. Carol Quinn, an archivist at the Boole Library, University College Cork, has addressed this very problem in her online introduction to Corkery's private papers which are housed at UCC. 'Because of his well documented association with Frank O'Connor and Seán O'Faoláin it would be presumed that researchers interested in these two writers should look to the Corkery collection for information', Quinn notes. However, any potential researcher should beware since 'the celebrated rift between Corkery and his 'gluggers' is apparent only through the paucity of references to them'.[25] This paucity of references is repeated in Corkery's published works, where there are remarkably few – if any – allusions to either of his protégés. Corkery refused to respond to O'Connor's Abbey Theatre lecture which was published in *The Irish theatre* (1939), for instance, and he chose not to comment on the various critiques which O'Faoláin also wrote about this time – including an essay for the *Dublin Magazine* in 1936, and the Proem to his biography of Daniel O'Connell, *King of the beggars* (1938).[26]

What is more, on one of the very few occasions when Corkery did attempt to publicly rebuke his former charges, his comments never made it into print. In May 1942, O'Faoláin attacked the aspirations of the Gaelic League in a feisty editorial for *The Bell*, and condemned Corkery for an article the older writer had submitted to the Catholic magazine the *Irish Rosary* on the subject 'What is wrong with Irish culture?'[27] Corkery's article was founded on the wearily familiar mantra that Irish culture was being contaminated by overseas influences, and that all Irish writing in English was neither natural nor national. The next issue of *The Bell* contained a short note which stated that the editors had received a reply from Corkery, but that they refused to publish the contents of this reply because they considered it too long and potentially libellous. The reply was never edited nor was it included at a later date in *The Bell*. For his part, Corkery declined to publish it elsewhere.[28]

Despite the apparent paucity of references in the work of O'Connor and Corkery, however, there was one occasion when the two writers together with Seán

---

25 http://booleweb.ucc.ie/search/subject/archives/corcora.htm. 'Glugger', the reader is informed, is 'a Cork term [which] means an egg which will not hatch and is needlessly nurtured by a hen'. **26** Seán O'Faoláin, 'Daniel Corkery', *Dublin Magazine*, 11:2 (April/June 1936), 49–61; Seán O'Faoláin, *King of the beggars: a life of Daniel O'Connell, the Irish liberator, in a study of the rise of the modern Irish democracy, 1775–1847* (London, 1938), 11–39. **27** Seán O'Faoláin, 'The Gaelic League', *The Bell*, 4:2 (May 1942), 77–86; Daniel Corkery, 'What is wrong with Irish culture?', *Irish Rosary* (Feb. 1942), 92–4. **28** Maume, *Life that is exile*, 130.

O'Faoláin did engage in something like a full-scale dispute in print. Little has been written about this dispute to date – it is mentioned in Maume's biography of Corkery, but it is omitted from the standard biographies of O'Connor and O'Faoláin and it is also overlooked in all of the critical surveys.[29] The dispute took place in the summer months of 1926, in the pages of a short-lived weekly newspaper, which was first entitled *The Tribune* and then, after four issues, the *Irish Tribune*. The editors never explained this change in title, but it would appear that it was part of a general attempt to re-launch the paper as a national rather than a local enterprise.

The Irish Tribune was based in Cork and was conceived as a nationalist alternative to George Russell's Dublin-based journal the *Irish Statesman*. During its short existence – it lasted only nine months – the paper provided the space for an uneasy alliance of republicans and disgruntled Free Staters and had the backing of several prominent Munster intellectuals, politicians and businessmen. Corkery was a prominent contributor to the *Irish Tribune* and served as its literary editor for several months. In the foreword to the first issue of the paper, the editors announced that their intentions included the revival of 'idealism', the reunification of the island, and the promotion of 'the needs and interests of provincial Ireland'. They also unequivocally declared their Irish Ireland credentials: 'we are opposed to anglicisation and alienisation alike in morals, culture, language and industry', they remarked, and 'our belief [is] that the ultimate and proper vehicle of Irish culture is the Irish language'. To this end, they intended to present a weekly commentary on current events 'which will be true to the traditional ideals of our people, which are now in greater danger than ever'.[30] The ethnic appeal to 'traditional ideals' and 'our people' is especially significant when it is considered within the context of the ensuing dispute, not least because it was with Corkery's use of the ideas of tradition and identity that O'Faoláin and O'Connor took issue.

The dispute began on 18 June, when the *Irish Tribune* published two articles, one by Corkery and one by O'Connor's friend Sean Hendrick. Hendrick's essay, 'The heart has reasons', was a rather oblique piece which declared that the cause of republicanism transcended intellect and reason since it was a mystical arrangement of soul and spirit. In support of this argument, Hendrick asserted his belief in a static idea of tradition – something which he claimed was unfashionable in a modernising Ireland, but which nonetheless supposedly strengthened and purified the sacred symbols of nationalism, republicanism and religion.[31] Corkery's

---

29 Ibid., 91–2. **30** 'Foreword' to *The Tribune* (18 June 1926), 4. **31** Sean Hedrick, 'The heart has reasons', *Irish Tribune* (18 June 1926), 19.

essay, 'A landscape in the West', touched on some of Hendrick's points, and was replete with the stock phrases 'the Spirit of the Nation', 'the mind of the race' and 'communion' with the land. The essay ostensibly provided a portrait of an abandoned estate which was once the property of an Anglicized Gaelic family, and detailed some of the improvements which were built onto the estate during the nineteenth century, at the time of the Young Ireland movement. However, all of these improvements came to nothing, Corkery argued, because a descendant of that family – a so-called 'pervert Gael' – was not prepared to submit to 'the National Spirit' and 're-establish contact with the mind of his fathers'. By refusing to succumb to this call, the imagined descendant of that family was said to have consigned himself to a life of deracination and exile. 'For homogeneity is the very principle of nationhood', Corkery ominously concluded, 'and to achieve it a nation ruthlessly casts out' anything that does not fit.[32]

In the correspondence page of the next issue of the *Irish Tribune*, O'Connor charged Hendrick and Corkery with 'sentimentalism' and 'muddy thinking'. The tone of O'Connor's piece was initially light-hearted. Hendrick was satirized for indulging in 'a deluge of drivel', whereas Corkery was characterized as 'a very Oisin, weeping after The Spirit of the Nation'. However, the tone changed as O'Connor proceeded with his attack. Although he acknowledged a certain respect for Corkery, he nonetheless also claimed that his former mentor had allowed emotion to outrun reason. If a nation does not accept what a person has to offer, irrespective of their politics, religion or tradition, he remarked, then it has only itself to blame if it is left destitute. Having made this point, O'Connor proceeded to unravel a central thread in Corkery's argument. 'I do not believe that the spirit of the nation [lower case 's' and 'n', the reader might note], any more than the spirit of the Catholic religion, is a permanent and unchanging thing'. Instead of holding to the view that tradition is something permanent and unchanging – something which the editors of *The Tribune* had declared in the first issue of their paper, and a theory which was fundamental to the informing ideology of Corkery's article and Hendrick's essay – O'Connor set forth an idea of tradition which was ever growing and always in process. A national tradition is necessarily inclusive and continually negotiates between the past and the present, he argued; it is only sustainable 'while it is absorbing life into itself'.[33]

Corkery's reply the following week was contemptuous. He claimed that

32 Daniel Corkery, 'A landscape in the West', *Irish Tribune* (18 June 1926), 20–1. **33** Frank O'Connor, correspondence, *Irish Tribune* (25 June 1926), 17–18.

O'Connor had not been able to understand the point of his essay on account of his 'immature mind'. Seemingly, Corkery's article had been intended as an appeal to the contemporary middle-classes and landed families who had grown disenchanted with politics and culture in the post-Treaty years. What is more, Corkery deflected the charge of emotionalism back onto his former pupil, remarking that 'if Mr O'Connor had more control of himself … he would not have written his letter'. Significantly, O'Connor's theory of tradition-in-process was dismissed out of hand as infantile.[34] At this point, O'Faoláin entered the fray and defended O'Connor's intervention; he also denounced Corkery as the embodiment of a provincial mentality which was fearful for its own safety. According to O'Faoláin, 'neither Mr Corkery nor anyone else is the custodian of the national tradition'. O'Faoláin was adamant that national traditions are part of a larger network of beliefs and cultural practices, and argued that the distinction between this expansive view of tradition and the insular view to which Corkery subscribed could be accounted for by their generational difference as writers of the Revival and post-Revival periods.[35]

O'Faoláin's involvement in this debate came at a time when he was writing a series of four articles for the *Irish Tribune* on the future of the Irish language. In the second of these articles, O'Faoláin launched a scathing attack on Corkery, in which he made the extraordinary claim that his former mentor's influential study of eighteenth-century Munster Gaelic poetry, *The hidden Ireland* (1924), had done 'more to retard Irish education than three centuries of foreign rule'.[36] Aodh de Blacam (another writer with Catholic, nationalist sympathies and, like Corkery, a member of the Gaelic League) leapt to the older writer's defence and argued that Corkery's book was invaluable since it had opened up new lines of inquiry and established the rules for future discussions of Irish literature.[37] A fortnight later, O'Connor responded to de Blacam with the remark that *The hidden Ireland* was 'valuable not for its principles but for its enthusiasm'.[38] This earned a further reproach from his former mentor. 'Some time since I had to point out to Mr Frank O'Connor that he suffered from immaturity of mind. Here he's at it again!', Corkery groaned, 'well, fools will step in'.[39]

With this rebuke, the only extended debate in print between Corkery and his

---

34 Daniel Corkery, correspondence, *Irish Tribune* (2 July 1926), 22.   **35** Seán O'Faoláin, correspondence, *Irish Tribune* (23 July 1926), 23.   **36** Seán O'Faoláin, 'The language problem 2: Irish – an empty barrel?', *Irish Tribune* (16 July 1926), 9.   **37** Aodh de Blacam, 'Have we a literature?', *Irish Tribune* (30 July 1926), 17–18.   **38** Frank O'Connor, correspondence, *Irish Tribune* (13 Aug. 1926), 23.   **39** Daniel Corkery, correspondence, *Irish Tribune* (27 Aug. 1926), 22–3.

two protégés came to a close. Neither O'Connor nor O'Faoláin rose to Corkery's insults, and Corkery, for his part, declined to respond to O'Faoláin's astonishing goad. Indeed, Corkery declined to respond to O'Faoláin at all – one of the most remarkable things about this dispute is the fact that Corkery only engaged with the younger and, according to Patrick Maume, 'more vulnerable' O'Connor.[40] Corkery continued to contribute regularly to the *Irish Tribune* until its collapse several months later; O'Faoláin ceased all involvement with the paper and left Cork to study at Harvard at the end of the summer; and O'Connor submitted only a few book reviews and two brief sketches, 'Sion' and 'The pedler', in the following months. The exchange ended in bitterness on Corkery's part and incomprehension on all sides. It also ended rather inconclusively, and there was a sense that the arguments – and the various issues which were at stake – weren't really resolved in any way.

In the months prior to the *Irish Tribune* debate, O'Connor began to move apart (physically and intellectually) from Corkery. Still shaken by his experiences in the Gormanstown camp, O'Connor took up his first position as an apprentice librarian in Sligo, in May 1924, and over the next few years he was transferred to Wicklow, then back to Cork, before finally moving to Dublin. It is no coincidence that James Matthews dates their first serious disagreements to this time, a time when O'Connor came increasingly under the influence of George Russell and William Butler Yeats.[41] O'Connor's first contribution to the *Irish Statesman*, a verse translation of 'Suibhne geilt speaks', was published in March 1925, and Russell and Yeats soon replaced Corkery as mentors and father figures. In the posthumous volume *My father's son* (1968), O'Connor alluded to the many difficulties which had developed with Corkery by late 1925. 'I found it impossible to talk to Corkery' by this time, he reminisced, 'he was too gentle and considerate to be rude, but he made it plain that he was taking sides and that I was on the wrong one'.[42] Silence, misunderstanding and an inability to communicate seem to have characterized the few occasions when the two writers reportedly met in the decades that followed.[43]

If O'Connor continued to struggle with the legacy of his 'first and greatest love' in his later years, however, he nonetheless also developed as a writer and critic in his own right. Interestingly, one of the theories that he developed was the idea that tradition is alive and always in process. This idea was initially sketched in the

40 Maume, *Life that is exile*, 92.   **41** Matthews, *Voices*, 42, 94.   **42** Frank O'Connor, *My father's son* (London, 1968), 53–4.   **43** Matthews, *Voices*, 313; Maume, *Life that is exile*, 138.

pages of the *Irish Tribune*, and it is something which O'Connor returned to time and again in his mature work. It is at the heart of the Abbey Theatre philosophy which O'Connor discerned in his essay 'Synge', 'that nothing is settled, that everything must be created anew', for instance, and it also informed the argument of his magisterial study *The backward look* (1967), where it is claimed that the only way to 'escape from the burden of tradition' is 'by confronting it and robbing it of its mystique'.[44] O'Connor's idea that traditions are alive is strikingly contemporary and, it could be suggested, anticipates the recent claims of many cultural theorists. According to one such theorist, Stuart Hall, for example, traditions and cultural identities 'undergo constant transformation' because 'far from being eternally fixed in some essentialized past, they are subject to the continuous play of history, culture and power'. That is to say, traditions and cultural identities are continuously produced and reproduced anew, and 'belong to the future as much as to the past'.[45] When O'Connor's theory is read with Hall in mind, one could argue that it gains a renewed relevance for a twenty-first-century Ireland which is re-negotiating concepts of identity and belonging.

The argument of *The backward look* is doubly significant, though, for if one only escapes a burden by confronting it, it is quite ironic that in spite of the many comments which have since been generated about the rift between Corkery and his most famous protégés, very few details of the actual confrontations between these writers have survived in print. Many reasons can be advanced to explain why these writers fell out so dramatically in the mid-1920s. It was certainly, at least partially, a consequence of the different political stances that were taken in the wake of the Civil War, as Corkery remained committed to a belief in ideals and principles which his young charges viewed with increasing scepticism and disbelief. This is how Seán Ó Tuama interpreted the situation when he praised Corkery for being 'one of the few writers/intellectuals who did not jettison his beliefs' in post-independence Ireland.[46] Ironically, it is also what Harmon and McKeon meant when they congratulated O'Connor and O'Faoláin for finally 'outgrowing' the influence of their mentor. The split was more personal than this, though (Corkery seems to have interpreted it as an act of personal betrayal, for instance, with O'Connor looking to other centres of influence and alternative father figures), and this perhaps explains the bitterness which underlies their only public

---

44 O'Connor, 'Synge', 34; Frank O'Connor, *The backward look: a survey of Irish literature* (London, 1967), 8. 45 Stuart Hall, 'Cultural identity and diaspora' in Patrick Williams and Laura Chrisman (eds), *Colonial discourse and post-colonial theory: a reader* (Hemel Hempstead, Herts, 1993), 394. 46 Ó Tuama, *Repossessions*, 237.

debate as well as the terrible silence which punctuated their relationship in the months and years that followed. Such theories aren't entirely satisfactory, though, because of the lack of confrontation, or the paucity of references, in each of these writers' works – the 'burden' was not confronted, at least publicly, by any of the writers involved, nor were their reasons for falling out ever fully articulated. This is perhaps the reason why O'Connor's famous 'fierce' dispute with Corkery has retained its air of 'mystique', as well as its apparent simplicity ('the pupil outgrew the master'), for subsequent generations of scholars, biographers and critics.

Frank O'Connor at Trinity: a reminiscence

PHILIP EDWARDS

As I look back over a long academic life, my relationship with Frank O'Connor at Trinity College, Dublin, in the early 1960s stands out with the greatest clarity as one of its most absorbing features.

I first met Frank O'Connor in the early summer of 1962. He was the guest of David Greene, professor of Irish, at Commons, and David introduced him to me. I was astonished by his confident and positive opinions on my own subject, Shakespeare, but I found his trenchant expression of them exhilarating. This was the beginning of a close personal relationship between Michael and his wife Harriet with my wife Sheila and myself until Michael's death in 1966. I had come to Trinity as a brash young Englishman in 1960 and there were three things in those early days that I wanted to do. Although I recognized that one of the strengths of English at Trinity was that it was always studied in conjunction with another subject, usually a modern language or Latin, there was no degree available in English literature and language as a whole and that seemed to me a weakness. It was not too difficult to introduce the major changes necessary for that innovation. The second thing I wanted to do was to experiment with what was still a novelty on this side of the Atlantic, a 'writer in residence', and thus associate the study of imaginative literature with its creation. The third requirement was to increase the Irishness of my department. I had been apprehensive in 1960 that my own knowledge of Irish literature – or Anglo-Irish as it was then called – would be wholly insufficient in an Irish university. I need not have worried.

My lectures on Joyce and Yeats seemed news in a department where the only course on Irish literature was James Walton's on the nineteenth-century Irish novel. My other colleagues, Fitzroy Pyle and R.B.D. French, were not in the least inimical to the study of Irish literature, but they accepted the syllabus as it had been handed down. My predecessor at Trinity, H.O. White, had been a student of the illustrious first professor of English literature, Edward Dowden, and there is no doubt that some of the latter's political prejudices about the provinciality of Irish culture and his determination to maintain Englishness in the canon of literature had remained in what I inherited. I wished not only to deepen the study of literature by creating a degree in English literature and language alone, but to widen it to include a much greater specifically Irish element, and also, by the establishment of a 'writer in residence', to link the study of literature with the power for creative writing already so evident among those whom I was teaching. And when I look back at those among my students who came to do so much as the poets and scholars of present-day Ireland – Brendan Kennelly, Derek Mahon, Eavan Boland, Nicholas Grene, John Kelly, Terence Brown, Edna Longley and others – I feel convinced I was on the right track. I still regard my appointment of Brendan Kennelly as a junior lecturer in September 1963 as one of the happiest moves of my time at Trinity.

Early in the session of 1963–4 I began to scheme to get Frank O'Connor attached to the English department as a 'writer in residence'. I had the strongest support from the provost and the board, although initially the provost, A.J. McConnell, said to me, 'Wouldn't you be meaning Seán O'Faoláin?' He thought I must have this 'safer' writer in mind; much more an establishment figure, less wild than O'Connor. At this time Frank O'Connor was going through a lean time financially and lucrative offers from the USA seemed very attractive. But the idea of being attached to an academic community in Ireland, especially Trinity College, Dublin, was much more attractive. As I have indicated, his attitude to the problems of literature was to be sudden and bold: the opposite of the cautious academic approach. Yet his knowledge of literature was profound, and he loved to be with those who had an academic training; perhaps he valued too highly what we academics brought to the study of a literature which he had taught himself. Anyway, his pleasure in a possible relationship with TCD was unalloyed. But he did not wish to be a 'writer in residence'. He had had enough of that in the States. He envisaged a series of lectures on the literature of Ireland, in Irish as well as in English, and he thought that TCD should take the lead in establishing a school of Irish studies, in which departments of language, literature, history, and archaeology could combine.

We compromised, of course. Michael (I always think of him by that name) agreed to spend an hour a week on a 'creative writing' course and I agreed he should give his course of lectures in literature in Ireland. Then there was the problem of his title; I think it was someone in the registrar's office who came up with 'special lecturer in the literature of Ireland'. And all that we could offer him, which he nobly accepted, was £500 for the year.

So began that fine series of lectures which were published after his death as *The backward look: a survey of Irish literature* (1967). I gave a detailed account of the giving of these lectures in an essay 'Frank O'Connor at Trinity', and this I now quote.

The weekly lectures were immensely successful. My honours students, for whom they had been chiefly intended, never formed more than a fraction of the big audience. The lectures were not public, and they were not advertised, but they soon began to draw in students from University College, as well as interested Trinity students whose subjects were anything but literature. Visiting American academics, young writers and unclassifiable members of the public used to drop in. There had been nothing like it since the great days of Dowden's lectures. The 'openness' of the lectures was highly irregular, but of course no one said a word.

O'Connor more or less gave up his year to the preparation of these lectures. He suffered financially and he suffered emotionally. He was always worrying about them. He was nervous before the start of every single lecture. He would come up to my room a quarter of an hour early every Tuesday, and we would talk, with much glancing at watches. Then the donning of gowns and the ritual procession to the lecture-theatre, myself as acolyte with the indispensable flask of water.

Nervous or not, he lectured magnificently. He stood at the lectern, black gown over bright blue tweed jacket, reciting in that deep voice his translation of an old Irish poem, reminiscing on something apropos which Yeats had said to him, or dogmatising on matters which made the Celtic scholars from the Institute for Advanced Studies turn and look at each other. He could never understand why at the end there were not more questions. I was always sorry that his own enthusiasm was not repaid by a good discussion. It was better when we reached the Anglo-Irish writers; few of my students knew anything of Old Irish literature – I think he assumed more knowledge than there was. At any rate, he quite rightly became dissatisfied with a series of lectures attended for their own interest and without any follow-up in the undergraduates' own studies, and he began to think out schemes for degree courses in the literature of Ireland.[1]

In some ways it was a great misfortune that just at this time I was invited to spend the session of 1964–5 as visiting professor at the University of Michigan at Ann Arbor. We put forward a great scheme for a school of Irish Studies, which we

[1] In Michael Sheehy (ed.), *Michael/Frank: studies on Frank O'Connor with a bibliography of his writings* (Dublin, 1969), 131–2.

hoped would be directed by Frank O'Connor. The board of the college accepted
the scheme and a committee was set up consisting of myself, David Greene, W. B.
Stanford (Regius professor of Greek) and Brian Spencer (professor of
Biochemistry). We produced a long document on the introduction of a school of
Irish Studies. This was accepted and, as I wrote back in 1969, 'we felt the excite-
ment of pioneers in a new academic adventure in Ireland'.[2]

O'Connor did not wish to be re-appointed in 1964–5 as special lecturer. His
refusal was partly because I would be absent in the States, partly because he did
not wish to repeat the lectures he had just given, and partly because he wanted to
wait for the initiation of the new school of Irish Studies. The provost assured me
that the new school *would* be introduced, but it was essential for the financing of
the scheme that additional money, chiefly for staffing, should come from the
government, and in the event this grant never arrived. At this time of greater pros-
perity in Ireland it is perhaps difficult to comprehend the very small budgets on
which academic life had to survive; contributions from public funds could offer
only minimal help towards new developments, and in this particular case, Trinity
was just unlucky.

In Ann Arbor, we had many letters from Michael and Harriet, filled with
gloom at the progress of negotiations and convinced that my return would help.
But when I returned in the late summer of 1965 it was quite clear that there was no
prospect whatsoever of an implementation of the scheme in the immediate or
indeed the foreseeable future. Michael accepted re-appointment to his former
position as special lecturer for the 1966–6 session, but he was too ill to do much
lecturing and in March 1966 he died.

In late 1966 I accepted an invitation to a post at one of the new universities in
England. In many ways, I still think that this acceptance was a mistake. Trinity,
with all its financial privations, had more to offer than affluent new universities in
England. I reflect, however, that the commitment to the literature of Ireland, so
evident in the work of the school of English in recent decades, must have owed
something to the early efforts of Frank O'Connor, the writer who dominated my
all too few years at Trinity.

2 Ibid., 134.

Frank O'Connor's American reception: the first decade (1931–41)

ROBERT C. EVANS

The importance of America to Frank O'Connor's practical success and literary reputation, especially in the first decade of his US publishing career, is hard to over-estimate. As an author working in and writing about a rather small and (at that time) rather poor country, O'Connor only stood to benefit if his work attracted the attention and support of readers outside his native land. Success in Britain was important, especially during the years of World War II, when O'Connor's finances became especially strained and when domestic censorship (and even political and social persecution) made it particularly difficult for him to earn a reliable living in Ireland. Winning success in America, however, was even more significant. With its vast and growing wealth, its huge and expanding population, its increasingly educated readership, and its large contingent of Irish immigrants, the US was a crucial market for any writer of serious fiction.

This was particularly true in the 1930s, when the world's economic markets were attempting to recover from the Great Depression and when O'Connor was trying to make his way as a professional writer. Fortunately for him, most of his first American reviewers responded enthusiastically to his work, and O'Connor's positive reception in America eventually helped ensure his status as one of the most influential Irish writers in the mid-twentieth century. Nevertheless, although scholarship on O'Connor's reception in the US in the 1940s, 50s, and 60s is relatively plentiful, this is less true of the first ten years of his American career.[1] Yet the 1930s are in fact a particularly interesting decade, not only because they provide the groundwork for everything that came later but also because they show O'Connor trying his hand at two genres (biography and the novel) he eventually

---

[1] For a very comprehensive list of items relevant to O'Connor's American reception from 1940 until his death in 1966, see: John C. Kerrigan, 'A bibliography of works by and about Frank O'Connor' and James D. Alexander, 'Frank O'Connor's *New Yorker* stories: the serious side' in Robert C. Evans and Richard Harp (eds), *Frank O'Connor: new perspectives* (West Cornwell, CT, 1998). Also important is James D. Alexander, 'Frank O'Connor in *The New Yorker*, 1945–1967', *Éire-Ireland*, 30:1 (1995), 130–44. In James Matthews' standard biography, *Voices: a life of Frank O'Connor* (1983), the entry on America in the index focuses exclusively on the period from 1951–61, further evidence of the relative neglect of O'Connor's initial reception in the US.

abandoned, even though his efforts in these genres received generally strong endorsements from most American critics. Critical reception of his work in this decade focuses on all aspects of O'Connor's output, including the two short-story publications – *Guests of the nation* and *Bones of contention*, both novels – *The saint and Mary Kate* and *Dutch interior*, a translation of Gaelic poetry – *The fountain of magic*, and O'Connor's biography of Michael Collins – *The big fellow*. This essay attempts to comprehensively present everything of substance said by nearly every American reviewer of O'Connor's work that I could trace in the years 1931–1941, as well as analyze the reputation established for O'Connor by the 1930s American periodical literati.

O'Connor's American success began with the acceptance, by the *Atlantic Monthly*, of his 1930 break-through story 'Guests of the nation', which appeared in the magazine in January 1931. 'Guests' is still, perhaps, the story by which O'Connor is best known and for which he is most respected; he thus had the good fortune of beginning his American career with a genuine masterpiece. It was not, however, until the publication later in 1931 of his first collection of stories, also titled *Guests of the nation*, that O'Connor began to attract the serious attention of American reviewers. For a first book of short fiction, the volume received wide attention, attracting reviews in the *Boston Transcript*, the *New Republic*, the *New York Times Book Review*, the *Saturday Review of Literature,* and the *Springfield Sunday Union and Republican* (Massachusetts).[2] No doubt the fact that the book was issued by a major house (Macmillan) helped ensure it a respectful welcome, but the genuine enthusiasm of most of the reviewers is unmistakable.

The anonymous writer for the *New York Times*, for instance, proclaimed, 'there is not a dull line in it' and described it as 'impartial and honest, with the clear-eyed, rather scornful impartiality and honesty of youth'. Quoting freely from touches of O'Connor's phrasing, the reviewer reported that the volume contained both 'harsh pictures' and 'lighter, mirth-making ones'. The *Times* reviewer also noted that the 'penury of Ireland south of Ulster, its inbred and ingrained Catholicism, its sentimentality and the essential chastity of its simpler folk are abundantly illustrated in story after story'. S/he found the volume 'most delight-fully, free from controversy; a book of deeds rather than talk'.[3] O'Connor could

2 For this and similar information throughout this essay I am indebted to the *Book Review Digest* reference series. The reports in this source are very brief and sometimes only the existence of a review is mentioned. For assistance in tracking down many of the reviews quoted in this article, I am indebted to the ever-industrious and always-pleasant Carolyn Johnson, Interlibrary Loan Librarian at Auburn University Montgomery. **3** 'The Irish rebellion', *New York Times Book Review* (20 Sept.

not have asked for a much more positive initial notice in one of America's most important newspapers. Less than a week later the volume was also positively reviewed in the *Saturday Review of Literature* (one of the most important magazines of the era). The anonymous review began by declaring (perhaps with Joyce in mind),

> This new artist out of Ireland has the health and simplicity and sanity of an older time. His materials are precisely those of which contemporary Irish novelists have wrought their fabric of negation, disgust, and despair. He deals with them honestly, without suppression or sentimentality. But there is love in his heart for the absurd or hapless children of men of whom his tale is, and the smile on his lips never goes slack with pathos or stiffens to a sneer. The fifteen stories and sketches in this volume are concerned mainly with Ireland of the Revolution, an Ireland piteously and often comically at odds with itself, inconsistent, fratricidal, preyed upon by enemies within and without: never quite ignoble or lost.

The reviewer remarked on O'Connor's tendency toward understatement and his artistic ability to present his facts in a detached manner: 'the elements of tragedy and comedy in them must be sorted and moralized by the spectator: the showman makes no comment'. The story 'Jumbo's wife' is cited as a particularly effective example of O'Connor's reticence, and the reviewer's concluding opinion is that it is 'a book of poignant beauty'. 'Æ, it seems, 'discovered' this writer, and we cannot wonder that he says "I haven't discovered any writer so good as O'Connor since I found James Stephens".'[4] Thus, in a magazine with a broad national circulation, O'Connor had been endorsed not only by the unnamed reviewer but by Æ himself. In early November, an anonymous reviewer for *The New Republic*,[5] an important journal of liberal opinion read across the country, also termed the volume 'excellent'. Just as laudatory was an unsigned review published in the *Springfield Sunday Union and Republican* (a typical local newspaper of the time with a diverse readership). Beginning with the claim that 'Frank O'Connor is considered an Irish writer of great promise', the reviewer asserted that 'the other stories [apart from 'Guests'] are less forceful, but there is not a weak piece in the book. The author has an intelligent conception of realism, his sense of values is sound and he writes with commendable restraint and economy.'[6]

1931), 22–4.   **4** 'A new voice from Ireland', *Saturday Review of Literature* (26 Sept. 1931), 147.   **5** 11 Nov. 1931   **6** 'O'Connor's stories', *Springfield Sunday Union and Republican* (17 Jan. 1932), 7E. For

The positive American impact of O'Connor's first volume reverberated for years to come. For instance, a review in 1932 by Signe Toksvig (of O'Connor's new novel) mentioned the 'rich promise' evident in his first collection of stories. Likewise, another review published in 1932, by May Lamberton Becker, retrospectively judged *Guests* a 'strong' collection. William Troy, writing in 1936, argued that the 'moral of the title story' of *Guests* 'is that anything less than a profound and all inclusive charity is madness and death', and it is clear from the context of Troy's more general remarks that he regarded the entire volume as very much worth reading. Meanwhile James Stern, in 1941, argued that O'Connor in *Guests* had 'established himself … as a writer of extraordinary power', and further asserted that '[*Guests*] along with Joyce's "Dubliners" and O'Flaherty's "Spring Sowing" … probably contain the highest achievements in the art of the contemporary short story in the English language'.[7] Within a single decade, then, *Guests* had won O'Connor real respect among influential American readers, and admiration for the book – and especially for its title story – continued for years to come.

More surprising, perhaps, is the enthusiasm with which American reviewers greeted O'Connor's first novel, *The saint and Mary Kate*, in 1932. O'Connor himself later spoke disparagingly of his two novels, but reviewers in the US, at least, seem for the most part to have welcomed his efforts in the genre, especially this first novel. Moreover, what is also revealed in the reviews of this novel is the beginning of the general establishment of O'Connor as a post-independence realist writer, who is uncovering the 'real' Ireland of this period. Thus Signe Toksvig began by proclaiming that

> [t]he real Ireland is finding voices at last, and among these the one with the warmest timbre and the subtlest inflections and the most convincing things to say is Frank O'Connor. His book of short stories, 'Guests of the Nation,' gave rich promise, and his first novel, 'The Saint and Mary Kate,' fully carries this out. It is written in firm, springy, elastic language, with idioms like the smell of turf-smoke, images as unforced as field flowers, and a lilt throughout it straight from Cork. He has the grace of

careful, hand-written transcriptions of this review and another, I am indebted to the exceptional kindness of Sharman Prouty, Associate Librarian of the Historic Deerfield Library in Deerfield, Massachusetts.   **7** Signe Toksvig, 'The real Ireland', *Saturday Review of Literature* (10 Sept. 1932), 89; May Lamberton Becker, 'The reader's guide', *Saturday Review of Literature* (8 Oct. 1932), 164; James Stern, 'Frank O'Connor as novelist', *New Republic* (20 Jan. 1941), 91; William Troy, 'The comic view', *The Nation* (29 Apr. 1936), 566–7.

beauty that is never affected, his irony is never heavy nor his tenderness sentimental or patronizing. His characters walk out of the pages into one's mind and stay there.

She expressed some dissatisfaction with the ending of the book, arguing that only 'a glimpse of hope is left that poor, good, intense, narrow Phil, who somehow resembles young, Republican Ireland, will come to his senses as well as out of the dark and smelly crypts, and end by embracing and accepting life in all its vivid fulness, life in the enticing shape of a moral, gay, fresh, and lovely Mary Kate'.[8]

Whereas Toksvig came close, in these final sentences, to reading the novel as a political allegory, an anonymous reviewer for the *New York Times Book Review* firmly stressed the realism of the book. 'Stories about the Irish', the reviewer began, 'have a tendency to be wild tales. They go in for riot and revolution, leprechauns and fairy rings, banshees and ghosts, Irish-tenor sentimentality. Frank O'Connor's novel is not like that. It has its feet firmly planted on the ground, in the cheaper streets of Cork'. Reacting perhaps to a perceived impression of Irish literature as previously romantic or fantastical, this reviewer seems to positively appraise O'Connor as presenting something 'new', something realistic. 'To be sure', the reviewer continued,

> there are mad, half-mad and slightly touched Irish in it, but they are presented in a matter-of-fact way, stripped of the usual mystical or senti-mental haloes … it is instead a straightforward, realistic narrative told in a lively style, spiced with wit, that makes the book hard to relinquish to some one else in the family reading it at the same time.

Nevertheless, the *Times* reviewer did register a few complaints, namely that the minor characters were better defined than the protagonists and, concurring with Toksvig, that O'Connor's story does not finish in any satisfying way for the reader.[9] In a review published on the same day as the one just cited, Norah Meade detected a darker realism in O'Connor's work than was present in previous Irish writers. She saw the difference between O'Connor's Mary Kate and the main char-acter in 'Mary, Mary', a story by James Stephens, as 'not so much the result of time or changing tastes as of a revolution in the Irish outlook as reflected in its litera-ture', with O'Connor offering a more sombre view of Ireland than Stephens had

---

8 Toksvig, 'The real Ireland', 89.   **9** 'Realistic Irish', *New York Times Book Review* (18 Sept. 1932), 6.

presented. Meade detected in O'Connor a darker voice that she thought more accurately represented the mood of the country in the post-independence period.[10]

In another rather brief review, Thomas F. Healy, writing in *The Commonweal* (a generally liberal Catholic journal), also favoured the realistic approach and admired O'Connor's sensitive depiction of Irish people: 'On the surface Mr O'Connor seems another O'Flaherty in carrying on the revolt against the saccharine sentiment of former Anglo-Irish literature; but save when he stretches the tenets of realism too taut, this author is *sui generis*. He brings his own gifts, prime among which is to draw characters who live as individuals, well-rounded and well-realized.' After summarizing the plot of the novel, Healy concluded: 'The author unfolds a picturesque panorama of Irish life, with colorful characters of tradesmen, tramps and tinkers whose prayers and maledictions are in the rich and abundant idiom of the Irish southland. The rich flashes of native humor that save the race in its darkest hours light up the tragedy, and make the poverty less drab. It is a novel of power and tenderness, and the author shows a deep understanding of his people.'[11] James T. Farrell, the noted author, also critiqued the novel and placed it in a discerned recent tradition of Irish writing which Farrell labelled 'confessional realism'. Farrell contended that there 'is a sensitive tenderness in Mr O'Connor's book that overrides its patches of irony. Likewise, because of his skillful use of indirection, he is able to portray that melodrama and extravagance so apparent in many Irish lives without being himself melodramatic'. For Farrell, the 'hopeful youth' of Mary Kate and Paul stood 'out in contrast to the frustrations of the older people' in the novel. After summarizing the plot, Farrell ended by saying that 'Mr O'Connor's book is serious and genuine. Its strongest pages are those which retail the pitiful and almost heart-breaking lives of the poor. He is, unquestionably, an Irish novelist who should be read'.[12] On the whole, therefore, O'Connor's novel was lauded for its sensitive, honest portrayal of Ireland and its people, and welcomed for its fresh approach to depicting Irish social issues.

The only strongly dissenting voice from this generally positive chorus appeared in the magazine *Catholic World*, where a reviewer, identified by the initials 'B.L.C.', took serious exception to the image of Catholicism portrayed in the novel, mocked Irish writers' efforts at 'sordid' Zola-esque works of realism and condemned the book ferociously, attacking

10 Norah Meade, review of *The saint and Mary Kate*, *New York Herald Tribune Books* (18 Sept. 1932), 8.   11 Thomas F. Healy, 'Irish realism', *The Commonweal* (19 Oct. 1932), 599.   12 James T. Farrell, review of *The saint and Mary Kate*, in the *New Republic* (26 Oct. 1932), 301.

the impure air of Frank O'Connor's pseudo-Catholic Ireland. If you want to wade in filth up to your eyes, read *The saint and Mary Kate*, his caricature of the Irish people. He is a realist of the Zola type, who wastes ink and paper by writing of the sordid tenements of Cork, as if they were inhabited solely by drunkards, gamblers, thieves and adulterers. Catholicity is made ridiculous in his hero Phil, who measures his religion by a multiplicity of outward observances, and in his heroine, Mary Kate, whose every word and deed give the lie to her faith.

When the French do this sort of thing they at least give a certain glamour to their nastiness, but when their Irish imitators venture into this same field, they simply disgust us by their foulness.[13]

Published comment on *The saint and Mary Kate* continued for several years after the novel was first printed in America. After 1940, however, references to the novel tend to drop from view; by the mid-1940s apparently most US reviewers, like O'Connor himself, tended to perceive the Irish writer as first and foremost an author of short fiction, rather than as a novelist.

This emphasis on O'Connor as a writer of tales was strengthened, no doubt, by the appearance in 1936 of *Bones of contention*, his second collection of stories. One of the first reviews, by Fred T. Marsh in the *New York Herald Tribune* Sunday 'Books' section, was generally positive but also somewhat mixed. Marsh found the tale 'Tears – idle tears', for instance, 'not to my way of thinking a very successful story', nor did he have anything especially glowing to say about 'In the train', a tale often admired by many of O'Connor's other commentators. Marsh also disliked the widely regarded 'The majesty of the law', calling it 'a trite little number for all its indirectness in the telling'. He found several stories too provincial, remarking, 'I am no special connoisseur of Irish dishes. Not when they go so Irish that I cannot relate them to a varied world of good cookery'. Marsh did, however, have good things to say about 'Peasants', and he declared 'Michael's wife' a 'recognizable little fragment of fine goods'. Although Marsh's review is not glowing by any means, it did end on a fairly positive note. Directly addressing his readers, he told them that: 'you should, I think, like these stories, for they are honest; they are keen in their quirks; they are clever; and they are Irish to the core. Some of them are even good'.[14]

13 C.B.L, 'New books', *Catholic World*, 136 (Jan. 1933), 495–6. 14 Fred T. Marsh, review of *Bones of contention*, in *New York Herald Tribune Books* (29 Mar. 1936), vii, 12.

Far more unequivocally positive was the substantial commentary on *Bones* offered a week later by Peter Monro Jack in the *New York Times Book Review*. Jack began by declaring that:

> Mr O'Connor's stories have the Irish in them and they still have the good old-fashioned way of telling a good story. Such forthrightness is out of favor at the moment, when one turns a page to discover that the story has ended with a sigh and a suggestion. But here are tales worth telling and characters worth remembering. The old country is the background, with its Irish manners, Irish morals, Irish whisky and Irish sentiment; and the old characters are to the fore, with their sturdy assertion and individuality. Mr O'Connor tells their stories as if he had just heard them at the pub or the street corner. They are authentic anecdotes turned into a literary form so artfully that one scarcely notices the transposition … It would be absurd, however, to suggest that Mr O'Connor is a sentimentalist … Mr O'Connor accepts his Ireland, half ruefully, half laughingly, but always for itself. He is likely to be a superb writer of the realistic-fantastic style, of the anecdote, the *fabilau* in prose, the *conte drolatique* … Mr O'Connor's bent seems to be for clear and open expression of the humors and pathos of his Ireland, brightly imagined and rightly expressed. He is an authentic voice in the tradition, and he does not need to pitch himself to the prevailing fashion.[15]

Like Jack, William Troy, writing in *The Nation* (a prominent left-wing weekly), also asserted the unfashionable nature of O'Connor's fiction:

> It is too bad that Frank O'Connor's books are not better known in this country, because they illustrate qualities likely to be forgotten in a period like the present. It is not only their humor, or their peculiar variety of humor, but also the qualities of sympathy and detachment. Sympathy is … rarely to be found as a function of the writer's whole vision of experience – a vision so complete as to include the writer along with his characters. Mr O'Connor is detached in the sense that he allows the observed experience to carry its own moral. And the moral is that

---

15 Peter Monro Jack, 'The admirable stories of Mr O'Connor', *New York Times Book Review* (5 Apr. 1936), 7.

anything less than a profound and all inclusive charity is madness and death.

Continuing, Troy further asserted that:

> The comic pattern demands objectivity, and the technical success of these stories arises out of the strict adherence to dialogue and situation ... The language is a realization of the improbable flights of Irish speech of a sort to make the more famous passages of Synge seem like the insincerities of a tired littérateur. It grows on the page, sprouting into lush foliage out of the materials of the situation. As for the situations themselves, they are rarely more than the common crises of living in the Irish town and countryside. What Mr O'Connor does with them, of course, is a result of his gift and his vision.[16]

Both Troy and Jack, then, saw *Bones* in particular, and O'Connor in general, as exemplars of a then-unfashionable but still highly valuable approach to fiction – one of honesty, humour, humanism and humility. Much the same note is also sounded in a review of *Bones* by Otis Ferguson, published in the *New Republic*, which concludes that the collection 'is about people in general and small-town Irish in particular ... simple and mostly uncouth people in the primitive state where they fight grandly among themselves but present a baffling solidarity at the first sign of intrusion, alternately garrulous and inscrutable, credulous and shrewd, barbarians and poets ... O'Connor [is] able to write about them successfully only by virtue of not being superior to them or maudlin about them ... [he] is a fine writer'.[17] What is interesting about these reviews of *Bones* is the obviously developing opinion of O'Connor as an old-fashioned, anecdotal storyteller. This reputation of being old-fashioned was one that 'stuck' and which perhaps led to a decline in readership in the latter decades of the twentieth century; yet, it was an evaluation that was evidently meant as a compliment in America's 1930s literary criticism.

The 1936 reviews of *Bones* also reveal that in the five short years since he had first been published in America, O'Connor had established a very solid reputation as a writer of fiction, both novels and stories. In 1937, however, O'Connor made

---

16 Troy, 'The comic view', 566, 567. **17** Otis Ferguson, 'O'Connor's Irish harp', *New Republic* (3 June 1936), 110.

his first appearance as an author of extended non-fiction with his biography of Michael Collins, alternately titled *The big fellow* (in Britain) or *Death in Dublin* (in the US). The first published American review, which appeared unsigned in the respected *Christian Science Monitor*, was anything but favourable. It began by asserting that this biography was not a satisfactory life of Collins and did not do him justice. Instead, it offered an inconclusive picture and lacked characterization, and the reviewer alleged that Collins' reputation as a 'playboy is over-stressed'. His verdict was that

> the book suffers from cloudy wordiness; names drift on and off the pages with no concise characterization and no attempt is made to present the historical background in perspective. Anyone knowing little of Irish affairs probably will not be much the wiser for reading it.

The review ended (rather inconclusively) with the complaint that the 'question of land ownership, so dear to the Irish heart, is never mentioned'.[18] Far more favourable was a review by Horace Reynolds a few days later in the *New York Times*. Reynolds, eventually one of O'Connor's most vigorous American champions, began by proclaiming that 'Frank O'Connor is one of the small band of significant young Irish writers who are attempting to define the new Ireland to this generation' by 'fighting to free the Irish intellect'. He praised O'Connor's strong and sensitive fiction and asserted that O'Connor had now 'written brilliantly' of Collins. 'The halos around the heads of the leaders of the 1916 Rising', Reynolds maintained, 'have not blinded O'Connor to their faults as thinkers or leaders of men', and he paid tribute to O'Connor's ability to compress complex historical events into vivid narrative; Reynolds ended succinctly: 'The book is good reading. There isn't a dull page in it'.[19]

Similarly glowing was a review by Maurice Joy in the *New York Herald Tribune*. Joy commended O'Connor for not denying the weaknesses of his 'dynamic hero' and found his portrait 'intimately and humanly convincing', although he lamented the 'maladroitly reminiscent title' of the American edition, greatly preferring the English title instead. He also registered misgivings that O'Connor might not be bothered by Collins' allegedly 'dictatorial ambitions'. On the whole, however, Joy praised the work unstintingly, as when he summed up his views by saying that:

---

18 'Playboy and revolutionist', *Christian Science Monitor* (8 Sept. 1937), 11.   **19** Horace Reynolds, 'Michael Collins, the hero of the Irish revolution', *New York Times Book Review* (12 Sept. 1937), 5.

One has no hesitation in recommending this book for the brilliant power of its narrative, the sharp and clear-cut, if somewhat acid, portraits of Collins himself and of the men who fought with and against him, the able presentation of their conflicting views. One may disagree with some of Mr O'Connor's theories or judgments, but one should be wary of tackling a writer so well equipped for his job.[20]

Equally laudatory was a review by Michael Sayers in *The New Republic*. Comparing O'Connor's account with others about Collins, Sayers argued that 'none has better succeeded in catching the man himself … [the biography] sharpens the drama of a novel with the fidelity of a history … and the personality of Collins emerges starkly'. Sayers continued: 'I know of no better book which moves so excitingly and perspicuously through all that ludicrous, tragic muddle out of which came contemporary Ireland', adding that:

> Even its faults, its overstatements, contribute to the atmosphere it evokes. In one rather astonishing passage, moving immediately from panegyric to flapdoodle, O'Connor compares Collins to another organizing genius who operated under circumstances apparently similar. Beside Collins, says O'Connor flatly, 'Lenin seems a child.' But this, after all, is the true native blarney, bred of insularity and cheek and the lack of a comprehensive political education.[21]

Despite this reservation, however, Sayers' overall assessment of the book was highly positive. Five days later, the widely-read *Time* magazine published an unsigned review that also seized on the quote about Lenin, calling the author of those words 'bristling'. Yet the *Time* review, although it had much to say about Collins, had little to say about the biography. It merely called O'Connor one of a number of 'gifted young Irish writers'.[22]

Far more extensive was the commentary offered by Horace Gregory in a review in *The Nation*, which discussed three recent books on Ireland and found some fault with them all. Gregory suggested that in two poems by Yeats 'the familiars of Irish life, which are madness, wit, self-betrayal, sentimentality, famine, and a sense of guilt, convey their reality with greater force' than in any of the books

20 Maurice Joy, 'A life of Michael Collins', *New York Herald Tribune Books* (19 Sept. 1937), 4. **21** Michael Sayers, 'The patriot', *New Republic* (22 Sept. 1937), 193. **22** 'Big fellow', *Time* (27 Sept. 1937), 69–70.

under review. Calling O'Connor's work 'a brisk melodrama disguised as biography', Gregory suggested that some of its flaws resulted from the fact that 'the real death in Dublin is too terrible to bear'. Although Gregory called O'Connor 'by no means one of the least able of the younger Irish writers', he found the biography 'a curiously elliptical life', arguing that 'the realities of Michael Collins's position as Minister of Finance in the Dail Eireann must be read between the lines of machine-gun narrative and Mr O'Connor's gratuitous opinions', including (once more) the comment on Lenin. From the Lenin comment forward (Gregory asserted), 'sensible disagreement with Mr O'Connor seems futile; Michael Collins becomes his property, his hero of an exciting legend, and it is not always possible to discern the moment when an extravagant claim for mere heroism shades into fact'. Although recommending 'O'Connor's chapter on the signing of the Treaty of 1921' as 'a warning to men of action in revolutionary tactics', Gregory's overall opinion of O'Connor's book seems sour; he ended his review by recommending a new Liam O'Flaherty novel in a way that reflected poorly on O'Connor: 'it would seem that he [O'Flaherty] is one of the few writers of his generation in Ireland who is at last fulfilling the promise of his earlier work'.[23] Next to Gregory's extended censure, the brief praise offered by Philip H. Williams in a review in *The Commonweal* seems almost perfunctory. More concerned with Collins himself than with O'Connor's book, Williams merely said of the author that 'truly he has brought out the living man'.[24] Although published in the 'Shorter notices' section of the November 1937 issue of the *Catholic World*, an unsigned review there was more substantive than Williams's comments. The review asserted that O'Connor had done 'a good job, for he gives us a living, speaking picture of a hero – not an idealized hero either'. However, the reviewer ended by complaining that '[o]ften enough Mr O'Connor goes out of his way to publish his disapproval of persons or policies with the certainty of giving offence, at the same time leaving us in the dark about his own opinions'.[25]

As the assessments just quoted demonstrate, although the American reviews of *Death in Dublin* were mixed, they were also numerous and were often lengthy and thus testified to the perceived importance of the book. Far less attention was paid to the publication, in 1939, of *The fountain of magic*, O'Connor's collection of translations of Irish poems. The *New Yorker*, for instance, merely noted that the book consisted of 'new versions of the traditional heroic songs, the classical poetry

23 Horace Gregory, 'The Irish "Trouble"', *The Nation* (2 Oct. 1937), 355–6. 24 Philip H. Williams, 'Republic and Free State', *The Commonweal* (8 Oct. 1937), 555–6. 25 'Shorter notices', *Catholic World*, 145 (Nov. 1937), 250.

of the bards, and post-seventeenth-century folk poetry'.[26] However, Horace Reynolds, who had praised *Death in Dublin* so emphatically, also offered a long and glowing assessment of the poems in the *Christian Science Monitor*. He described the translations as superb: 'More literal than those of Mangan and James Stephens, for instance, they combine respect for the original with poetic feeling … Mr O'Connor measures his powers against the finest of the translations and adaptations from the Irish, and comes off creditably'. Reynolds concluded on an emphatic note: 'Excellent in selection, sympathetic in feeling, certainly this is the finest volume of translations from Irish verse since Hyde's 'Love Songs of Connacht".[27] Reynolds, however, was highly unusual in devoting so much attention to this collection; for most periodicals, then as now, poetry was simply not a major interest. Thus the review by Ruth Lechlitner in the *New York Herald Tribune* consisted of one paragraph, in which the translations were simply called 'excellent'.[28]

In contrast, O'Connor's next novel, *Dutch interior*, attracted significant attention, much of it extremely positive, although there was disagreement about the perceived influence of Joyce. In the space of three days in November 1940, for instance, the novel was reviewed in five important periodicals. Thus, Ruth Byrns, writing in *The Commonweal*, declared O'Connor to be a gifted and sensitive writer and argued that the novel was 'written beautifully'.[29] However, Clifton Fadiman, a major critic writing in the *New Yorker*, was far more dismissive in a brief but stinging review. 'The talented Irishman Frank O'Connor' (wrote Fadiman):

> has applied a Chekhovian technique, not too successfully, to an overbrief novel of middle-class Irish life called, for no very good reason, 'Dutch interior.' He touches his people so glancingly that one never really gets to know them, but the effect is to give an impression of the hopelessness and dreariness of contemporary Ireland. As a matter of fact, everything O'Connor is trying to say was said better long ago by James Joyce. Still, there are certain fugitive pages of quiet perception that give the author a place of his own, though he has yet to write a book genuinely worthy of him.[30]

26 Review of *The fountain of magic*, *The New Yorker* (27 May 1939), 84.   27 Horace Reynolds, '1,000 years of Irish poetry', *Christian Science Monitor* (17 June 1939), 10.   28 Ruth Lechlitner, 'Poetry, ancient, modern', *New York Herald Tribune Books* (6 Aug. 1939), 7.   29 *Ruth Byrns,* review of *Dutch interior*, in *The Commonweal* (15 Nov. 1940), 106.   30 Clifton Fadiman, Review of *Dutch*

Ironically, an anonymous and equally brief review in *The Nation*, published on the same day as Fadiman's, almost seems designed to counter the latter's comments. The *Nation* reviewer called the novel a 'series of scenes' offering 'a realistic composite picture of the Irish temperament and of life in a modern Irish city. These vignettes', the reviewer concluded, 'recall 'Dubliners,' but they are warmer, more full-bodied than Joyce's work'.[31]

Far more substantive than any of the reviews just mentioned, however, was the lengthy commentary by Horace Reynolds published (alongside a large photo of O'Connor) in the *New York Times Book Review*. It would have been hard for Reynolds to begin more positively than he did:

> Let me say at the outset that this is the deeply felt and beautifully executed work of a sensitive artist. All those who read to understand and comprehend life more fully will profoundly enjoy this book. Here are warmth and compassion and irony, both tenderness and cruelty. It is a book to be read slowly, to be savored, to be read more than once.
>
> The title is significant. O'Connor has eschewed the vivid coloring of an O'Casey or an O'Flaherty, avoiding the strong dynamics which crash flamboyant humor against flamboyant tragedy ... For the superficial distinctnesses of local color O'Connor has substituted what impinges itself again and again on the Corkonian consciousness ... [so that the city described in the novel might seem] any small provincial city anywhere.

Reynolds felt that both O'Connor and his friend Seán O'Faoláin, both from Cork, 'write about [Cork] with more affection than hate', and he asserted that 'there's a streak of genius in each, and they both honestly seek to comprehend and express the poverty and pride of contemporary Irish life'. Like the anonymous reviewer for *The Nation*, however, Reynolds also considered the book 'episodic, a series of loosely related sketches, a form which appears to be everywhere the residuum of Joyce's influence upon the structure of the novel. Discursiveness and economy are its advantages; loss of concentration and the power of an integrated structure its drawbacks'. However, Reynolds found also much to praise in O'Connor's style and extolled his writing for being natural and free of affectation.[32]

Almost as positive as the review by Reynolds was the assessment by Thomas

interior, in *The New Yorker* (16 Nov. 1940), 84. **31** Review of *Dutch interior*, *The Nation* (16 Nov. 1940), 485. **32** Horace Reynolds, 'Frank O'Connor's "Dutch interior"', *New York Times Book Review* (17 Nov. 1940), 6.

Sugrue, in the *New York Herald Tribune*. Although Sugrue contended that the book offered 'few leading characters' and 'little or no plot', he admired its dark depiction of middle-class life and maintained that O'Connor sketches his characters and action swiftly and effectively. Sugrue claimed that 'O'Connor produces a mood, subjective and impressionistic … As the pages go by, the story evokes mental shudders; not because it is ugly, but because it is true. It is a sensitive, delicately woven book, to be read for profit, not fun'.[33] All the reviews of *Dutch interior* just cited appeared within a few days of each other in November 1940. In the following month an unsigned review appeared in the *Springfield Sunday Union and Republican*, which admired the novel for its playing with light and shadows and its beautiful prose (it quoted a long passage to illustrate the effectiveness of O'Connor's phrasing). The review summarized that "Dutch Interior' is a book to be read slowly and to be reread'.[34] One month later yet another review of the novel was published, this time in the *New Republic* and written by James Stern (who would eventually become another one of O'Connor's greatest champions in the US). Stern began by hailing O'Connor as an author who, in *Guests of the nation*, had shown himself to be 'a writer of extraordinary power'. Although suggesting that the tales in *Guests*, as well as collections by Joyce and O'Flaherty, 'probably contain the highest achievements in the art of the contemporary short story in the English language', Stern lamented that nevertheless 'the name of Frank O'Connor does not appear to be well known in this country'. Partly, he suggested, this was because publishers and readers favoured novels over short stories, and he even raised the possibility that O'Connor, perhaps succumbing to this pressure, had presented, in *Dutch interior*, 'a series of very loosely related chapters, some of which are themselves superb, self-contained stories. The technique', Stern continued, 'has its advantages: every word has to be read; but in a novel the constant introduction of new characters is hampering and confusing and requires great concentration from the reader'. In his final paragraphs, Stern not only offered a general assessment of the novel but also suggested a possible new direction for O'Connor's art:

> 'Dutch Interior' – an unfortunate title, for surely a Vermeer, a Ter Borch, does not suggest the squalor, drabness and the everlasting domestic crises of O'Connor's Ireland – is a very sad book. There are passages of great

---

33 Thomas Sugrue, 'Hunters and shadows', *New York Herald Tribune Books* (17 Nov. 1940), 10.
34 'Incisive portrayal of Irish characters: Frank O'Connor's "Dutch interior" pictures people and environment', *Springfield Sunday Union and Republican* (15 Dec. 1940), 7E.

beauty; too many, perhaps, just as there are too many characters, for so brief a novel. And there are many moments of such rhetorical dialogue, of such drama, that the reader who knows his Irish Players feels he is seeing the characters on the stage ... Ireland has produced great dramatists, and this novel leaves the impression that Frank O'Connor has in him all that is required for first-rate theatre.[35]

Perhaps Stern was being ironic; his tone here is hard to discern. What seems clear, however, not only from Stern's comments but from many of the other reviews of O'Connor's works published in the first decade of his American career, is that in those first ten years O'Connor had established a very solid reputation in the US – not only as a writer of short fiction (which is how he is mainly remembered today) but also as a novelist, biographer, poet, translator, and even as a potential dramatist. His ear for dialogue is one of the traits most often praised in his work of the 1930s and early 40s, and praise of this skill is closely related to praise of a trait that is even more frequently emphasized in American commentary of this decade: praise for his 'honesty' and 'realism'. Again and again reviewers commended O'Connor for depicting life as it was actually lived, and in the few instances when O'Connor's writing was censured, it was criticized for being unrealistic, whether because of improbability, affectation, trickiness, melodrama, superficiality or unconvincing dialogue. Far more often, however, O'Connor was extolled for his ability to depict life in realistically credible ways. Related to this emphasis on realism, moreover, was a tendency among many reviewers to commend O'Connor for the balanced tone of his writing – for his ability to blend humour and pathos, sympathy and irony, sentiment and detachment. More than one reviewer commented that O'Connor rarely either condemned or condescended to the people he described, and the strongest complaints his writings provoked during this first decade of American reviews came from commentators who felt that O'Connor had sacrificed his objectivity for bias of some sort (as in the charges against his biography of Michael Collins). In general, though, O'Connor had received the kind of attention from major American periodicals that any young writer could envy. He was regarded not simply as a short-story writer but as a comprehensive man of letters, and by 1941 the stage was set for the even warmer welcome that would soon develop and would make him one of the best-selling and most respected of all serious Irish authors in the United States.

35 Stern, 'Frank O'Connor as novelist', 91.

Frank O'Connor: reluctant realist

MAURICE HARMON

Frank O'Connor belonged to that post-colonial, post-revolutionary generation of Irish writers who in their youth were deeply affected by romantic nationalism and then as emergent writers by the reality of life in the new society of the 1920s, 30s and 40s. While he did not speak about forging the uncreated conscience of his race, he and his contemporaries – Liam O'Flaherty, Francis Stuart, and Seán O'Faoláin – were in effect the pioneers of their time. The young poets of the period – Austin Clarke, Padraic Fallon, Patrick Kavanagh, Denis Devlin, and Brian Coffey – had to find new subject matter and idiom to distinguish them from W.B. Yeats and poets of the Irish Literary Revival. For the novelists and short-story writers there was a comparable need to identify new subject matter and to develop techniques to encompass the changed reality of Irish life in the decades after the revolution. While they might have thought about the example of Russian novelists who represented a society of aristocrats and peasants much like their own, most of them found the shorter compass of the story more congenial as they examined an embryonic society. The revolution in fact had virtually destroyed the model of Big House and peasant. In its place were the peasantry and an indemnified middle-class who were linked to the countryside economically, culturally and linguistically. They spoke the same language with a large Hiberno-English component; O'Connor's stories are particularly interesting for their varied uses of dialect and non-dialect narrators. They were loyal to the same conservative Catholic Church, were undisturbed by intellectual questions, and had horizons that were confined largely to the island of Ireland. There were exceptions – the small town intellectual, the social misfit, those who sinned against the Catholic light, some of whom appeared in the work of Seán O'Faoláin. The big sin was sexual. It appears in many of O'Connor's stories. Other means of possible regression – cheating, greed, lying, swearing – were hardly worth mentioning from the altar.

Nationalism was part of the romance of youth. Participation in the revolution was something one might claim. If a man had been 'out' during the Troubles – the Civil War was less readily mentioned – that was good enough for most people, good for loyalty, good for a recommendation, something handed on in the family.

Romantic Ireland hung on and it is significant that Frank O'Connor may just mention revolutionary involvement as a motive for loyalty. No other justification is required. He had little to guide him. Irish life had changed so much that the attitudes and values of writers of the Irish Literary Revival had little relevance, being generally romantic and/or backward-looking. The revolution made him an adherent to the cause of independence so that although he drew back from its emotional excesses, and reacted to the nationalistic appeal of Daniel Corkery, his early work about life in the country is infused with romantic colour and excitement. The Irish Literary Revival had its iconography of round tower, Irish wolfhound, Cathleen Ní Houlihan and leprechauns, but these were out of place in the grimmer climate of revolution and its aftermath. In O'Connor's stories they have been replaced by his evocative commemoration of traditional life, reflected in peasants and landscape, with particular attention to the iconography of the kitchen, the centre of domestic life. When post-revolutionary society came into being he had realism thrust upon him as he sought to portray its values. The tension between romanticism and realism gives some of O'Connor's stories a particular interest. Moved instinctively to respond to traditional, rural life with affection, he wrote story after story in which he created a colourful and attractive version of peasant life. His strong emotional nature gave vitality and vividness to these depictions of a vanishing world, but it is noticeable that they give no sense of the actuality of life, of how people lived and worked. Then he tried to contrast the old and the new, the world of the West, of Ummera, Farranchreest or Carriganassa with the urban world of Cork, Dublin and the small towns. Turning more directly and critically to the new society of shopkeepers, shop girls, clerks, priests, bachelors and strong mothers – the milieu of piety, respectability, caution and greed – he described the world with some distaste but also with delight in its comic absurdity, its timidity, its knee-jerk support of nationalism, its passive morality. O'Connor's fondness for exuberance, drama, attractive dialogue, colour and vitality determined the texture and tone of his work.

In the clash between parish priest and parishioners in 'Peasants', O'Connor established one of the concerns that would occupy him for much of his literary career. Why do people behave in particular ways? Why do they have one set of responses rather than another? The conflict in this story is based on a relatively simple event. A man has stolen the funds of the local Club. Fearful for the shame this will bring to his family and to the community, the Club members want to send him to America until the incident has been forgotten and he can return. The parish priest has other ideas. As far as he is concerned the young man has done

wrong and should be tried in a court of law. The committee members are aghast.
They reason with him.

> 'Maybe so, father,' said Con Norton, the vice-chairman, who acted as
> spokesman. 'Maybe you're right, but you wouldn't say his poor mother
> should be punished too and she a widow woman?'
>
> 'Serve his mother right!' said the priest shortly. 'There's none of you
> but knows better than I do the way that young man was brought up. He's
> a rogue and his mother is a fool. Why didn't she beat Christian principles
> into him when she had him on her knee?'
>
> 'That might be, too', Norton agreed mildly. 'I wouldn't say but you're
> right, but is that any reason his Uncle Peter should be punished?'
>
> 'Or his Uncle Dan?' asked another.
>
> 'Or his Uncle James?' asked a third.
>
> 'Or his cousins, the Dwyers, that keep the little shop in Lisnacarriga,
> as decent a living family as there is in County Cork?' asked a fourth.
>
> 'No, father,' said Norton, 'the argument is against you.'[1]

The argument becomes heated, but the priest is obdurate. The Committee will
not give up. They make a collection, bring the money to the priest and ask him to
give the boy a character reference so that the judge will 'leave him off and there'll
be no stain on the parish' (159). When that fails they offer to raise a contribution to
the parish fund. Faced with perjury and bribery the priest's anger and despair are
easily understood. He has spent his whole life, he tells them, preaching honesty,
truth and justice and they still do not understand.

The weakness in the story is that although the priest comes from only fifteen
miles away, he does not understand their argument. This failing is essential to the
dramatic mode of the story but it is unconvincing. At its heart is O'Connor's
interest in values. By upholding the principle that the thief is responsible for his
own actions the priest adheres to English/Roman law that was introduced into the
country by invasion and conquest. By upholding the idea that a disgrace to the
individual stains his family, including the cousins and the community, the peasants respond to a traditional concept. Through the priest's attack on the
long-tailed families he subverts a central force in modern Irish society – the

1 Frank O'Connor, *The stories of Frank O'Connor* (London, 1953), 156. Further citations are given in
the text.

network of kinship and connection that affected decision-making, influenced appointments, and undermined objective evaluation.

The issue is found even more clearly in one of his best stories 'In the train' which has a more complex structure, a more particularized and contrasting characterization, a steadier style, and an inherent dignity. His mastery of form and organization in this story makes it a joy to read. The focus of attention moves from one compartment to another, from one set of characters to another, one topic of conversation to another, linked by the meandering of the drunk, and signifying the influence of east coast, alien law weakening as the train makes its way westward from Dublin to Farranchreest. Once again it is a question of values which have been tested in a court of law. In the story a woman from the west, accused of poisoning her husband, is protected by her neighbours who will commit perjury rather than give evidence against her. As the elder among them says, 'What else could I do, woman? There was never an informer in my family' (172). He reflects sadly on the changes that have come about.

> 'Did any of ye ever think the day would come when a woman in our parish would do the like of that?'
>   'Never, never.'
>   'But she might do it for land?'
>   'She might.'
>   'Or for money?'
>   'She might so.'
>   'She might indeed. When the hunger is money people kill for the money; when the hunger is land people kill for the land. But what are they killing for now? I tell ye, there's a great change coming. In the ease of the world people are asking more. When I was a boy in the barony if you killed a beast you made six pieces of it, one for yourself and the rest for the neighbours. The same if you made a catch of fish. And that's how it was with us from the beginning of time. But now look at the change! The people aren't as poor or as good or as generous or as strong.' (173)

It might seem that the woman gets away with her crime, but the signs are against that assumption. She travels alone, subjected to the attentions of the drunk. She has escaped hanging but she will not escape the law of the people.

> 'Well now,' said Kendillon darkly, 'wasn't it great impudence in her to come back?'

'Wasn't it indeed?' echoed one of the women.

'I'd say she won't be there long,' he went on knowingly.

'You'll give her the hunt, I suppose?' asked Moll politely, too politely.

'If no one else do, I'll give her the hunt myself. What right have she in a decent place?'

'Oh, the hunt, the hunt,' agreed a woman. 'Sure, no one could ever darken her door again.' (172)

By the end as the isolated woman knows well she cannot go back to the life she had. The man she wanted is of no interest to her now. 'The flame of life had narrowed in her to a pinpoint, and she could only wonder at the force that had caught her up, mastered her and then thrown her aside' (178). It is a story alive with vignettes, contrasts and flexible dialogue, but more than anything it is a moral narrative of contrasting sets of values in which the law associated with the invader and colonist will not be supported by the rural population who will put their own justice in place, in defence of traditional values, now under attack.

The contrast between east and west is central to a number of stories. It is heard with particular emphasis in 'Uprooted' where two brothers, one a teacher in Dublin, one a curate in County Wicklow, return to where they were born and raised and where their parents still live. The story is seen through the eyes of the teacher whose search for an alternative life in Dublin has not resulted in satisfaction. The description of his life in a bed-sit in Rathmines resembles the settings and the tentative manner of some stories and characters in *Dubliners*. When the brothers arrive at their old home they step into time's pocket, a place where life goes on timelessly, unchanging, formulaic, colourful. The kitchen is as it was.

> Nothing was changed in the tall, bare, whitewashed kitchen. The harness hung in the same place on the wall, the rosary on the same nail in the fire-place, by the stool where their mother usually sat: table under the window, churn against the back door, stair without banisters mounting straight to the attic door that yawned in the wall – all seemed as unchanging as the sea outside. (198)

Listening to the voices of his parents, it seems to Ned that he was interrupting a conversation that had been going on since his last visit. Conscious of the gap that has opened between him and this childhood world he is deeply aware of its elements – the timelessness, its completeness in itself, the language used. He sees with intensity so that everything speaks of his loss – the colours of the landscape, the sea, the clouds, the habits of the people. It adds to his pain that their father is totally unaware of how the boys are feeling. He shows them off to the neighbours – two fine sons, one a priest, the other a teacher. 'Uprooted' is a wonderful, well-realized recording of western life which has its own rhythms and values. Nobody does this better than O'Connor in language that is pictorial in its depiction of indoor and outdoor settings, in its portraits of people who are part of the land-scape. The story creates a deeply moving connection with the local, even though that connection ignores the day to day realities of work, or the hardships of this western world.

The journey out to the island is a further trip back in time. Not only does the father want to boast about his sons to his wife's people but to demonstrate what he has achieved through them. He, a landless man, married a girl from the island, although her family were not pleased – 'They were an old family and I was nothing only a landless man' (204). Now he can prove himself through his sons. Once again the iconography of a kitchen epitomizes the blessings of the old life – 'The dim blue light poured down the wide chimney on their heads in a shower with the delicacy of light on old china ... the fire burned a bright orange ...' (210) – as do the mysterious ways of the island girls. Ned is deeply aware of the beauty of one of the girls. She is his *aisling* girl luring him back to what he has lost, evoking mystery and romantic possibility, increasing his sense of 'exultation and loss' (212). Morning brings reality. Tom confesses that he is lonely and isolated as a priest. Ned knows they can never go back: 'We made our choice a long time ago. We can't go back on it now' (214). He goes outside.

> There was a magical light on everything. A boy on a horse rose suddenly against the sky, a startling picture. Through the apple-green light over Carriganassa ran long streaks of crimson, so still they might have been enamelled. Magic, magic, magic! He saw it as in a children's picture-book with all its colours intolerably bright; something he had outgrown and could never return to, while the world he aspired to was as remote and intangible as it had seemed even in the despair of youth. (214–15)

Despite the high-spirited manner of the story real feeling comes through: the rift between east and west looked into with pain and that realisation of absence made all the more powerful because of the colourful, exaggerated yet deeply felt evocation of the beauty of what has been left, while the dream that lured the boys away remains unrealized. The ending with its unnecessary flourish is spoiled by O'Connor's editorialising, a weakness that grew. He does the reader's thinking for him, instead of allowing the insights to emerge naturally. His formula stories have these intrusions in abundance. 'Uprooted' like O'Connor's best stories about the west reaches out beyond itself, beyond the issue of men uprooted, to rich, magical evocation of place, people and culture. The issue of such displacement and loss, including the dream of success elsewhere in urban settings is common to western civilization. Behind cities everywhere lies the uprooting of people from rural, traditional life.

It was one thing for O'Connor to commemorate traditional life in warmly imagined narratives but quite another to take on the emergent life of towns and cities. The question of values by which one might live is examined in two stories, in particular, 'The Luceys' and 'The idealist'. The former was written to a formula that O'Connor had worked out by the 1940s: state the theme, tell the story, re-state the theme in the conclusion. The story which is told by an omniscient, non-dialect narrator focuses on members of a family. Tom Lucey, the elder, is a shopkeeper, a bookish, opinionated man whose son, Peter, swindles clients and then runs away to escape prosecution. Tom's brother Ben has a job with the County Council. His son Charles, a friendly, easygoing, adaptable man, also works for the Council. How the family deals with Peter's disgrace is the issue on which the story and its revelation of values turn. Prim and straight-laced, Tom expects his son to behave with probity by facing the music. Trapped within the rigidity he has framed for himself, he is unable to do anything practical to help his son. Charles who has the flexibility that is needed, is not shocked by Peter's lapse, thinks how the problem might be handled by pressure and influence, but knows he cannot do this on his own. He tells Tom his father might be able to use influence to get Peter off but his father refuses to become involved. Tom never forgets this nor does Charles realize the hopes he has raised.

> Tom Lucey's mind was in a rut, a rut of complacency, for the idealist too has his complacency and can be aware of it. There are moments when he would be glad to walk through any mud, but he no longer knows the way; he needs to be led; he cannot degrade himself even when he is most ready to do so. (302)

When Peter dies in England Ben goes to see Tom who refuses to accept his hand-shake of condolence.

'Ben,' said his brother, squaring his frail little shoulders, 'you disrespected my son while he was alive. Now that he's dead I'd thank you to leave him alone.' (304)

He becomes a misfit, more isolated than ever, more introverted, his oddness magnified. Then, years later, when Ben is dying and longs for Tom to visit him, Tom refuses. The old row and its legacy of bitterness lives on, exerting its distorting effects. Charles appeals to Tom to come to his father and to forgive him, but his uncle stands by his principles. 'I forgave him long ago for what he said about one that was very dear to me. But I swore that day, Charles, that never the longest day I would live would I take your father's hand in friendship' (311). Tom's wife accuses her husband: 'Even the wild beasts have more nature' (311).

That is the key. O'Connor's standard of behaviour is the decent man who is capable of feeling and able to rise above disagreements. Not to accept his brother's hand at a time of death goes against human nature. Not to visit his dying brother is a further outrage, one the townspeople will not forgive or forget and he knows it. O'Connor makes too much of the 'hysteria' in the town and of the pressure it puts on Charles. The story does not need this extra element. The question of how one behaves is in itself sufficient to the story. O'Connor judges the situation in terms of wholeness or deficiency. The decent man has sympathy and effective consideration. The deficient man narrows reality beyond its normal human range and is a source of evil.

The question of how one should behave is also central to 'The idealist' which dramatizes the issue through the figure of the schoolboy Larry Delaney, an avid reader of stories about English schoolboys. English boys, he saw, always stuck together. They never told lies and would not talk to anyone who did. If they were caught doing something wrong, they always told the truth. But Irish boys 'sucked up' to the teacher, tried to blame somebody else if they were caught, even if it meant telling lies, and howled shamelessly if they were punished. Delaney begins to behave like an English schoolboy – tells the truth when he is late for school, is beaten for being late but doesn't show his pain; when caught talking in class, he admits it and is again beaten, more severely this time, because the teacher suspects he is defying his authority. Again Delaney refuses to show his pain. Then, one day, he notices a boy named Gorman taking something from another boy's coat. When the teacher questions the boys, asks each in turn if he stole money or saw someone doing so, Gorman denies all knowledge of the incident and says he saw nobody else doing it. Delaney is trapped. According to the rules he cannot throw the blame on someone else. The teacher in a rage at his refusal beats him fiercely. Eventually, Gorman is exposed by one of the other boys but Delaney has had enough. English rules just do not work in Irish contexts.

The story is not entirely satisfactory. It has the feeling of being manipulated and the use of the word 'hysteria' to describe Delaney's feelings, and those of the teacher and the boys is exaggerated. The psychological analysis is too adult for the boy-narrator whose coy tone is nauseating. Furthermore in the final confrontation between Delaney and the teacher, the latter's way of speaking is false: 'There's no need to lose control of yourself, my dear young fellow, and there's no need whatever to screech like that. 'Tis most unmanly. Go back to your seat now and I'll talk to you another time' (51). This is not the teacher's way of speaking.

'The custom of the country' also deals with the influence of English ways on Irish values. On one side is English independence of mind, reliance on logic or reason, and belief in man's right to practise whatever religion he wishes. On the other side is Irish Catholic complacency, emotionalism, a reliance on faith and the Pope, not to mention concern for what the neighbours might think. Ernest, an Englishman, falls in love with the innocent Anna and tries to seduce her but without success. Anna's mother points out that since Ernest is not Catholic she cannot marry him, unless he 'turns', that is, converts to Catholicism. After a number of incidents he is baptized, received into the church and marries Anna. But it is too good to be true. On the boat to England he tells her he already has a wife and two children but, he declares, he loves Anna and knew from the beginning of their relationship that she is the only woman for him. True to her upbringing Anna refuses to go with him and returns home. There she has to endure the commiseration and gossip of the townspeople, while Ernest writes to her regularly. Suddenly, in rebellion against middle-class mores, she realizes that she has a husband who loves her, whose child she carries and to whom she now writes telling him when to expect her. O'Connor's characters who try to live by English values are faced with an amiable, charming but corrupt society. The theory behind this is that there is something wrong with Irish life, but in fact O'Connor likes Irish life, its complex, contradictory, exasperating and unpredictable ways. Instead of fighting it, he sets out to describe it.

In 'The house that Johnny built' he looks at romance, Irish-style. Johnny Desmond, a countryman, owns the best general shop in town. Impressed by the style and attractiveness of a new woman doctor, he orders a new brown suit and a new soft hat, puts on a new gold watch chain and goes to see her. His purpose is

marriage, but she turns him down. But Johnny is not easily foiled. He builds a fine
house and a chemist shop and advertises for an assistant. When she arrives he
meets her at the station, takes her home, wines and dines her, telling her, when
she asks, that there is no Mrs Desmond but that the post is still vacant. He is
mystified when she suddenly decides to visit the chapel. He waits in growing
anxiety but when a car pulls up outside it is the doctor who comes in. The young
chemist has come to her, in tears. Johnny does not understand but the doctor
makes it clear.

> 'At your age oughtn't you know damn well that in a town like this you
> couldn't bring a girl just out of school to live with you.'
> 'God above!' Johnny said in an anguished whisper, his hands clasped,
> his face gone white. 'I meant no harm to the girl.' (256)

Next morning he asks the girl to marry him: she has seen his house – he tells her
how much it cost – and he'd like her to choose the pictures for the walls. But he
cannot win. He knew she would not have him. It baffles him. O'Connor uses
humour to reveal character and to comment on Irish life. Perhaps it is the only way
he can capture its absurdity and pervasive ignorance. Desmond is an extreme case,
hence the broad humour, but stands for men who foolishly think they can buy
happiness. Love does not enter into it.

By contrast 'The holy door', a romantic novella of some fifty-five pages, is
more restrained, its humour subordinated to comical and complicated relationships between Charlie Cashman and a number of women – Polly Donegan and
Nora Lawlor, both of whom he marries, Mollie the servant whom he makes pregnant and his mother, an old battle-axe who believes in ghosts and is reputed to cast
spells. Her big regret is that her husband left the business to Charlie and not to her
other son. The catch is that if Charlie has no children it will pass on his death to
his brother's children. Charlie wants to marry Nora but she turns him down, so he
marries the prudish Polly who doesn't bear him a child.

At the heart of all this are the 'facts of life' which Nora is curious about and
ignorant of and which Polly will not tell her about, particularly after the shock of
her marriage night. When Polly realizes she may not conceive and sees the consequences for the business she consults Nora who advises her to go on pilgrimage to
Rome, to the holy door, opened once every seven years. She and Charlie go to
Rome, but it does not work. There is no sign of a child. Then Nora suggests that
since Charlie is so unattractive she should replace him in her imagination by a

handsome man. She remarks that Carmody the young teacher is good-looking. Word gets out, as it always does in O'Connor's stories, and Charlie realizes people are laughing at him. Word is that their not having a child is his fault. So Molly the servant comes into the picture and he proves his manhood, but that leads to even worse complications. He spirits her away to another town, but she becomes remorseful for her sin and wants him to tell all to his wife. And so the complications develop.

Typically in an O'Connor urban story people are given to backbiting, envy, intrigue. So too is ignorance of sexual matters and the authority and cunning of the priest who is as interfering and nosey as the rest of his flock, as clever a schemer as any of them and a good man to patch up disagreements. Ironically, his exercise of power is more secular than spiritual. Life according to O'Connor is complicated by intrigues, rivalry, envy and gossip. His belief that this is the way the world is informs his fiction, justifying its air of unending comedy. The human race, as he sees it, or at least the Irish part of it, is always good for a laugh or at least a prolonged chuckle. In the process he often exaggerates, making people ignorant, simple-minded and one-sided.

'The mad Lomasneys' also deals with romantic complications. Social pressure is not an issue, but individual contradiction is. Although Rita Lomasney and Ned Lowry have been close friends for years, first of all Rita falls in love with a seminarian, then on a whim, in a reckless gamble, marries an older man even though Ned has already asked her to marry him. She makes a choice that will dog her for the rest of her life and Ned, losing his composure and air of indifference, marries someone else a month later. It is a form of 'madness', of reckless behaviour, in which Rita's confused quest for love ends in pain. O'Connor concentrates on the girl's own nature, because of which she ends up with a man she does not love and loses the one man she respects, her measure of her own behaviour. When O'Connor writes at his best he develops the story in such a way that the emotional high-point is finely brought into focus, as when Ned in 'Uprooted' is drawn to the island girl and then realizes he cannot undo the past, or the poignant figure of the brother in 'The Luceys' with the bottle of whiskey and two glasses by his bedside as he waits in vain for the arrival of his brother, or the predicament in which Rita Lomasney lands herself through her own irresponsible nature. There is less emphasis here on social pressures. Rita's own temperament makes her behave as she does. O'Connor says this is human nature; these are the foolish ways we behave at times. He was trying to make sense of what he saw and if he did not like it, he used humour and comedy as a mode of comment on it. Central to his approach was the need to entertain, to dramatize, to create colourful character and he displayed a strong feeling for oral narrative. Above all, underlying his work is the endemic question of the difficulties of self-knowledge which we also find in writers from George Moore to Mary Lavin.

Inside out: a working theory of the Irish short story

JOHN KENNY

> These things are external to the man; style is the man.
>
> Comte de Buffon, *Discourse on style*.

There would seem to be a close parallel between the relative generic youth of the short story and the frequency with which it is scolded for its immature ways. Here, for instance, is one of the most entertaining chidings ever inflicted on an entire literary genre:

> Short stories amount for the most part to parlor tricks, party favors with built-in snappers, gadgets for inducing recognitions and reversals: a small pump serves to build up the pressure, a tiny trigger releases it, there follows a puff and a flash as freedom and necessity combine; finally a celluloid doll drops from the muzzle and descends by parachute to the floor.

With his synonymic indication of diminutive stature, the American critic and practitioner, Howard Nemerov, thus confined the short story to the play-pen of literary history.[1] This is a particularly facetious version of a view of the genre widely held – if sometimes only colloquially – by both readers and writers of short fiction. Simple length is accepted as automatically indicative of a grander, more adult aesthetic ambition in and for the novel; the very shortness of the short story is taken as a potential admission of smaller, more confined artistic intentions. Even during what is considered to be its heyday in Ireland, this was the suspicion voiced by Seán O'Faoláin: 'I suppose no university in Britain thinks the short-story other than a modern toy.'[2] Fourteen years after O'Faoláin's extended response to the suspected critical diminution of the short story, a second Irishman provided a second and much more influential formal defence while being equally mindful of the potential for a negative translation of shortness into a kind of less-ness: 'the conception of the short story as a miniature art is inherently false'.[3] Frank O'Connor's rejection of any critical description of the short story as a miniature and therefore minor form is writ large throughout *The lonely voice*.

1 Quoted in Ian Reid, *The short story* (London, 1977), 2.   2 Seán O'Faoláin, *The short story* (London, 1948; repr. Old Greenwich, CT, 1974), 26.   3 Frank O'Connor, *The lonely voice: a study of the short story* (Cleveland, OH, 1963; Repr. London, 1965), 27.

While the individual chapters on writers in *The lonely voice* are rarely read so frequently or closely as the introduction, where O'Connor provided what has turned out to be an eminently portable theory of production for the short story, some crucial points are scattered outside of those opening pages. There is, for instance, the almost throwaway remark in the opening sentence of his study of D.H. Lawrence and A.E. Coppard: 'Though the short story does not seem to me to be an English form ...'[4] Paralleled with O'Faoláin's comment on the contemporaneous attitude to the short story in the literature departments of British universities, the basic operational implications for Irish writers dependent for decent fame or income on the British publishing industry becomes clear from O'Connor's quick dismissal of the English writer's short-story talents. It has long been a phenomenon, especially in Ireland where we are yet assumed to be especially solicitous of the form, that young or new fiction writers launch their careers with a collection of stories and quickly follow this with a novel that is usually part of a two-book deal with British publishers who, if O'Connor is to believed, are rarely likely to be natively disposed to nurturing short-story talents in the long term. Very few writers who start out in this way later return to shorter fiction. The short story is presently automatically thought of as the generic domain of apprenticeship, of somewhat unprofitable childish party games before the writer matures into the more serious version of the saleable fiction writer – which is the novelist. In terms of sheer material profitability, the international short story, even in the more lucrative domain of American periodicals, no longer has the close mutually supportive relationship with magazines that provided for John Updike's wistful recollection of supporting himself and his family during his twenties by the sale of just six stories per year.[5]

In terms of aesthetic prestige, unprofitableness was equally not the perceived case with the volume generally taken to be the foundation-stone of the modern Irish short story. George Moore's *The untilled field* (1903) was laid down, at least in Moore's retrospective self-assessment, as 'a landmark in Anglo-Irish literature, a new departure', a book written in the not inconsiderable hope of 'furnishing the young Irish of the future with models'.[6] O'Connor was confident that 'Irish literature has gone Moore's way'.[7] As matters have progressed, however, the young Irish have not always been grateful to Moore for his example. After his first book, *Long lankin* (1970), a thematically cohesive collection of stories that practised a

4 Ibid., 30.   **5** John Updike, *More matter: essays and criticism* (New York, 1999), 256.   **6** George Moore, Preface, *The untilled field*, intro. Terence Brown (London, 1903; repr. Dublin, 1990), xxiii, xix.
7 O'Connor, *The lonely voice*, 37.

conscious version of the scrupulous meanness of the Moore-influenced *Dubliners*, John Banville for instance published just two further uncollected stories later in the 1970s and has never returned to the form. Banville's judgment that the short story, though ironically a 'splendid' form with 'a far higher success rate than the novel', was essentially 'an easy form' was emphatic; it would, he was arguing by the age of thirty, be 'foolish to expect to derive from short stories the same satisfaction to be had in the novel'.[8] And this was from a young writer already devoted to the fiction of Henry James, one of the major figures who passed on to the twentieth century a concept of the short story as a component part of the art of fiction, as 'a form delightful and difficult'.[9] While Banville's seemingly natural inclinations in prose are the exact opposite of O'Connor's admitted difficulties in writing novels, and while others of the handful of Irish names internationally recognized as masters of fictional prose (John McGahern and William Trevor for instance) are equally known for their abilities in short and long forms, Banville is easily our most articulate and uncompromising novelist-critic and his regularly voiced practitioner's aesthetics of fiction are sophisticated even by world standards. As such, his view of the short story as a form vis-à-vis the novel is an indication of the current danger for the short story to find itself *in extremis* in the most influential of Irish writing circles.

A combined material and aesthetic diminution in overall status reflects, and further produces, a dearth of short-story theories and generic specifications in Ireland and elsewhere. Too often, what is said about the novel is taken to apply to fiction generally, and thus, by subsumption, to the short story. The standard relegation of the short story in the minds of contemporary editors and readers is exemplified in Carmen Callil and Colm Tóibín's *The modern library: the two hundred best novels in English since 1950* (1999) which subsumed under its generic banner important story collections by Alistair MacLeod, Raymond Carver and Mary Lavin.

While the variety of types and the volume of individual examples of the short story provide their own warnings against interpretation and reductive classification, I want to suggest here that one of the short story's key inherent elements (inherent in the criticism if not always in the stories themselves) is implicated in the pervasive view of the genre as an immature variety of fiction. For present serviceability, I want primarily to focus on ideas about the short story as a genre, on its

8 John Banville, 'A sense of proportion', *Hibernia* (30 Jan. 1976), 26. **9** Henry James, 'The storyteller at large: Mr Henry Harland. Comedies and errors' (1898) in Roger Gard (ed. and intro.), *The critical muse: selected literary criticism* (London, 1987), 333.

theories. Lest that word raise an early groan I should point out that what is intended here is not any external imposition of a Procrustean critical template – I am not interested for the moment in typologies or morphologies – but the elicitation of a short story theory mainly from the formal ideas practitioners have had about their own short-story writing, certain generalisations they have made based on their own developing experience of the craft. These working theories are usually explicitly expressed outside of the work proper, but they are also sometimes organically figured as actual themes within certain stories, as in the prime examples from Ireland's two major relevant theorists: Frank O'Connor's 'The idealist' and Seán O'Faoláin's 'How to write a short story'. Rather than anything survey-like or comprehensive, I intend merely a focus on a basic but crucial dialectic that generally surfaces when we speak of the short story in general and of the Irish short story in particular.

Almost all of the few major practitioners' theories we have of the short story's emergence and development mention its *lyrical* constitution. The two dominant and still prevalent theories tend to focus on either the stylistic composition of stories, as with Poe's originative theories, or, instead, on the pervasive social conditions that seem to foster the growth of story writing, as in the theories of Henry James and their development in Frank O'Connor, Seán O'Faoláin and, less programmatically but nonetheless crucially, in John McGahern. These separate tendencies in short-story criticism – the one more formalist, the other more sociocultural – can be usefully integrated by a consideration of the respective ways in which they define and develop what they variably call the lyrical element. The important initial distinction here will be between a standard sense of the lyrical as a style of language, where the meanings of words are poetically overdetermined, and a more metaphysical sense of the lyrical as a disposition towards the world regulated by social circumstances that may or may not be communicated in what we conventionally call poetic language. Such a disposition is often taken to be a matter of ethnic inevitability. In his chapter on 'The Irish school' in a survey of the modern short story whose usefulness was somewhat occluded by the stronger working generalisations of O'Faoláin's and O'Connor's subsequent studies, H.E. Bates attributed a large part of the success of the Irish short story to a 'natural genius for dramatizing life', to a 'naturally poetic' mode of expression.[10] While this may be partly a version of the familiar subscription to the idea of John Bull's Irelanders as more poetically than empirically inclined, there would appear to be reasonable plausibility in Bates's suggestions. O'Connor was especially keen to

10 H.E. Bates, *The modern short story: a critical survey* (London, 1941; repr. London, 1943), 148–9.

align the short story with the lyric disposition. 'I write my stories as though they were lyrics', he said: '... I would call myself a spoiled poet.'[11] Seemingly natural native inclinations to the poetic dramatisation of Irish life equally have their crucially conscious side however. The resolution here will be that while the lyrical as a defining term in both senses involves the idea of the free individual – whether alienated or proudly alone; whether as the person within a society or the writer within linguistic-artistic tradition – certain organic alignments of the living individual and social context, and of literary form and content, seem always to prevail. O'Connor's widely credited theory that a preference for the short story comprises an attitude, an ideological pre-disposition, among submerged population groups that subsequently seek a natural formal home for spontaneous expression can be allowed continue its dissemination since we still have little else on the short story to cling to critically. Further flotation can be aided however by a nuancing of the theory both in terms of its contexts and implications.

It is a commonplace that the historical evolution of short fiction is formidably heterogeneous. Despite this, the theory of short fiction that is widely taken to have inaugurated the modern short story, or at least extended reflection on the artistic possibilities of the genre, was very particularized. We tend to have an enduringly generalized conception of Edgar Allan Poe's foundational theory of the genre as the single-sitting effect, where the well-composed story is presumed to be similar to poetry in its achievement of 'unity of impression'. O'Connor additionally encapsulated the author's own act of composition within this theory of sitting and frequently commented that he found the writing of a short story absolutely analogous to the writing of a poem: 'I write my stories, as I've suggested, as a lyric poet would write his poems – I have to grasp all my ideas in one big movement ... novels require meditation and a more plodding day-to-day kind of energy.'[12] While there is the obvious problem with the basic premise of this theory that, as William Saroyan once remarked, some people can sit for much longer than others, it is worth reverting to the detail of Poe's arguments to point to his close alignment of poetry with the short story (what he at this stage calls a 'tale').

The important text is Poe's 1842 review of Hawthorne's *Twice-told tales*.[13] Here, Poe starts from the position of an already supreme confidence in the short fictional form:

11 Michael Longley, 'Frank O'Connor: an interview', *Twentieth Century Literature*, 36:3 (Fall 1990), 273. 12 Ibid., 273. 13 Edgar Allan Poe, *The complete tales and poems of Edgar Allan Poe, with selections from his critical writings*, intro. and notes Arthur Hobson Quinn, with Edward H. O'Neill (New York, 1992). All quotations are from 946–50.

> We have always regarded the *Tale* … as affording the best prose opportunity for display of the highest talent. It has peculiar advantages which the novel does not admit. It is, of course, a far finer field than the essay. It has even points of superiority over the poem.

In face of the ongoing interest in anthropologically inclined tales, Poe encouraged the transformation of residual folkloric content into an aesthetically self-conscious form. In essence, Poe's single-sitting compositional protocol is an extension of a poetic principle downwards to what he seemed to simultaneously suggest was a lesser and superior kind of writing. The 'unity of effect or impression' that rhymed poetry best achieves can be striven for in short stories; short stories must aspire to the condition of poetry. The implication of Poe's principle is that there is poetry, and there is prose, and 'poetic sentiment' can, in supreme cases, be found in either. Despite an accumulatively slippery distinction between genres, it becomes clear that Poe places the story, in terms of the values he outlines, exactly between poetry on the upper and the novel on the lower elevation. In thus distinguishing between story and novel, he imposes on the short story the Romantic organic imperative:

> In the whole composition there should be no word written, of which the tendency, direct or indirect, is not to the one pre-established design … The idea of the tale has been presented unblemished, because undisturbed; and this is an end unattainable by the novel.

In this alignment of the composition and effect of the ideal short story with lyric poetry, Poe was asking the short story generally to grow up as a genre fully conscious of its aesthetic possibilities.

Sometimes unspoken, and sometimes with local inflections, Poe's theory has remained a constant in short story criticism; any discussion of the genre as a serious art characterized by an adult concentration on form and unity echoes his idea of the single lyrical effect. Terms analogous with Poe's appear again and again. One of the best known descriptions of the organic relations between form and content in this lyrical effect is Flannery O'Connor's:

> When you can state the theme of a story, when you can separate it from the story itself, then you can be sure the story is not a very good one. The meaning of a story has to be embodied in it, has to be made concrete in it.

> A story is a way to say something that can't be said any other way, and it takes every word in the story to say what the meaning is.[14]

In the Irish case, Poe's and Flannery O'Connor's compositional obsession with the inseparability of form and content, if not the actual supremacy of form over content, has applied with equal weight. O'Connor's preferential treatment of architecture as opposed to materials is clear: 'It's the design of the story which to me is most important ... I'm always looking at the design of a story, not the treatment.'[15] Elizabeth Bowen had clearly attended closely to Poe's advice when, introducing her own stories, she emphasized that 'the short story revolves round one crisis only – one might call it, almost, a crisis in itself. There (ideally) ought to be nothing in such a story which can weaken, detract from, or blur the central, single effect.'[16] John McGahern's facility as a social chronicler was enabled by a similar concentration on organic form. 'Material and form are inseparable', he insisted in admiration of Joyce's *Dubliners*: 'So happy is the union of subject and object that they never become statements of any kind, but in their richness and truth are representations of particular lives – and all of life.'[17] Declan Kiberd provides a domestic version of the lyrical theory where the older forms of Gaelic literature (accepted as a vital influence generally on the emergence of the short story in Ireland) feed into contemporary stories in this specific way. Kiberd argues that the Irish short story's 'real generic affinities' are with a 'favoured form of Gaelic tradition, the lyric poem'. This means that, as with the stories from the Irish language Kiberd is introducing, there comes a 'moment of revelation, when the actual surfaces of things take on a wider symbolic meaning, as in a moment of poetry'. Far from the story being an 'easy' form as is sometimes argued, Kiberd argues that 'at its best it has the intensity and lyric power of a symbolist poem'.[18] As Kiberd has more recently shown, this lyrical Gaelic background and the resultant form of writing 'that is poetic, even though it is formally offered as prose' is a major factor in John McGahern.[19]

14 Flannery O'Connor, 'Writing short stories' in Sally and Robert Fitzgerald (selec. and ed.), *Mystery and manners: occasional prose* (New York, 1969), 96. 15 Anthony Whittier, 'Interview with Frank O'Connor' in Malcolm Cowley (ed. and intro.), *The Paris Review interviews*, 1st ser. (London, 1958), 151. 16 Elizabeth Bowen, 'Stories by Elizabeth Bowen' (1959) in Hermione Lee (selec. and intro.), *The mulberry tree: writings of Elizabeth Bowen* (London, 1986), 128. 17 John McGahern, '*Dubliners*' in Augustine Martin (ed.), *James Joyce: the artist and the labyrinth* (London, 1990), 71. 18 Micheál Ó Conghaile et al., *Fourfront: contemporary stories translated from the Irish*, intro. Declan Kiberd (Indreabhán, Conamara, 1998), 9. 19 Declan Kiberd, 'John McGahern's *Amongst women*' in Maria Tymoczko and Colin Ireland (eds), *Language and tradition in Ireland: continuities and displacements* (Boston, 2003), 195.

This theory of the modern short story as a genre devoted in its higher manifestations to concentrated lyrical moments, since it is a matter of assiduously applied effects, is the more difficult of our two ideas of the lyrical to accuse of any kind of childishness. A second version of the lyrical, which concentrates on the distillation of experience rather than the distillation of language in the short story, is more problematic and potentially divisive. One of the key artistic tensions of the modern world that emerged just when the short story itself was developing into a new form is at issue here. The dominant practitioners' sociocultural version of the lyrical theory argues that the short story is a prime generic reflection of the immature existential retreat into the self in the face of an increasingly imperious and complex reality: as the novel is to extroversion, so the short story is to introversion. As O'Connor put it in his generic distinction: 'A novel requires far more logic and far more knowledge of circumstances, whereas a short story can have the sort of detachment from circumstances that lyric poetry has.'[20] *The lonely voice*, where O'Connor solidified and handed down a working theory of the short story that remains, despite a paucity of reprints, strangely compelling even to those practitioners or critics who find his stories themselves outmoded, is the acme of the sociocultural approach to short-story theory. O'Connor's renowned theory of the short story defers absolutely to the eponymous idea of the lonely, lyrical voice somehow detached from a surrounding society: 'Always in the short story there is this sense of outlawed figures wandering about the fringes of society.'[21] And the continued relevance of this basic view of the short story is rarely questioned, in the Irish context or otherwise. The most direct testament to the continued impact of the lonely-voice theory is Richard Ford's introduction to *The Granta book of the American short story* (1992). Ford, whose own stories have been much admired in Ireland in turn, not least by John McGahern, takes *The lonely voice* to be 'the most provocative and attentive' work available on the genre and restates a claim, widely held, that O'Connor was, in 1962, writing 'from a country where the short story was *already* the national form'.[22] While many have refused the short story the luxurious title of 'the national form', O'Connor contrived at all opportunities to claim it as such and, further, to argue that the form best reflected post-independence national introversion and displaced the theatre's claim to be the quintessential national art:

> After him [O'Casey], writers like O'Flaherty, O'Faoláin, Mary Lavin, and myself turned from the theatre and adopted fiction – mainly the short

20 Whittier, Interview with Frank O'Connor, 148. **21** O'Connor, *The lonely voice*, 19. **22** Richard Ford, Introduction, *The Granta book of the American short story* (London, 1992; repr. London, 1998), vii.

story – as our medium. There were, of course, other reasons for this than purely literary ones, like the difficulties O'Casey himself encountered in dealing with a moribund theatre – but there was also, what is always to be understood in the short story, a turning away from the public to the private thing.[23]

While O'Connor's individual analyses of short story writers have much to offer, the lengthy introduction to *The lonely voice* arguably proves far too limited in its backward look and far too restrictive for any younger writers interested in developing their own working theories of both what the short story has been and what it might still do. That extraordinarily influential introduction should always be read, at least in part, as O'Connor's theories about himself:

> I had always wanted to write poetry, but I realized very early on that I didn't have much talent that way. Story telling is a compensation; the nearest thing one can get to the quality of a pure lyric poem. It doesn't deal with problems; it doesn't have any solutions to offer; it just states the human condition.[24]

The same can be suggested about the related theories Seán O'Faoláin proposed in *The short story* (1948) which informed O'Connor's more incisive and better-phrased judgments. Michael MacLaverty reacted particularly strongly to both O'Faoláin's and O'Connor's theories and went so far as to portray them as falsifying romantics 'out on the cod'.[25] The widespread acceptance of the lonely-voice theory would suggest, nevertheless, that the situation of the modern Irish short story was, local motivations aside, somehow symptomatic of the nature of the genre in certain wider contexts. The short story has flourished in those cultures where older, usually oral forms, are met head on with the challenge of new literary forms equipped with the ideology of modernisation. The short story is the genre of the cusp between tradition and modernity, and in this it is intimately related to the social motivation of lyric poetry. Post-Romantic nineteenth-century developments, as with Poe, are central here.

---

23 Frank O'Connor (selec. and ed.), *Modern Irish short stories* (London, 1957), xii.   **24** Frank O'Connor in Michael Steinman (ed.), *The happiness of getting it down right: letters of Frank O'Connor and William Maxwell, 1945–1966* (New York, 1996), 14.   **25** Michael McLaverty, 'The novel and the short story' in Sophia Hillan King (ed. and intro.), *In quiet places: the uncollected stories, letters and critical prose of Michael McLaverty* (Dublin, 1989), 112–13.

The traditional ideal of the lyric, Theodor Adorno has pointed out in an important essay on lyric poetry and society, is to remain 'unaffected by bustle and commotion'; it is a 'sphere of expression whose very essence lies in either not acknowledging the power of socialization or overcoming it through the pathos of detachment, as in Baudelaire or Nietzsche'. The lyrical attitude to experience is the quintessence of the experience of modernity; the demand that the lyrical word should be untainted by the world is itself, says Adorno, social in nature:

> It implies a protest against a social situation that every individual experiences as hostile, alien, cold, oppressive, and this situation is imprinted in reverse on the poetic work: the more heavily the situation weighs upon it, the more firmly the work resists it by refusing to submit to anything heteronomous and constituting itself solely in accordance with its own laws.[26]

The paradox is that the lyrical motivation absolutely accepts the reality of the anti-lyrical: in order for the lyrical to emerge as a justified privacy, the alienating modern must be – even if absolutely immanently – recognized as a gross reality. As Adorno puts it simply: 'the lyric work is always the subjective expression of a social antagonism'.[27] This is in direct agreement with one of O'Connor's most humorously delivered remarks on the unavoidable origins of the Irish lyrical disposition in an idiosyncratic 'national attitude' toward society, at least as it prevails among the educated:

> In America as in Czarist Russia one might describe the intellectual's attitude to society as 'It may work,' in England as 'It must work,' and in Ireland as 'It can't work.' A young American of our time or a young Russian of Turgenev's might look forward with a certain amount of cynicism to a measure of success and influence; nothing but bad luck could prevent a young Englishman's achieving it, even today; while a young Irishman can still expect nothing but incomprehension, ridicule, and injustice.[28]

The validity of the socially antagonistic lyrical voice in Ireland was accepted wholesale in the first half of the twentieth century, the decades immediately

---

26 Theodor W. Adorno, 'On lyric poetry and society' (1957) in Rolf Tiedemann (ed.), trans. Shierry Weber Nicholsen, *Notes to literature*, 1 (New York, 1991), 37, 39–40.   **27** Ibid., 45.   **28** O'Connor, *The lonely voice*, 20.

following Independence. In his introduction to the literature of the mid-twentieth-century decades in *The Field Day anthology*, Terence Brown underlines the validity of O'Connor's analysis and repeatedly emphasizes the 'defining lyricism' of the Irish short story:

> In a submerged population, where the provincial mind senses its own social impotence, definition of selfhood must perforce involve private feeling, romantic imagination and defeat. A lyric form is an aesthetic acquiescence in the general sense of powerlessness, an artistic making-do.

Working through O'Faoláin's similar views, Brown continues in the same vein:

> So the characteristic Irish short story deals in an oppressive, authoritarian environment, where law, politics and the iron regimen of economic life determine existence. The tale itself achieves a moment of lyric definition, an epiphany, in which protagonist, narrator, author and reader all share, as if momentarily transcending the bleak condition of life to which the story itself is attentive.[29]

While the Irish case is thus ample illustration of general theories on the lyric, with an awkward and unformed society proving discomfiting for the fiction writer, the practitioner-theorists who emerged in this period widened the social specificity of their situation into a general theory of the short story that has remained widely influential even where the exact same social conditions do not necessarily pertain. While O'Connor's theory about submerged population groups has continued potential validity in the social sense in that marginalizations of various kinds are cruelly imposed on, and sometimes carefully nurtured by, various demographic groups, the enduring influence of the theory surely also has something to do with the way in which it helps cultivate the popular Romantic image of the writer that we especially cater to in Ireland. Despite his best suspicions at the time of the overly subjective nature of modern art, O'Faoláin's propounded ideal of the short story was unrelentingly privatized and lyrical-minded:

> What one searches for and what one enjoys in a short story is a special distillation of personality, a unique sensibility which has recognized and selected at once a subject that ... is of value to the writer's temperament

---

29 Terence Brown, Introduction, 'The counter revival: provincialism and censorship 1930–1965' in Seamus Deane (ed.), *The Field Day anthology of Irish writing*, 3 (Derry, 1991), 93.

and to his alone – his counterpart, his perfect opportunity to project himself.[30]

If the Irish case is symptomatic, what seems to happen in a case where the writer feels driven into existential privacy by an alienating society is that Poe's kind of idea of the short story as an autonomously perfectible lyrical form is seen as a natural reaction. Thus both versions of the lyrical theory merge. The tension that can result is famously prominent in Joyce, whose emphases on poetic stylisation and on the cherished lyric moment of epiphany operate curiously alongside his realist instincts in *Dubliners*. An extreme version of this combined social and formal lyrical attitude is captured in one of Liam O'Flaherty's self-reflexive dialogues in *Shame the devil* (1934), and it is perhaps no accident here that O'Flaherty was heavily influenced by Nietzsche's rugged high Romanticism in the conception of his stories:

> I'd cut off your hands and feet in order to write a phrase. I'd have you annihilated for the sake of creating something really perfect. What you call the holiest thing in life is holy when it is the food of the imagination. When it ceases to feed the imagination it ceases to be holy.[31]

Regardless of background, this attitude has been particularly ingrained in our short story writers. Elizabeth Bowen, even in career retrospect, continued the pattern:

> Man has to live how he can: overlooked and dwarfed he makes himself his own theatre. Is the drama inside heroic or pathological? Outward acts have often an inside magnitude. The short story, with its shorter span than the novel's, with its freedom from forced complexity, its possible lucidness, is able, like the poetic drama, to measure man by his aspirations and dreads and place him alone on that stage which, inwardly, every man is conscious of occupying alone.[32]

Poe would have been proud of such obliterations of the external in favour of the aggressively perfectionist private imagination.

The potential working endgame in this dialectic of the lyrical disposition,

---

30 O'Faoláin, *The short story*, 30.   **31** Liam O'Flaherty, *Shame the devil* (London, 1934), 101.
32 Elizabeth Bowen (ed. and intro.), *The Faber Book of Modern Stories* (London, 1937), 16–17.

both in its compositional and social senses, is unsurprisingly provided by the case of Samuel Beckett. Beckett's short fiction, for reasons of obvious generic uncertainty, has received relatively little attention, particularly among students of the Irish short story, even though the hitherto ignored Irish import of his work has at this stage been generally well established. Given his status as the stylistically supreme chronicler of self-conscious existential privacy, Beckett's stories are crucial to any contemplation of the limits of the lyrical. Though Beckett had famously little to say by way of extended generalisations on his own or anybody else's fiction, short or otherwise, one of his pieces, titled 'neither' (1979), is especially relevant here. Originally a libretto piece which Beckett considered to be the very essence of his self, 'neither' contains only eighty-six words and was originally and subsequently published with line breaks that seemed to suggest that it was intended as a poem. When Beckett's British editor, John Calder, included 'neither' in preparations for Beckett's *Collected poems* however, Beckett took it out of the collection arguing that it was a story, not a poem. Here is the complete story:

> To and fro in shadow from inner to outershadow
> from impenetrable self to impenetrable unself by way of neither
> as between two lit refuges whose doors once neared gently close,
> once turned away from gently part again
> beckoned back and forth and turned away
> heedless of the way, intent on the one gleam or the other
> unheard footfalls only sound
> till at last halt for good, absent for good from self and other
> then no sound
> then gently light unfading on that unheeded neither
> unspeakable home[33]

Just as we have yet really to come to generic terms with the ways in which Beckett pushed at the bounds of the short-story form, we still have to appreciate fully the lyrical heritage of the genre as a whole. Equally importantly, we must

---

33 Samuel Beckett in S.E. Gontarski (ed, intro. and notes), *The complete short prose, 1929–1989* (New York, 1995), 258. For an account of the quirky publishing history of 'neither' see xii and 284. For variant accounts of the story's operatic origins, see Anthony Cronin, *Beckett: the last modernist* (New York, 1997), 583; and James Knowlson, *Damned to fame: the life of Samuel Beckett* (London, 1997), 630–2.

recognize the extent to which critical thinking about the genre has frequently limited itself to one dismissive version or another of the broad lyrical theory we have touched on here. The problem, really, centres on whether we continue, in the great anti-literary, anti-fiction sweep of our age, with its overweening confidence that prosaic historicist method and social bad conscience are the intellectual keys to the communally real, to equate lyricism with a kind of introverted irresponsible childishness. Far from being given to childish tricks and devices, far from being turned immaturely away from the world, Beckett's distillations of the short story are, metaphysically and stylistically, one of the highest points of development so far in the genre. The limits of the lyrical, in both the senses we have been dealing with, is Beckett's theme in 'neither': as a form, this work seems to have reached the final fine line between poetry and story, and its story is, in perhaps Beckett's own most distilled version, exactly about the tension between the inner and the outer, between impenetrable self and unself, between society and the lyrical disposition as figured in distilled language.

Beckett may thematically and figuratively have put an end to it on paper, but the lyrical theory of the short story remains remarkably tenacious and refuses to be confined to its points and periods of origin. Influence has come from all sides. A key volume for any Irish reader under fifty, Augustine Martin's short-story school anthology, *Exploring English I* (1967), was the first introduction for most of us here to O'Connor and other masters of the form. Devised within earshot of *The lonely voice*, Martin's introduction to the anthology largely propagated the Poe and O'Connor theories, naturally watered down for young minds.[34] More recently, seeing parallels between his Ireland and Alistair MacLeod's Nova Scotia, John McGahern takes up the O'Connor line again. While the novel is the most social art form, and is closely linked to 'an idea of society, a shared leisure, and a system of manners', McGahern argues that the short story 'does not generally flourish in such a society but comes into its own like song or prayer or superstition in poorer more fragmented communities where individualism and tradition and family and localities and chance or luck are dominant'.[35] It is ironic that the individualistic thrust that is the essence of the lyrical in both the senses we have dealt with here has become the homogenising basis of the favoured theory of national short-story tradition. McGahern, realizing this, has crucially argued in his essay on *Dubliners*

34 Augustine Martin (ed. and intro.), *Exploring English I: an anthology of short stories for intermediate certificate* (Dublin, 1967), 1–13. **35** John McGahern, Introduction, in Alistair MacLeod, *Island: collected stories* (London, 2002), xiii–xiv.

that 'remarkable work in the short story has come continually out of Ireland, but it is likely that its very strength is due to the absence of a strong central tradition'.[36]

However childish the individualizing lyrical disposition may be, some root aspects may be worth holding on to if received theories about the national characteristics and uniformities of the short story are not to stymie continued remarkable work. While O'Connor took the socially reforming function of honest writing seriously, one of his most revealingly levelling anecdotes against himself simultaneously encourages a deliberate elemental return to the essential freedom of the lyrical and suggests a major reason why his own stories are currently not taken as seriously as they might. O'Connor is at a major Harvard conference on the novel, sitting onstage alongside Anthony West, and an unnamed writer begins to speak about the serious responsibilities of the novelist. O'Connor begins to get hysterical:

> It's never happened to me before in public; I was giggling, I couldn't stop myself. And, 'All right,' I said at the end of it, 'if there are any of my students here I'd like them to remember that writing is fun.' That's the reason you do it, because you enjoy it. You don't read it because of the serious moral responsibility to read, and you don't write it because it's a serious moral responsibility. You do it for exactly the same reason that you paint pictures or play with the kids. It's a creative activity.[37]

Thus did one writer work it out. For himself.*

---

36 McGahern, '*Dubliners*', 63.   **37** Whittier, Interview with Frank O'Connor, 155.

*I gratefully acknowledge funding from the Irish Research Council for the Humanities and Social Sciences under their Post-Doctoral Scheme which provided for the research and writing of this essay.

Merry men: the afterlife of the poem

DECLAN KIBERD

Oscar Wilde once said that the future is what artists already are. Yeats expressed the same idea in more lyrical style when he asserted that the arts lie dreaming of what is to come. By this linking of art to futurology, both men seemed to suggest that all great works of literature have a sort of ideological surplus which derives more from the future than the past. If art often takes the shape of a dream, as indeed Brian Merriman's vision of the midnight court surely does, then behind that dream is a sort of wish-fulfilment, in the course of which the dreamer hopes to awaken in a world which more closely resembles his desired future than did that fallen, frustrating world in which first he fell asleep.

The playwright Synge took a similar view. 'What is highest in poetry', he wrote, 'is always reached when the dreamer is leaning out to reality, or when the man of real life is lifted out of it, and in all the poets the greatest have both these elements.'[1] Although the past history of the Irish might have seemed to the young James Joyce as a nightmare from which he was trying to awake, that past also carried, in the utopian possibilities folded within it, a claim upon the future. For such men, as for Merriman, poetry is less about the Celtic twilight than the *fáinne geal an lae* – the moment of clarity reached when the dreamer rises from sleep and finds a transformed world. This world also became the very model of modern psychoanalysis: 'every night the sleeper abandons himself to the ranks of the dead', joked Sigmund Freud, 'but with high hopes of a daily reprieve'. Merriman was both a major poet and a deep psychologist, who knew just how valuable dreams could be in charting a way forward to a better state of things. But he was also a strong materialist who had a profound sense of the material realities within which people are asked to live their lives. Being both a materialist and a magical thinker, he understood that genius was a way by which the lost, buried energies of a pre-modern world could be joined to the conscious life of a contemporary poem, in such a way as to create a new energy which would blast open the hope of a revolutionary future – and that the artist was one who could achieve this dream-like vision while still awake.

1 J.M. Synge, in Alan Price (ed.), *Collected works: prose*, vol. 2 (London, 1966), 397.

Frank O'Connor, himself a romantic realist, was attracted by these elements of Merriman and his poem, *Cúirt an mheán oíche*. O'Connor was a good illustration of the fact that the translator may be 'a character in search of an author', one who in finding the author without liberates the hidden author within. Ireland in the 1940s was an introverted, rigid place, which had lost its revolutionary view of tradition. It was no longer (in the words of Seosamh Mac Grianna in *Mo bhealach féin*, 1940) 'inchurtha lena dhúchas' (compatible with its heritage). What passed for Gaelic values were often no more than a prim moralism in the drag of native tradition, something that Samuel Beckett as early as 1934 had castigated as 'the Victorian Gael'. O'Connor took the view that in connecting people with their buried past, texts of the Irish language could help to create a more liberal and tolerant society. 'Look back to look forward', he would later say to his children in the dedication to *The backward look*. A writer grappling in his stories with such themes as unmarried mothers, love-children, and sexually-active priests had much to learn from Merriman's poem, which treats these matters with a novelist's eye for detail.

So many of our journalistic debates in today's Ireland seem to have been interpreted in the poem – the major importance of sexual energy, the debate about clerical celibacy, the commodification of the female body, the need for a reconfiguration of the laws about family and upbringing. All of which suggests that Merriman was a prophet as well as a poet – not really because of any flashy predictive power, but simply because he saw so deeply into the culture of his own time that the shape of its future became dimly discernible. We are, in truth, still learning how to be Merriman's contemporaries. In this essay, I hope to show just how many of the themes and techniques of the later masterpieces of Irish writing are latent in the lines of the poem, assess Frank O'Connor's engagement with *Cúirt*, and also examine how much of the radical politics of modern Ireland may also derive from its inspiration. But first let me excavate for a moment the prehistory of the *Cúirt* – for it itself was once a future bringing into definition the potentials of the cultural past.

The whole poem is formed as a dream of surreal intensity – but the underlying idea of a court or parliament convened in secret opposition to the prevailing social order is of ancient lineage. Chaucer had his parliament of fowls and Gaelic Ireland by 1703 had its *Parlaimint na mBan,* a text based on a French original which interpreted the *Cúirt* by suggesting that the world would be a happier place if women had control of it. In that fictitious world, set a few years earlier in 1697, the convenor objects to the relegation of women to the purely domestic world out of the public sphere:

Do chítear daoibh go léir go mbíd a gcomhairlí agus a gcomhthíonóil ag
na fearaibh go laethúil ag déanamh a ngnótha agus ag tabhairt aire do
gach ní bhaineas riu féin, i gcás, an uair bhíd said ag trácht orainne, gurb
amhlaidh bhímid mar chaitheamh aimsire, mar chomparáid, nó mar stoc
magaidh acu de ló agus d'oíche.[2]

She proposes the establishment of just the sort of virtual assembly described by
Merriman about eight decades later. In the intervening period, women's roles
remained largely domestic and decorative, as Jane Austen lamented in *Northanger
abbey*: 'there remained those for whom imbecility in females was a great enhance-
ment in their charms.'[3]

The Gaelic *cúirt filíochta* was also a formalized alternative structure set up as a
kind of parallel reality within the official colonial scheme – rather like the 'cúirt
bhreá oirirc' described in *Parlaimint na mBan*. Daniel Corkery took the view that
there was little or no parodic intent – that country people had through force of
practice come to associate all forms of authority with the law courts, whose
mighty procedures they took with a sort of deferential awe. But it's hard to believe
that a sophisticated intellectual such as Merriman didn't have a lot of his tongue in
his cheek. His use of formulae connected with courts and magistrates was, of
course, a mocking reminder that in ancient Ireland the role of the *file* and
breitheamh had been overlapping – his own powerlessness and lack of awe,
mocked repeatedly through the poem, is a confession of just how magical such
authority had become. But the alternative authority claimed by the English law is
not fully secure either, leaving him free to jeer at its self-important procedures.

The main point surely is the notion of a virtual assembly, set up between the
real world and the fantasy world, between the despised English law and the lost
Gaelic tradition – in that liminal zone called Creag Liath, the place frequented by
fairies. Angela Bourke has shown how fairies, though enjoying only a low status in
lore, offered a mirror on real life, sharing space with the human population but
using it differently:

> they are forever outside human culture, exempt from control by its rules.
> But they do hope to be saved, so instead of ranging themselves in opposi-
> tion to human society, fairies are always prowling on its edges, looking
> above or below it, marking its boundaries ... [4]

---

2 Anraí Mac Giolla Chomhaill (ed.), *Díolaim próis, A.D. 1450–1850* (Dublin, 1971), 131. **3** Jane
Austen, *Northanger abbey* (London, 1965), 143. **4** Angela Bourke, 'The virtual reality of Irish fairy
legend', *Éire-Ireland*, 31:1&2 (Spring & Summer 1996), 9–10.

They are also known to abduct people from the human world who may be unfortunate enough to wander into the liminal zone – rather in the way in which a resistance army might capture hostages. Indeed, Angela Bourke in her magnificent book *The burning of Bridget Cleary* goes so far as to suggest that the fairies can function as a sort of unofficial counter to the colonial police, being everywhere and nowhere at once, on the lookout, eager to store intelligence to be used in future confrontations with officialdom.

If this is so, then Merriman's poem, reissued in 1912 by Risteárd Ó Foghludha, may come at a telling moment, providing in its parody of the law a powerful example of how best to resist, not by direct opposition to the colonial authority but by setting up a parallel state or system within the prevailing one. This was an ancient tradition which Frank O'Connor had recognized in work published in his second collection of short stories, *Bones of contention* (1936) – the fact that there was in rural Ireland, stronger than any statute, an unwritten, customary law by which people resolved social problems. In his short story, 'In the train', characters refuse to inform on a woman of their community in a Dublin court, despite the fact that she had poisoned her husband and apparently become the lover of a much younger man. As far as they were concerned, she will undergo her punishment within her own village upon returning to it, most of all by virtue of her own remorse and adverse self-judgment, in keeping with the notion, widespread in rural Ireland, that one is not so much punished for one's sins as by one's sins.

There is a sense in which this move had already been rehearsed, before 1912 of course, by the very act of establishing the Abbey as a national theatre in an occupied land. The theatre, by insisting that the conditions of the world are forever plastic, and by teaching people how to impersonate their betters, is itself a place in which revolution can be rehearsed and it is a fact that many who went on to take part in the Easter Rising and War of Independence served part of their apprenticeship in the national theatre, in whose green room the printing press on which the Proclamation of the Republic was written was hidden. The very theatricality of the rebel's demeanour underlines the connection.

The Abbey as a virtual republic within the monarchical scheme was followed later by the proclaimed republic of 1916, fought for by up to 70 women soldiers. If successful, would have had in Hannah Sheehy Skeffington the first female government minister anywhere in the world – a full year before Alexandra Kollontai in Moscow. It is interesting to read in Colm Ó Gaora's great autobiography *Mise* of how he taught Irish to inmates of Lincoln Jail after the suppression of the Rising, using Ó Foghludha's text of the *Cúirt* as a basis for some of the classes. One of his students was Éamon de Valera, who astonished his fellow captives by memorizing every line. He repaid the intellectual debt many yeas later by subscribing to the memorial for Merriman commissioned in the late 1940s.

But an even more direct imitation of the virtual institution embodied by the *Cúirt* within the colonial scheme was, surely, the convening of the first Dáil Éireann in 1919 – and, of course, those Dáil Courts which gave their allegiance to it, set up during the War of Independence in 1920. The object was not so much to seek independence from the British as to assume it as of right – power was not to be given but taken anyway. The deputies sought to show the wide world that they were capable of self-government: as Yeats told the Oxford Union in 1920, it was not law but British law which had broken down in Ireland. The Dáil Courts were, of course, every whit as subversive as that of Merriman, subversive of the British naturally enough, but also of the rather macho militarists who dominated the resistance movement. The courts were often improvised in backrooms of hotels or bars, or even in domestic kitchens – and though the work done was dangerous and ill-rewarded, the lawyers and clerks were seldom thanked by the militarists. Cathal Brugha, that most stern of men, had no doubt that power was passing through the medium of each Dáil Court from the military élite into the hands of ordinary people, and he thoroughly disliked that development. It wasn't long before what Mary Kotsonouris calls the 'retreat from revolution' had begun, as lawyers read-opted the wigs and gowns of the old British system, showing how keen the rulers of the new state would be to apply all the once-despised devices of the old regime upon themselves. Yet even in the most censorious years of the new state, the spirit of Merriman lived on. In his recollections, John McGahern describes how young people in the 1940s created a virtual world of their own in which freedom was still possible – after the barn dances every July, he recalls, there wasn't a hay rick safe for miles around the dance-hall, but the youth of the parish were making full use of the ricks: 'the whole lot of them going off like alarm clocks'.[5] He suggests that the Irish were as adept at subverting their own institutions as once they had subverted those of the occupier. Frank O'Connor's own translation of the *Cúirt* might be a prime example of that tactic, since it subverted the rather abstract pastoral Ireland of Éamon de Valera's 1943 radio broadcast with a more flesh-and-blood version of what athletic youths, nubile maidens and old men might actually be thinking and feeling in a land which seemed to have lost not just sexual energy but the very will

5 John McGahern, 'Change in Ireland', lecture at the University of Notre Dame, Keough Institute for Irish Studies, Dublin, Irish Seminar (10 July 2003).

to procreate itself. O'Connor probably knew that de Valera once had listed the *Cúirt* as a favourite poem, and so he used it to call the leader's bluff. For, at the time when he worked on the translation, he became convinced that he had been put on an unofficial blacklisting by the Fianna Fáil government. As if to confirm that diagnosis, his version of the poem was banned, even as the original in Irish remained on sale with government subsidy.

It is worth emphasising all of this, because too many commentators have sought, especially in the years of compulsory revisionism, to delink Merriman's poem from nationalism or the national idea, seeing in its parody of the *aisling* mode a rejection of all nationalist politics. Not so. The year of publication of Ó Foghludha's version in 1912 should alert us to these other possible meanings – it was also, by the way, the year in which *Parlaimint chloinne Tomáis* was published, with its mockery of parliamentarianism – a mockery that would probably be more to the taste of the Cathal Brugha's wing of the movement. But the image of de Valera, escaping from Lincoln Jail just days after he had learned the poem, got up in the garb of a woman, remains long in the mind.

As an image, it brings us to another issue raised by the *Cúirt*, the question of female impersonation, of a male author presuming to speak for women. The *aisling* mode was clearly sexist – a passive, wilting *spéirbhean*, awaiting liberation by a male deliverer who might prod her back to life, would not today seem incongruous as the centrefold girl of a pornographic magazine. It can be argued that Merriman's great achievement in the *Cúirt* is to undo all that by restoring agency to women, who are eloquent and in charge of things. But it is also symptomatic of the obstacles disabling women at the time that the literary case for them should have had to be made by a male author.

This was in fact common enough in the literature of the period. In 1702, just a year before Dónal Ó Colmáin produced *Parlaimint na mban*, Daniel Defoe published *Good advice to the ladies*, which called for female presence in government. Defoe would also become famous as the author not only of *Robinson Crusoe* but also of *Moll Flanders*, a book which purports to represent the memories of a prostitute. Moll Flanders is presented as something of a modern hero – she is upwardly mobile, good at acquiring cash, unburdened by strong or lasting emotional commitments, and willing to move from place to place in pursuit of comfort. All of which suggests that she may be less a portrait of any real woman and more a version of Defoe's own autobiography – the story of a male merchant capitalist in the drag of a female adventuress.

Why do so many men feel this need to impersonate women or to represent the female role? One explanation is the patronising, predictable one: through the sexist centuries, they may have felt about women what Marx felt about the peas-antry – 'these people cannot represent themselves – and so they must be represented'. But there may have been a deeper agenda at work here, an attempt by male authors to locate the *anima*, the creative element within themselves. After all, since the legends of Greece and Rome, the Muse has been imagined as female. But there is an element of danger in all such transactions. They take a toll on the energy and vitality of the male artist, as can be deduced from vision-poems such as Keats' 'La belle dame sans merci', in which the poet is finally left spent and wasted. At such moments, the Muse of poetry may not be the inspiratrice one wishes to fly towards, but rather a potential killer one might prefer to flee from. Yet, no matter how hard the poet tries to escape from poetry and poetry-making, he may find, by virtue of his vocation, that the escape is impossible.

The problem is then posed, however, that the female impersonator may be left feeling unmanned by what has been disclosed. There is an old Italian proverb which says that deeds are masculine, and words are feminine. A male artist who gives untrammelled expression to his female element may discover that the world does not greatly respect his achievement – and that even women may demand from him some final proof (as was asked of Merriman) that he is nevertheless reas-suringly male. Shakespeare was the first major modern artist to explore the underlying problem. In his comedies, women such as Viola or Portia impersonate men and only good things happen, – Viola fights more bravely than any man; Portia shows more wit in court than any male lawyer, all while dressed as a man. The disguise allows the women to observe their lovers as they truly are among other men and not just when posturing or posing in the presence of the women. Hence the marriages at the close of the plays are seen as images of true, honest bonding. And better still, the woman who finally returns to female clothing is shown to have enhanced herself by exploring her male side – even to the discovery, replicated by the modern fashion industry, that hip-hugging tight trousers will show off a woman's figure better than any dress can do. In the tragedies however, Shakespeare switched his investigation to the plight of the womanly man – but his adoption of feminine qualities led only to disaster. Macbeth is 'too full of the milk of human kindness' to live up to his dirty deeds, unlike his macho wife; Hamlet is 'passion's slave'; Lear gives up power and is ruined. The female dimension in the male, if articulated, leads only to suffering. After Shakespeare, the male imperson-ation of womanhood was relegated to such debased, caricature versions as the drag show – and boy actors were replaced by real women to play female parts – or the impersonation was relegated to ventriloquized literary performances such as those supplied by Defoe or Merriman.

I want to suggest now a more profound and occluded intention behind the *Cúirt* and other such performances: that when men are afraid to confront their inner uncertainties directly, they will often project them onto a woman figure in a literary text. It may even be possible that some translators of the *Cúirt*, like Frank O'Connor, were using the poem in a similar way, to explore doubts which they were reluctant to express more directly themselves. A man may be least himself when he talks with his own face, but give a man a mask and he might just tell you the truth. That is why Stanislaus Joyce could joke that in the end, men always blame women for being exactly what it is men have made of them. In other words, they ask women to live out on their behalf a fear which all too often they fail to confront or else suppress in themselves.

Merriman seems to have been worried about male inadequacy: his own and that of others. It is sometimes suggested that he was spurned in a marriage proposal made in his youth to a woman who considered him not good enough for her. His male narrator does not speak a word of dialogue at the court, suggesting a figure who was invincibly shy. His anxieties about his inadequacy are placed, as I've argued in *Irish classics*, on the lips of his woman characters as well as on the mouth of the elderly male cuckold – and the close of the poem has the quality of a catharsis in the Freudian analysis, a self-administered therapy. As Brian's body is bound and flayed in a sort of bondage fantasy by the amazonian women of the court, the poet in effect confesses that he is as guilty as anyone of repressing natural instinct; and with that recognition he is saved and declared fit for a return to the world.

This reading of the poem could probably not have been made without Frank O'Connor's translations; and it suggests other elements which may have permitted O'Connor to treat his version as an occluded autobiographical work. At the time he worked on the *Cúirt*, O'Connor was himself before a semi-official court, a victim of blacklisting who, in the effort to support a family, had to live and work in England. There he had a son born out of wedlock. It might not be stretching things to interpret his lines as a call for understanding and leniency, as well as for a proper appointed place for love-children within the official scheme of things.

The celebration of sexual energy of bastards makes sense in this context as does the pragmatic rather than idealistic view of human sexuality. The suggestion is that sexual energy outside of wedlock is more in keeping with the authentic traditions of ancient Gaeldom, which was more liberal on such questions:

Cuirfidh an dlí seo gaois a nGaelaibh
Is tiocfidh an brí mar bhí ina laochaibh;
Ceapfaidh sé com is drom is dóirne
Ag fearaibh an domhain mar Gholl Mac Mórna.[6]

The scholar Sarah McKibben has shown in a brilliant doctoral thesis that such an
anxiety about the ongoing manliness of the Irish male was raised as early as the
bardic poems of the 1500s, such as 'Fúbún fúibh, a shluaigh Ghael', written to
rebuke those cowardly princes who had surrendered without fight after 1541 to the
policies of the Crown. Against that backdrop, Sarah McKibben says, Merriman's
poem, far from subverting Gaelic tradition, seems to uphold it.

Even in its inaccuracies, as when it laments a fall in population, at the end of a
century in which the number of children born was steadily rising, the *Cúirt* pursues
its theme of lost manhood, lost procreativity, lost self-belief. The theme was all too
real for Frank O'Connor and his generation of veterans of the War of
Independence, who had once said 'revolution or death' but who were now facing
the death of their revolution. This, as I've hinted, is a problem compounded for
those men who love words over deeds, words being seen as the weapons of the
disarmed. Male writers who achieve a degree of prominence in macho cultures
often feel secretly ashamed of their artistic gifts – hence the notorious brawling of
Eoghan Rua Ó Súilleabháin or Robbie Burns, as if fighting for them helped to
reassert an imperilled virility. Hence, also Norman Mailer's love of boxing matches,
or Hemingway's love of bull-fighting, or Behan's of pub crawling. It was as if each
man, fearing emasculation by the very fact of being a writer, sought to compensate
by wearing lots of false hair on his literary chest. For men who 'admit' a feminine
side often feel impelled to reassert by way of balancing a more traditional, even
obnoxious form of masculinity. This would help to account for some of the more
unpleasantly sexist passages which come all the more surprisingly from Merriman
in a poem otherwise rightly seen as sympathetic to women – for instance, the old
cuckold's misogynistic outbursts, or the young woman's resort to such foreign frip-
pery, 'húda', 'púdar' or stiletto heels. For the poem in this aspect is an allegation not
just of male but also female inadequacy. As in so many other colonies, from the
Americas to India, the eighteenth-century woman is accused of being anglicized…
for in Merriman's world, England was fashion-smart, Ireland not.

It's remarkable to me just how many of these themes were reprised by Joyce in

6 Liam P. Ó Murchú, *Cúirt an mhean oíche* (Dublin, 1982), 36.

Ulysses – though I can't prove that he used a copy of the *Cúirt*. The Oxen of the Sun chapter chronicles what Joyce called the crime against fecundity and is built around the old bardic suggestion that the Irish race is in danger of dying out. There is a sense in which *Ulysses* was written for much the same reason as was given by Desmond FitzGerald for the Rising of 1916 – as one answer to the fact that the very idea of Ireland was about to go under and disappear. As early as 1907 in a Triestine newspaper article, Joyce voiced the fear that Ireland might evaporate and five years later Desmond Fitzgerald, Joseph Mary Plunkett and Pearse voiced a similar claim. The Oxen of the Sun chapter celebrates the birth of a bouncing baby but is filled with nervous, hysterical joking by medical students about procreation, and a narrative voice which rebukes Leopold Bloom for leaving a seedfield unploughed and fallow, because of his addiction to masturbation. This fear of infertility, aging bachelors and spinsters, sexual frustration and masturbation appears again in the concerns of Irish writers in mid-century Ireland. Frank O'Connor was directly involved in getting sections of Kavanagh's *The great hunger* first into print in 1942, just a few years before the appearance of his *Cúirt* translation.

The Circe episode of *Ulysses* climaxes in just the sort of literary show trial that Merriman had made possible, just like one of the Dáil courts. It is held, as they often were, in an anonymous place, the bar of a brothel in Tyrone Street; and Joyce must have known that these brothels often served as safe-houses for republicans on the run. In the episode, Bloom expresses and exposes his own uncertain masculinity (perhaps as a self-administered punishment for having masturbated while eyeing Gerty McDowell on Sandymount Strand – for if she was on display there, he is on sexual display here). Under the petticoat government of the whoremistress, Bella Cohen, he becomes abject, a pig-like animal. She masculinizes herself as the male Bello and threatens, as in the *Cúirt*, to have him whipped and chastised for his many infractions of the manly code.

Perhaps these overlaps were inevitable: like Merriman, Joyce dug deep into the male consciousness of his culture and came up with many similar things. A lot of the technical mysteries posed by *Ulysses* for its scholars would make more sense if we were to read them along Merrimanian lines. Many feminists have problems with the fact that a writer as apparently sympathetic to women as Joyce chose to dramatize not the consciousness of a sophisticated intellectual woman but of a silly airhead like Gerty McDowell, who is a prisoner of old folk pishogues and the advice columnists of popular magazines. But in that she has everything in common with the young woman of the *Cúirt*, who said:

Níorbh áil liom codladh go socair aon uair dhíobh
Gan lán mo stoca do thorthaibh fám chluasa
In aghaidh na srotha do thomainn mo léine
Ag súil tréim chodladh le cogar óm chéile[7]

Likewise, Gerty has her hair cut on the day of a new moon and wears certain items of clothing inside out, in hope of getting a man to wed. But, if Joyce is to be read as really recreating the technique of Merriman, then Gerty's voice is not really her own so much as an ascribed soliloquy, to be seen as attributed playfully to her by Bloom as he watches the young woman among her friends on the beach. It may even be that the far-famed Molly Bloom monologue could also be interpreted in this way, as Bloom's own confection, in which (much like Merriman with the voice of the women) he uses the persona of his wife as a way of exploring his own inner self – his maidenly bashfulness (for what attracts Molly to him is the fact that he is 'not to be had for the asking'), his desire to be courted and dominated by a strong female, and so on. Brenda Maddox may have been wrong, therefore, to say that the life of Nora Barnacle was the secret life of Molly Bloom (the subtitle used in the American edition of her biography of Mrs Joyce) – that privilege was reserved for Joyce's own *anima*. Writing at that level of depth, he had no consciousness but his own from which to glean the implied portrait of Molly, just as Merriman had no choice but to dramatize his own inner self, even when he evoked the words of the young supplicant woman and those of Aoíbheall, queen of the *Cúirt*.

The subsequent afterlife of the poem is, if anything, further proof of my theory. For all its feminist reputation, it has not to my knowledge attracted a woman translator, in the way (for instance) that *Caoineadh Airt Uí Laoghaire* called on the talents of the late Eilís Dillon. The reason is, I think, that women do not feel fully at ease with the underlying stunt. As Joyce's own Molly says, thinking back to Daniel Defoe, 'I don't like books with a Molly in them ... Oh Jamesy, let me up out of this.' The poem instead has been seen as a challenge by various male translators, each of whom has used it to pursue an agenda. Frank O'Connor's is justly famous for its brio and swagger, based on his desire to challenge and transgress the censorship laws. O'Connor saw the poem as one way of proving to puritanical nationalists that they had no real interest in a revival of authentic Gaelic tradition: and they duly obliged him by burning his translation, even as the

---

7 Ó Murchú, *Cúirt*, 26–7.

Gaelic original remained on sale in the government's own bookshop. Perhaps the censors were subtler than they realized. The transgressive note in O'Connor's version suits only those minds whose self-censors have already been activated – there is enough of a swagger in his breach of the rules to suggest a mind still very keenly in their grip. That note of violation would have little or no meaning for someone raised solely within the Gaelic tradition. A generation and more earlier, J.M. Synge had shrewdly observed that Douglas Hyde would in his books get away with using a word like 'léine', but that when he used the equivalent word 'shift' in English, there was a riot. 'May God damn the bloody Anglo-Saxon language', added Synge, 'in which a man can't swear without being vulgar!'[8] O'Connor's version of the *Cúirt* is mighty – but also mighty vulgar.

Both Coslett Quinn and Arland Ussher offered renditions which managed to lodge the claims for a more humanist attitude to sexuality within the constraint of well-mannered metrification – as if to suggest that in the Ireland of the second half of the twentieth century, with a little toleration on all sides, freedom and system might yet be reconciled. Like Vivian Mercier, they drew on a protestant or liberal humanist background to come up with readings into which were coded a polite insistence that they had as valid a claim on Gaelic tradition as any other social group on the island. O'Connor reviewed Ussher's translation in the *Irish Statesman* and his comments reveal some of his own underlying reasons for translating *Cúirt*. O'Connor admired Ussher's translation: 'in the main I must congratulate Mr Ussher on performing a very necessary task in a very delicate way. In a period when so few are writing poetry in a manly way – Synge's way – we feel that there should be all the more demand for a book like his'. He praised Merriman: 'He, more than any of the poets of the time, is safe from the charge of provincialism. He had a live theme and he made it live, using … the speech of the people'.[9] It is not inconceivable to think that O'Connor saw the *Cuirt* as a way to explore his own masked fears at the time (which included the charge of provincialism) as well as to explore his female element, all hidden underneath his 'manly' translation. O'Connor returns to this point of authenticity in his introduction to his own translation. He describes Merriman as 'supremely a realist' and criticizes Corkery's interpretation of Merriman as a court jester; there 'is nothing remarkable about [the poem] which a romantic critic like Professor Corkery can seize on; no extravagance of imagery or language which you can translate'. Instead, when

8 David H. Greene and Edward M. Stephens, *J.M. Synge, 1871–1909* (New York, 1959), 107.
9 Frank O'Connor, review of *The midnight court, translated from the Gaelic by Percy Arland Ussher*, in *Irish Statesman* (9 Oct. 1926), 114.

'the character of the woman drops away ... we are face to face with Bryan Merryman'.[10] Aside from some of O'Connor's more questionable critical claims in the introduction, what is also clear is that literary realism, simplicity of language and a subversion of social norms had obvious attractions for him as a translating project. Included in O'Connor's 1945 publication was a number of his other translations of Gaelic poetry that deal with frustrated sexual needs, the interference of religious beliefs with obtaining sexual satisfaction, and frustrated love in varying contexts.[11]

The first Merriman school in 1968 was, in its way, a measure of the liberalisation of Ireland – a year earlier, as a young minister for Justice, Brian Lenihan had lifted the ban on many books of literary value and a year later another minister, Charles Haughey, would proclaim a tax holiday for writers. But the most strategic and tactical of the recent interventions is surely *The midnight verdict* by Seamus Heaney. This offered a lucid translation of the opening and closing passages, placed cunningly between versions of Orpheus: in the Underworld and the dismemberment of Orpheus by enraged women as retold from Ovid. At the Merriman summer school of 1993, Heaney gave a lecture on the poem, not long after the ferocious critique of *The Field Day anthology of Irish writing* had led its general editor Seamus Deane to apologise for not including a single woman in his editorial team. Deane had been summoned to a trial by Eavan Boland and others, to be conducted at the Irish Writer's Centre, but had not shown up. Instead, he offered a general apology in the media, adding that the omission had been all the more regrettable for being unconscious. Heaney's lines often seem to bear closely on the controversy:

> Her words were grim when she got started
> 'Get up', she said, 'and on your feet!
> What do you think gives you the right
> To shun the crowds and the sitting court?
> A court of justice truly founded,
> And not the usual rigged charade,
> But a fair and clement court of women
> Of the greatest stock and regimen.
> The Irish race should be grateful always
> For such a bench, agreed and wise,

---

10 Frank O'Connor, *The midnight court, a rhythmical bacchanalia from the Irish of Bryan Merriman* (Dublin, 1945), 6–10. 11 'Liadain', 'To Tomas Costello at the wars', 'A girl weeping', 'To the lady, with the book', ibid., 53–61.

> In session now two days and a night
> In the spacious fort on Graney Height.'[12]

In his lecture, Heaney observed that from being an element of the mid-twentieth century war against sexual censorship, the poem has become a paradigm of the war initiated by the women's movement for female empowerment and for a restoration of women to the centre of language and consciousness and society. Yet by juxtaposing its seemingly tame ending with the violent conclusion of Ovid's story – in which Orpheus is accused of loving only his dead Muse and rejecting the actual needs of contemporary woman and is thereby torn to pieces by the 'court of aggrieved women' – Heaney seemed to be offering his own verdict on the feminist verdict on the anthology, in whose shaping he played a major and influential role. The hopes of the editor that the anthology might be adopted by such publishers as Norton or Faber in a cheap paperback format were effectively dashed by the controversy – and that, as much as the conclusion of the *Cúirt*, was for Heaney the real story of Orpheus in Ireland.

In this way, the Merriman school contributed to Heaney's foregrounding of the poem as a specimen of world literature (transmitted to that world by the inclusion of his talk in the Oxford Lectures titled *The redress of poetry*). The school has also played a part in enabling the most recent complete version, which came in 2005 from Ciaran Carson. All translations come at the mercy of their immediate occasions, one might say – hence the rather noisy audacity of O'Connor, the restrained bitterness of Heaney's idiom, or the rambunctiousness of Behan's. What strikes most about Carson's is its tonal range, which admits that none of his predecessors erred in finding any of these elements but that a combination of them all, in a narrative which moves through an astonishing variety of moods, will capture the totality of the experience, from visionary to satire, from feminist and misogynist, from bardic to personal. In his introductory note, Carson effectively suggests that his is a reading not just of the poem but, inevitably, of its English language versions – and he emerges in many ways as its ideal translator, a character who finds in Merriman the enabling author without, even as he uses his text to liberate his own Carson within.

This rendition is but the latest to prove what Quinn, David Marcus and Kinsella already have shown us: a good translator is like a good lover – faithful

---

12 Seamus Heaney, *The midnight verdict: translations from the Irish of Brian Merriman and from the 'Metamorphoses' of Ovid* (Oldcastle, Co. Meath, 1993), 25.

without seeming to be so. The style honed by Carson in his immense Dante project – itself an *aisling*, as he wryly observed – has found an even more expressive text here: and not least because Carson has found in Merriman's lines the rhythm of the song tradition of Clare and the way in which, though music, it reconciles the structures of poetry with, as O'Connor had insisted sixty years earlier, the cadences of everyday speech:

> 'Twas my custom to stroll by a clear winding stream,
> With my boots full of dew from the lush meadow green,
> Near a neck of the woods where the mountain holds sway,
> Without danger or fear at the dawn of the day.
> The sight of Lough Graney would angle my eyes,
> As the countryside sparkled beneath the blue skies,
> Uplifting to see how the mountain were stacked,
> Each head peeping over its neighbouring back.
> It would lighten the heart, be it listless with age,
> Enfeebled by folly, or cardiac rage –
> You wherewithal racked by financial disease –
> To perceive through a gap in the wood full of trees
> A squadron of ducks in a shimmering bay,
> Escorting the swan on her elegant way,
> The trout on the rise with its mouth to the light,
> While the perch swims below like a speckled sprite,
> And the billows of blue become foam as they break
> With a thunderous crash on the shores of the lake.[13]

---

13 Ciaran Carson, *The midnight court: a new translation of 'Cúirt an mheán oíche' by Brian Merriman* (Oldcastle, Co. Meath, 2005), 19.

Frank O'Connor and the Abbey Theatre

HILARY LENNON

From a very young age Frank O'Connor displayed a keen interest in the theatre. His active involvement did not begin until 1927 when, as a result of encouragement from Micheál MacLiammóir, O'Connor, Seán Neeson (head of RTÉ broadcasting in Cork) and J.J. Hogan (a director with Cork Opera House) founded the Cork Drama League. Despite proclaiming an intention at the debut performance on 20 February 1928 to stage 'the best of Southern thought and emotion'[1], O'Connor focused most of his attention on productions of works by writers such as Ibsen and Chekhov. The League instead attended to the second intention expressed at the same performance, to give a platform to those international playwrights whose work was 'unknown' in Cork. The only Irish playwright that was staged during O'Connor's time with the League was Lennox Robinson. O'Connor greatly admired Robinson as a dramatist. His other production choices – it was O'Connor who primarily selected – were undoubtedly influenced by his own strong interest in world literature at the time as well as the Dublin Drama League's more internationalist programme.

However, O'Connor's general eschewal of Irish plays also stemmed from his own literary-political opinions. He asserted soon afterwards that he had 'no use for a theatre that leaves out literature ... the Abbey should do Tchehov [sic] and Ibsen and Hauptmann instead of Brinsley McNamara'. Irish writers, in his opinion, were too involved in the politics of the country:

> he [Daniel Corkery] who was the finest artist of us all goes and writes blithering articles for the Irish statesman [sic] ... The business of the artist is with his art and not with the problems that will be decided far more finally and successfully by the illiterate mussolinis [sic] of the world.[2]

---

1 James Matthews, *Voices: a life of Frank O'Connor* (Dublin, 1983), 50. 2 O'Connor, Letter to Sean Hendrick (20 July 1929), Harriet O'Donovan Sheehy's private collection of O'Connor papers (hereafter referred to as HODSC). O'Connor rarely dated any of his letters and the vast majority of the letters in HODSC have been comprehensively dated by Prof. Ruth Sherry and Harriet O'Donovan Sheehy.

Rather than genuinely espousing an 'arts for arts sake' ideological framework, and notwithstanding his own contribution of nine articles by this stage to the same periodical, O'Connor was in reality reacting more to Corkery's cultural protectionist arguments and, most likely, the introduction of the Censorship of Publications Act in July 1929. He feared this would lead to a disregard for literary merit. O'Connor advocated similar sentiments just a few months later, to what he perceived as a hijacking of Irish-language drama by government-sponsored cultural nationalism, and in Arnoldian terms called for 'the fiercest criticism of everything second-rate, that will tolerate nothing but the best in literature and drama and art'.[3] O'Connor's selection of plays during his stint with the Cork Drama League appears to be an oppositional act to state-imposed literary standards. His time with the League was brief, however, as he moved to Dublin on 1 December 1928 and took up the position of librarian in Pembroke District Library, a post he was to hold until 1938. By the early thirties O'Connor's attitude towards the staging of Irish drama had completely changed and he became instead a champion of Irish playwrights; this change in attitude was something that he was to bring into full force by the time he became a director of the Abbey Theatre in 1935.

The closing down of the *Irish Statesman* in 1930, the poor condition of Irish libraries, the increasing social conservatism that was becoming prevalent in post-independence Ireland – these were just some of the issues that served to increase his frustration with the new establishment and ignited a burning desire to do something about it. In a loving letter to Nancy McCarthy (the woman O'Connor proposed to on several occasions in the early 1930s), he expressed the fear that he was afraid of her getting 'injured by my writing … This thing is going to get worse and not better'. He tellingly revealed in the same letter that he 'feels like a soldier on leave from the front'.[4] O'Connor's vanguard reaction to what he saw as a stultifying affiliation between an anti-modernist church and a conservative state and culture was beginning to set in. Through his friendship with George Russell (Æ), O'Connor was introduced to W.B. Yeats. Becoming acquainted with Yeats was a significant encounter for the young writer from Cork as the famous poet involved O'Connor in such projects as the campaign against the Censorship Act and the setting up of the Irish Academy of Letters in 1932. More importantly, it was Yeats who invited O'Connor to become a director of the national theatre.

---

3 O'Connor, Letter to the editor, *Irish Statesman* (16 Nov. 1929), 212.   4 O'Connor, Letter to Nancy McCarthy (7 Sept. 1933), HODSC.

The general history of the Abbey has by now been well delineated and its state of decline, by the time O'Connor joined, will be familiar to most. Previously, the 1920s had witnessed the development of an alliance between the theatre and the Cumann na nGaedheal government. The campaign by Yeats and Lady Gregory for state financial support for the Abbey was a crucial factor in the transpired affiliation. On the government's side, the newly formed state sought to create a stable society in the aftermath of revolutionary upheaval. The theatre's valuable ideological role in Irish culture, alongside its perceived association with the Anglo-Irish minority, served to develop the government's consideration of the theatre as a significant legitimising ally. Moreover, the Abbey's institutional support for the new Irish Free State was believed important for the government as it sought to rein in republican anti-Treaty opposition.[5] In August 1925, an annual subsidy of £850 was granted to the Abbey. The mid- to late 1920s saw the strengthening of this alliance and

> several of the most notable plays ... work either to sentimentalize the rela-
> tionship between Cumann na nGaedheal and southern unionism or to
> advocate support for the 'national' government of the Irish Free State as
> opposed to the recalcitrant and anti-modern forces of republican
> opposition.[6]

Despite the succession of Fianna Fáil into power in the 1932 elections and its winning of an overall majority in the 1933 elections, there was a continued, pronounced avoidance of major conflict between the Abbey Theatre and the government.[7] The theatre was in financial difficulties due to the economic depression of the thirties (it was £2,500 in debt), plus its annual subsidy from the government had been temporarily cut to £750 a year. In order to address these financial pressures the period 1932–5 saw a resumption of the theatre's American tours, but the overall standard of its Dublin repertoire remained poor. Instead of becoming an important cultural arena which could engage critically with Irish

---

5 See Lionel Pilkington, *Theatre and the state in twentieth-century Ireland* (London, 2001), 87–97; R.F. Foster, *W.B. Yeats: a life, II: the arch-poet, 1915–1939* (New York, 2003), 233–6, 302. 6 Pilkington, *Theatre and the state*, 107. 7 O'Connor was unusually reticent when reflecting on the relationship years later: 'it would not be unfair to say that the Establishment had a more than adequate voice in the running of the theatre', O'Connor, 'Quarrelling with Yeats: a friendly recollection', *Esquire* (Dec. 1964), 157; a copy of this article is held in the Denis Johnston Papers, Trinity College, Dublin, MS 10066/54/48.

social and political issues, the Abbey was being reduced to playing to an audience that wanted to eschew uncomfortable conceptions of what constituted 'Irishness' and whose expectations converged on perfunctory images of the country. It ran the risk of becoming a substandard theatre that catered to an audience who perceived a visit to the national theatre as mere entertainment. This decline was mirrored at an internal level in the Abbey Theatre by Lady Gregory's death in 1932 and the subsequent inefficient management by Lennox Robinson.

Yeats attempted to do something about it and in December 1934 announced that there would be a change of policy within the Abbey due to the 'slackening of activity among Irish dramatists'. What he was planning was the 'revival of lesser-known Irish plays' as well as an inclusion of regular productions of modern continental plays, to compete with the thriving Gate Theatre.[8] After Yeats' announcement of a 'fresh start' for the Abbey, Frank O'Connor and Seán O'Faoláin wrote to the *Irish Times* complaining about the production proposals. They believed that this exemplified the Abbey's shabby treatment of aspiring Irish dramatists and both writers strongly objected to these new intentions:

> In the first place, we doubt that there has been any real slackening of activity among Irish dramatists, and we cannot, therefore, agree that the theatre was compelled to fall back on the revival of old plays … To fall back on the revival of old plays is merely a confession of incapacity to encourage. In the second place, we consider it bad policy on the part of a National Theatre to set out on a scheme for the production of Continental plays. This is, surely, a pitiable confession of defeat.[9]

O'Connor had already written at least two plays that are still in existence, *A night out* and *Rodney's glory*. One of them had been rejected by the Abbey in 1934 (it is not known for certain which play was rejected but the evidence from his letters seems to point to *Rodney's glory*). The rejection appears to have had a deep effect on O'Connor and fuelled his conviction that the Abbey should do more to encourage and advise budding dramatists (it sparked his five-year-long battle with the Abbey board for improved treatment of young Irish playwrights). However, O'Connor's objection to Yeats' new policy of staging continental drama did not arise from purely personal playwriting ambitions. It also stemmed from his growing conviction that a national theatre should challenge and confront the dominant

---

8 Hugh Hunt, *The Abbey: Ireland's national theatre, 1904–1978* (Dublin, 1979), 149; the interview was expanded and republished in the *Irish Times* (23 Feb. 1935).   9 *Irish Times* (26 Feb. 1935).

orthodoxies, as opposed to the Abbey's strategic avoidance of so doing. He therefore began supporting the staging of contemporary Irish plays as, he argued, it
could help extirpate the doctrinaire from Irish cultural representations. O'Connor
would later admit that he had been attracted to the theatre in the 1930s because he
felt that it was the 'quickest and surest way of stinging the country alive'.[10] He
viewed modern Irish drama as the art form that would best encompass a subversive agenda; the theatre, he was to claim in Yeatsian tones, was 'a challenge to the
mob'.[11] Writing at a time when the threat of theatre censorship was rumoured,
O'Connor asserted that it was the arena that could best stage a combative stance
against the government's control of public opinion: 'the theatre is the only art
form than can directly influence opinion, particularly now that the censorship of
books is acting, more or less effectively, as a gag on the novelist'.[12]

O'Connor contention was that by staging plays that the audience could
socially and linguistically relate to, fresh realistic portrayals of Irish society might
possibly unsettle the predominately Catholic middle-class audience out of their
comfortable notions of what constituted 'Irishness'. The influence of Daniel
Corkery on his opinions is pronounced. Corkery's evaluation of the audience's
reaction to a play – that they always relate it their own contemporary situation,
hence the inherent instrumental nature of dramatic art, alongside his emphasis on
the educational importance of protecting and producing a native literary tradition
– is echoed in O'Connor's theatrical theories.[13] O'Connor also argued that the
staging of classical drama (unadapted for a contemporary audience) was akin to
staging 'museum theatre', as a playwright wrote with her/his audience in mind
and this in turn influenced a playwright's writing.[14] An Irish audience could more
easily access deeper meanings in contemporary Irish drama, where 'a line must
explode like a fragmentation bomb and hit a thousand people simultaneously'.[15]
O'Connor's combative language, on the subversive potential of language itself,
held the premise that contemporary Irish drama would succour a manumitting
effect whereas classical or continental plays would forestall a liberating agenda. In
a Hamletian sense, O'Connor saw plays as confrontational devices that could

---

10 O'Connor, Letter to Denis Johnston (1939), Trinity College, Dublin, MS 10066/287/2287.
11 O'Connor, 'Synge' in Lennon Robinson (ed.), *The Irish theatre: lectures delivered during the Abbey
Theatre festival held in Dublin in August 1938* (London, 1939; repr. New York, 1971), 34.   12 O'Connor,
'The future of Irish literature' in Cyril Connolly (ed.), *Horizon*, 5:25 (Jan. 1942), 63.   13 See
Corkery, *Synge and Anglo-Irish literature* (Cork, 1931; repr. 1955), 71–3; O'Connor, BBC broadcast,
'Curtain up! What is drama?', *The Listener*, 25 (23 Jan. 1941), 126; O'Connor, *The art of the theatre*
(Dublin, 1947), 26–9.   14 O'Connor, *The art of the theatre*, 25–8.   15 Ibid., 29.

provoke reaction, reveal truths and inspire action. While O'Connor's 'museum theatre' premise is critically interesting, in terms of the importance he attaches to the material conditions of reception, it would appear that his vanguard agenda in mid-century Irish cultural debate also underpinned his theatrical theories. This idealism stimulated his support for realism as opposed to abstraction. His desire to initiate social change in Ireland via the stage augmented his stance against experimental drama and cemented his support for theatrical realism, and he wanted it staged without compromise. The national theatre, O'Connor argued, should be disencumbered from acceptable social mores and ethics and this would lead to disturbing the audience into engaging with contentious issues. As he later said (with perhaps Synge and O'Casey in mind):

> The theatre has two great charms for me: one is the sense of freedom from considerations of circumstances; the other is its contemporaneity ... A storm in the theatre may very well mean the author's ahead of his time. The audience may not like the picture he gives of them because it's truer than the convention they want to have in their minds.[16]

O'Connor was ultimately objecting to what he saw as conservative, conventional attitudes in 1930s Ireland and the state's hegemonic mediation of art to the Irish public. When O'Connor joined the Abbey board, he did so with an oppositional agenda in mind.

O'Connor's actual joining was due to tension and divisions within the board itself. In the summer of 1935 Yeats and Sean O'Casey settled their quarrel over the Abbey's earlier rejection of *The silver tassie* and the play opened in the theatre on 12 August. *The silver tassie*'s political underpinning represented an inanity in undertaking violence for an idealistic end, while it condemned the collaboration of society, church and state in the sacrificing of young men to protect the status quo. A storm of protest based on religious grounds erupted and angry denouncements of the Abbey, O'Casey and Yeats ensued. Opposition also came from within the Abbey as Brinsley MacNamara joined the attack. Aroused by the charges of blasphemy that were directed at the play, he issued a statement to the press whereby he deprecated the 'vulgar and worthless' plays of O'Casey and proclaimed his powerlessness, as the only Catholic board member, to prevent the play's production.[17] Despite his refusal to resign MacNamara was eventually forced out. Yeats offered

---

16 O'Connor, BBC broadcast, 'Curtain up! Classical & contemporary theatre', *The Listener*, 25 (20 Feb. 1941), 268.   **17** *Irish Independent* (29 Aug. 1935). MacNamara was mistaken in his assertion that he was the only Catholic board member as Walter Starkie was also Catholic.

his place to O'Connor and he was subsequently elected on to the board on 9 October 1935. Various reasons have been offered as to why Yeats wanted the inexperienced O'Connor on the board of the Abbey. According to Peter Kavanagh, Yeats would have asked O'Connor a lot sooner but for the fact that he was a 'discovery' of George Russell's.[18] If this was true, Russell's death on 17 July would have removed Yeats' reason for hesitating. Some critics have argued that it stemmed from Yeats' belief that ex-gunmen were running all successful businesses at that time and O'Connor's history in the Civil War fitted the bill.[19] O'Connor's biographer has claimed that Yeats 'knew from disputes with Michael on the Academy Council that he could be depended upon to keep things stirred up and fight for the best interests of Irish artistic expression'.[20] There is an element of truth to both assertions. O'Connor's anti-Treaty credentials from the time of the Civil War, as well as his Catholic background, would have helped dissuade criticism leveled at the Abbey board that it had become a coterie of Ascendancy-related Protestants. Yeats also knew that O'Connor would fight for a more combative repertoire in the theatre, not just from his experience of O'Connor on the Academy Council but also from O'Connor's regular public skirmishes as a literary and cultural critic throughout the previous ten years. Moreover, O'Connor had already developed a reputation as a noted translator of Old Irish poetry and this interested Yeats in him (during O'Connor's time with the Abbey they worked together on numerous translations).[21] His strong approval of O'Connor's oration at Æ's funeral would have also increased the old poet's liking for the younger man.

In 1935 O'Connor's only real theatrical experience was from his brief time with the Cork Drama League. From the beginning, his innocence and inexperience served to put him at odds with the rest of the board members – Ernest Blythe, Richard Hayes, F.R. Higgins, Lennox Robinson and Walter Starkie. Their sagacious methods of conducting business were in direct contrast to O'Connor's youthful impatience and enthusiastic idealism, but it was with Robinson that O'Connor battled the most. By this stage Yeats, in his attempt to implement the new Abbey policy, had also engaged a young English producer, Hugh Hunt, as play director. Hunt's understanding of the Abbey's situation was very close to O'Connor's own beliefs at the time.[22] It set the stage for successful dramatic

18 Kavanagh, *The story of the Abbey Theatre* (New York, 1950), 127.   **19** Sylvan Barnet et al. (eds), *The genius of the Irish theatre* (New York, 1960), 245; Maurice Wohlgelernter, *Frank O'Connor: an introduction* (New York, 1977), 169.   **20** Matthews, *Voices*, 127.   **21** See Matthews, *Voices*, 98–9.   **22** Hunt, *The Abbey*, 153.

collaborations between O'Connor and Hunt, numerous disputes with Robinson, as well as O'Connor's antagonization of the already fractious board.[23] One of O'Connor's first discoveries on joining the board was the realization that it was Robinson who was mainly responsible for the rejection of new plays by Irish writers, as he had managed to persuade the board that no works of any real substance or value were being submitted. His incurring alcoholism, his demoralized state, and insecurity in the face of new talent played a dominant part in his directorial decisions. Whenever a new play appeared in the boardroom, Robinson 'reduced it to rubble with ingratiating smoothness'.[24] O'Connor's theatrical aspirations were threatened by this attitude. His discovery would augment his increasing frustration with the directorial decisions that were being taken as he wanted to represent the 'true Ireland' on stage.

O'Connor's desire to represent the 'true Ireland' on stage was not unique. Nicholas Grene has identified the importance of representations of Ireland within Irish drama since the Abbey was first founded, whereby it:

> has remained self-consciously aware of its relation to the life of the nation and the state … Every dramatist, every dramatic movement, claims that they can deliver the true Ireland, which has previously been misrepresented, travestied, rendered in sentimental cliché or political caricature.[25]

O'Connor's theatrical idealism was no different; he believed that one could utilize the national theatre as a 'fighting weapon' whereby the problems of the country could be thrashed out on stage.[26] O'Connor did not want Irish drama to merely reflect the surface of social life but to push instead for a deeper probing into Irish people's disparate beliefs and actions, and he therefore began to turn the Abbey away from Yeats' new policy. One of the final productions as part of this policy was Shakespeare's *Coriolanus* (13 January 1936). As Europe was in the grip of the rise of Fascism, the production of *Coriolanus* in Paris had caused a riot over the use of coloured shirts. Yeats wanted a similar reaction in Dublin and demanded a similar staging. His attraction towards the Irish Blueshirt movement in the previous few

23 These disputes obviously left Robinson with a lasting dislike of O'Connor. His only mention of O'Connor in his history of the theatre was to briefly record the dates for his appointment to the board, the staging of O'Connor's plays and his resignation – Lennox Robinson, *Ireland's Abbey Theatre* (New York, 1951), 149–50. **24** Matthews, *Voices*, 127. Also see Christopher Murray, *Twentieth-century Irish drama: mirror up to nation* (Manchester, 1997), 118. **25** Nicholas Grene, *The politics of Irish drama* (Cambridge, 1999), 1, 6. **26** O'Connor, *The Listener* (20 Feb. 1941), 269.

years was partly behind this desire, but his overt and rather outrageous reasoning was that a riot would help regenerate interest in the theatre. O'Connor refused to support the idea. His conciliatory gesture towards Yeats was a production of *Coriolanus* in Renaissance costume but it cost the theatre a lot of money. The new trend of staging classical and continental drama similarly failed in its attempt to capture the attention of Dublin's theatre-goers and the policy was thereafter dropped.

Instead, O'Connor began a process of actively promoting dramatists such as Teresa Deevy, Paul Vincent Carroll and Denis Johnston at board meetings and his methods began to be slowly felt. The board had rejected Carroll's *Shadow and substance* and Deevy's *Katie Roche* in 1935, but Deevy's play went on to be staged in the Abbey to critical acclaim on 16 March 1936 and Carroll's was staged on 25 January 1937. He had also 'gone the round begging for plays and had a few prom-ises, one from Seán O'Faoláin and another from Brinsley MacNamara'.[27] O'Faoláin's play, the only one he ever wrote, was *She had to do something* (27 December 1937). MacNamara's play was possibly *The grand house in the city* (3 February 1936). The staging of O'Faoláin's piece produced more personal conse-quences for O'Connor in that the players objected to Evelyn Bowen getting the leading part. O'Connor's relationship with the married Bowen (who went on to become O'Connor's first wife) was very unpopular with the rest of the board. He offered his resignation but Yeats refused to accept it, so O'Connor continued to assiduously attempt to create his 'fighting weapon'. He 'began screening the manuscripts submitted, approving and sending into production plays that turned the Abbey away from the fantasies which Yeats favoured. The Abbey thus began to emphasize dramatic fare … which dealt with either current social problems or with historical events'.[28] Hugh Hunt has described this period as something of a re-birth of Irish drama and D.E.S Maxwell has written that 'the truly remarkable fact is that noteworthy dramatists did emerge'.[29] Lionel Pilkington has also noted that in the mid-late 1930s 'the Abbey Theatre appeared to resume a more combative role in relation to nationalist majority views'.[30] This would seem to be directly attributable to Frank O'Connor's efforts. Robert Welch has highlighted that O'Connor was 'proving to be a dynamic force on the Abbey board', and Peter Kavanagh has credited O'Connor with being solely responsible for the attempts at revitalizing the Abbey: he 'was the only man whose genius might hold out against

27 William Tomory, *Frank O'Connor* (Boston, 1980), 52.   **28** Tomory, *Frank O'Connor*, 52. **29** Hunt, *The Abbey*, 157–8; D.E.S. Maxwell, *A critical history of modern Irish drama, 1891–1980* (Cambridge, 1984), 136.   **30** Pilkington, *Theatre and the state*, 131.

the ever-present deteriorating influences on the Abbey's integrity'.[31] While Kavanagh's account is somewhat laudatory, it is true that O'Connor played a leading role in encouraging new voices in Irish drama in the mid-late 30s, helped succeed in getting the theatre out of debt, and dominated an undertaking to shift the Abbey away from its theatre-state alliance during this period.

O'CONNOR'S STAGED ABBEY PLAYS

O'Connor of course was also involved in playwriting and several of his dramatic works, which included collaborations with Hugh Hunt, were staged by the theatre in the same period. In fact, O'Connor saw his joining the Abbey as an opportunity to become more involved in playwriting. 'The Abbey job is a help because it compels me to write something for the theatre', he wrote to his friend and fellow librarian, Dermot Foley, 'and as you know I've always had a shy and timorous passion for that'.[32] His initial efforts had already begun in the late 1920s. Ruth Sherry has pinpointed *A night out* and *Rodney's glory* as being two of his earliest plays, these plays were completely unknown until they were donated to the National Library of Ireland in March 1989. In 1928 O'Connor also referred to having written a three-act comedy about the Civil War with a view to staging it with the Cork Drama League but, to date, a manuscript of this play has not been found.[33] His third dramatic effort was the Kiplingesque entitled play, *The lost legion*.[34] Not counting his radio plays, he wrote eight plays in total – four were staged by the Abbey (three were collaborations) and the final one, *The statue's daughter*, by the Gate Theatre in 1941. This article concentrates on his staged Abbey plays.

In the train was O'Connor's first staged play and it turned out to be a successful venture, helped perhaps by the fact that it was a collaboration with Hunt. It was based on his similarly titled short story, previously published in *Bones of contention* (1936). While it is difficult to ascertain the exact extent of O'Connor's involvement in the dramatization of *In the train*, Hunt has written that during their collaborations, while there was no set pattern, O'Connor provided the characters and plot and Hunt shaped it into scenes and wrote some rough drafts of dialogue, which O'Connor then completely polished.[35]

31 Robert Welch, *The Abbey Theatre, 1899–1999: form and pressure* (Oxford, 2003), 130; Kavanagh, *The story*, 173. **32** Letter to Dermot Foley (Jan. 1936), HODSC. **33** Sherry, 'The manuscript of "Rodney's Glory" by Frank O'Connor', *Irish University Review*, 22 (Autumn/Winter 1992), 219–20. **34** O'Connor, *The lost legion* (1936, my date), Trinity College, Dublin, MS 10899a. **35** Hugh

The play opens with a voice-over by the judge informing the audience that Helena Maguire is alleged to have poisoned her much older husband. The action on stage is set in various compartments of a train where the people involved in the case (Helena, the local guards and Helena's neighbours) are on their way home to Farranchreesht, a small village in the West of Ireland. A wandering drunk carries information between the compartments. The audience learns from the guards' compartment scene that contradictory accounts have been given by the witnesses – the local guards and neighbours – and the implication is that the neighbours have committed perjury and will perform their own local punishment: 'standing for her in court and standing for her in Farranchreesht are two very different things'.[36] In the compartment filled with the country people, the gulf between rural and urban life is stressed. They are joined by the guards and joke about their brazen lies in court. The audience is given more details of the case by the voice-over and the drama moves to the compartment that Helena occupies. Quickly joined by most of the locals, they openly bait her about committing the murder so she could be with her younger lover, Driscoll; one guard ridicules her innocence: 'You wanted him, Helena. Your people wouldn't let you have him, but you have him at last in spite of them all'.[37] Helena angrily responds that Cady Driscoll means no more to her now than sea salt, and the play finishes with the judge's voice-over giving a 'not guilty' verdict.

In the train is a powerful and dramatically intense one-act play. Characters are adeptly honed, through dress and dialogue, and a compelling picture of life in rural Ireland emerges. The narrative illustrates the divisions between rural and urban life, between community law and official law. As the train travels westwards it symbolizes the departure of the people from a more modern way of life in Dublin, and traditional ways of maintaining authority are re-established on the journey back to Farranchreesht. The train's compartments symbolize the social order of the village community but do not privilege any one perspective. It is a self-contained culture with its own customs and values and appears immune to the modernizing forces of the state, this 'submerged population' will not sacrifice one of their own people to an 'outside' law but will decide on their own rural disciplining of Helena. The possibility of being branded an informer (a theme that materializes even more strongly in O'Connor's 1937 play, *The invincibles*) was

Hunt, Letter to Ruth Sherry (12 Sept. 1981), quoted in Sherry (ed. & intro.), *Moses' rock by Frank O'Connor and Hugh Hunt* (Washington, 1983), 36. **36** O'Connor, *In the train* in Barnet et al., *The genius of Irish theater*, 254. The version of the play used here is O'Connor's own; Hunt published his own version in 1973. **37** Ibid., 260.

something that would not be entertained and the villagers steadfastly respond to the unwritten laws within their own community. Because of this, O'Connor does not allow Helena to control and satisfy her sexual desires. Helena enacts her own self-punishment at the end of the play with the hardening of her heart toward the man she loves and this lonely individual now returns to social alienation. *In the train* was based on a true murder case being tried in the Four Courts in April 1935, of a woman from West Clare accused of poisoning her husband (in order to be with her lover). Her neighbours commit perjury to avoid 'informing'.[38] The ending of the play is O'Connor's own and while powerful in itself, it is not unsettling for a 1930s Abbey audience as it reinstates the woman back into conventional social laws concerning female behaviour. Instead, there is a dramatic containment of female autonomy, which counters emerging social 'problems' such as women's emancipation that threatened the official gendered idealization of the nation. O'Connor's first staged effort at 'disturbing' acceptable social mores achieves little in this context. The drama also continues the Literary Revival's depiction of 'true' Ireland, in that it maintains the Revival's anti-modern, wild Irish peasant stereotype, a sign that O'Connor had not left the sway of the Revival behind.

First staged in the Abbey on 31 May 1937, as a one-act preceding O'Casey's *The shadow of a gunman,* it received a positive response from the critics. The *Irish Press* praised the acting and production and hoped that 'it will be the forerunner of many such efforts'.[39] David Sears applauded the production, the stage design and the 'greatness' of the adaptation: a 'first-class' short story was transformed into a 'first-class one-act play'.[40] Hunt's dramatic technique of using a chorus to chant the rhythm of the train did not sit favourably with Joseph Holloway but he praised the acting and found it 'an interesting experiment'.[41] *In the train* was subsequently part of the Abbey's repertoire during the American tour in 1937 and was performed as part of the Abbey festival in 1938. It also enjoyed a revival when it was performed in the Abbey in August 1970 as part of a programme that included Yeats' *Purgatory,* Lady Gregory's *The rising of the moon* and Beckett's *Krapp's last tape.*

Due to its success, O'Connor and Hunt went on to collaborate on two more plays, *The invincibles* and *Moses' rock.* These were to become part of a dramatic trilogy by O'Connor that dealt with important events in Irish history (the third was *Time's pocket* but Hunt did not collaborate). In the case of *The invincibles,*

---

38 Matthews, *Voices,* 111–12.   39 *Irish Press* (1 June 1937).   40 *Irish Independent* (1 June 1937). 41 Robert Hogan and Michael J. O'Neill (eds), *Joseph Holloway's Irish theatre, Vol. 3, 1932–1937* (California, 1968), 70.

O'Connor claimed (in a preface written for a planned publishing of the play that never materialized) that the idea came to him while researching for his biography on Michael Collins (*The big fellow*, 1936).[42] In his autobiography he said he wrote the play because 'for years [he] had been haunted by the subject of the Invincibles'.[43] It is also possible that his idea for the play was impacted by his reading of *Ulysses*, which mentions the event in detail. This Joycean influence seems more likely when the title, *Moses' rock*, and background subject, the fall of Parnell, of his next play is taken into consideration (as discussed later in the essay). The Phoenix Park murders occurred on 6 May 1882 when Lord Frederick Cavendish, the newly appointed chief secretary for Ireland, and his under-secretary, Thomas H. Burke, were assassinated by a group calling themselves the Invincibles, a splinter Fenian group. The result was a condemnation of the murders by Parnell as he wanted to avoid any suggestion of involvement (the *Times* forgeries in 1887 would famously try to implicate Parnell in the event), and a betrayal by one of their own men who 'informed'. Five of the Invincibles were hanged in Kilmainham Jail and popular national sentiment in the country had held the view that the men were brave patriots betrayed by a hated informer.[44] It was a politically delicate subject to tackle and it was perhaps for this reason that O'Connor decided to attempt a dramatization of it. He drafted a play and Hunt joined him as collaborator in order to put 'real theatrical bones into my dramatized history'.[45] The result of their efforts was a seven-scene play that was first performed in the Abbey on 18 October 1937.

The play opens to a pub scene of squabbling and raillery between various Fenian factions, language that the Abbey audience would have been familiar with and comfortable listening to. The Invincibles, after their secret meeting in the pub, eventually receive their orders from their headquarters to kill Foster, the then Chief Secretary. In Scene Two, amid complaints of Parnell's negotiations with the British Liberal government, they express fears that the possibility of an Irish republic will dissipate. They had failed in the previous six months to assassinate Forster and Carey wants to forget it in light of Cavendish (who was better liked) taking over as Chief Secretary. When they hear the news that a twelve-year-old child has been killed by a soldier's bayonet as they dispersed a street-crowd celebrating Parnell's release from Kilmainham Jail, they angrily decide to carry out the assassination and the scene finishes with the words that 'Steel they gave us, and

42 Matthews, *Voices*, 403–4, fn. 46. **43** O'Connor, *My father's son* (Dublin, 1968), 172. **44** Senan Molony, *The Phoenix Park murders: conspiracy, betrayal & retribution* (Cork, 2006), 248. **45** O'Connor, *My father's son*, 173.

steel we'll give then back'.[46] In the opening lines of the next scene, set in a pub near the park, the Abbey audience listens to posturings by an English fisherman that the Irish as a race 'deserve nothing but drowning'. Cavendish and Burke have been killed and the scene focuses on revealing the men's uncertainty before committing the deed and their explanations for committing the assassinations; their remorse and panic is made clear. In Scene Four, the audience learns that the church, the Fenians, and Parnell have strongly condemned the murders. Brady and Tim Kelly are very disillusioned in Scene Five in Brady's sitting room. Carey drops in and all three men are subsequently arrested. In Scene Six, through the clever trickery of Inspector Mallon, Carey dramatically transforms himself into an informer. A year passes and the final scene of the play is set in Brady and Carey's lonely jail cells. The condemned men await their execution in the morning while outside silent crowds have gathered. Brady is bitter and defiant and dismisses the Irish for their hypocrisy. After talking to a nun (the sister of one of the assassinated men, Burke), Brady repents and begs for forgiveness. Tim Kelly's voice in a nearby cell begins singing the hymn 'Hail, Queen of Heaven' and the whole prison chorus joins in. Carey shouts to be hanged with the others (in real life, Carey was shot dead while ship-bound for Australia). While listening to the hymn, Brady changes his mind again and reasserts that his actions were right; he sadly comments that it is Ireland's shame, 'Poor Ireland with slavery in her blood',[47] he forgives Ireland, Tim continues singing and the play ends.

The staging of this episode in Irish history generated quite a bit of interest in Dublin circles and rumors on the opening night of a protest demonstration circulated. The appearance of Maud Gonne in the foyer only added to the rumor. Peter Kavanagh noted a 'tense and eagar' atmosphere and Joseph Holloway recorded 'an air of eagerness and excitement'.[48] No such protest materialized. The reaction of the critics was mixed. In his positive review, Kavanagh praised the acting, stage-settings, the historiography and the portrayal of Carey; one could now understand why he turned himself into an informer: 'his weakness is vanity and a foolish pride'. Kavanagh also admired the 'extraordinary emotional appeal of the play', illustrated by the fact that 'the audience joined ... in singing [the hymn]'.[49] David Sears' review, appearing a day after Kavanagh's, had an almost complete opposite reaction. Sears took issue with the historiography: 'When one indicts a nation it is hardly fair to leave the case for the defence to be presented mainly through the clowning of two

---

46 O'Connor & Hunt in Ruth Sherry (ed.), *The invincibles: a play in seven scenes* (London, 1980), 31.
47 Ibid., 74.   48 *Irish Press* (19 Oct. 1937); Hogan & O'Neill, *Joseph Holloway's Irish theatre*, 75.
49 *Irish Press* (19 Oct. 1937).

fools in a public-house bar' (a reference to two local Fenians whose reactions are idiotic and who serve as a comedic element in the fourth scene). While praising the acting and stage-setting, Sears admired the final scene where 'not even the rather irrelevant community singing which retards the action towards the end could spoil it'.[50] The very brief *Irish Times* review noticeably commended only the acting and production.[51] Holloway dismissed it as the 'crudest of melodramas ... cheers rang out from the audience. It was evidently more impressed than I was by the crude picture they had just seen limned of a very painful episode in our country's history'.[52] General public interest in the dramatic piece and its subject matter was further reflected in the various references to it in the 'Irishman's Diary' and letters page in the *Irish Times* during the staging of the play.[53] In addition, Robinson's public support of criticism of O'Connor and Hunt by the Actors' Guild (for dramatizing a subject painful to the Invincibles' relatives) nearly resulted in his being removed from the board.[54] A revival was planned for the Abbey festival in 1938 but Robinson succeeded in getting it dropped; it was subsequently reproduced in the Gaiety Theatre in February 1943 by Louis D'Alton.

O'Connor and Hunt's attempt to open up national memory of the historical event is an interesting effort, but it does result in the play being more dramatized history than theatrical creativity. It suffers from a lack of economy in its melodramatic language, and O'Connor's aim to provide background social and political context produces wearisome dialogue in places. It would seem that part of O'Connor's intention was to use the events of history to illustrate the pattern of repetition in Irish social conditions. This is particularly evident when the piece refers to the role of the church in Irish politics and a perceived passive acquiescence of Irish people to dominant social forces. The frequent references in the play to Irish people's fear of words could also be a rebuke at the prevailing strict censorial conditions that writers had to operate within during the thirties. However, the narrative of the play is carefully aligned with popular nationalist sentiment and it would seem that O'Connor and Hunt were directing the play at a particular audience, the dominant Catholic nationalist establishment. Scene one posits local political bickering and ineffectual republicanism against patriotic action. The second scene paints a picture of confusion and division within the Invincibles and a rather sympathetic and credible portrait of the men is drawn.[55] This splinter

---

50 *Irish Independent* (20 Oct. 1937). **51** *Irish Times* (26 Oct. 1937). **52** Hogan & O'Neill, *Joseph Holloway's Irish theatre*, 75–6. **53** *Irish Times* (21, 22, 26 Oct. 1937). **54** See O'Connor, *My father's son*, 174, and Letter to Evelyn Bowen (Aug. 1938), HODSC. **55** The pointed references to 'steel' at the end of the scene suggests O'Connor's own sympathy for the men if one considers a Joycean influ-

Fenian group is not displayed as simply a bloodthirsty violent faction and their final incentive for committing the murders is represented as a protective reaction to English force. Nationalist sentiment within the Abbey's audience would have fully approved of this portrayal, and this fortifies the impression that O'Connor and Hunt were consciously attempting to mitigate the murders and delineate the rationale behind them. O'Connor and Hunt switched the focus of the drama in the final two scenes, from the assassinations to the attitude within Irish society towards an informer.[56] The scenes where Carey is cast as the duped informer are the most powerful in the play. They bring the action to an emotional climax and conservative social order is reassuringly restored. Carey as the villain would have been comfortably received by most of the Abbey audience in the 1930s. But the play also displays a criticism of nationalism and the Irish nation. O'Connor and Hunt attempted to portray a basic dichotomy between outside and inside the jail cell, between nationalist ideology and individual experience. National memory might well have blamed the informer for the Invincibles' executions but the play, while not condoning, explicates Carey's actions and interjects the point that these men had already been abandoned by the nationalist movement and the public at large. O'Connor and Hunt's play does not indict the Invincibles. Instead, questions as to what constitutes 'heroism' in nationalist rhetoric and in Irish society are confrontationally posed throughout the drama.

Just a few months after the Abbey production, O'Connor and Hunt's next and final collaboration was *Moses' rock*, which was staged on 28 February 1938. The focus again was on Irish history and this time the political downfall and death of Charles Stewart Parnell serves as a structuring device for the plot. It is a three-act play and each act is connected to important events during this time – the splitting of the Irish Parliamentary Party, Parnell's by-election defeats, and his funeral. Act I takes place in December 1890 and is set in Cady O'Leary's house, a wealthy Catholic butter merchant. Ned Hegarty has just been released from prison and Cady, Jer Coughlan (his lawyer) and Dr Jackson, the local intellectual, are cele-

ence. In the 'Eumaeus' chapter in *Ulysses*, while Stephen and Bloom sit in the cabmans' shelter (owned by Skin-the-Goat, James Fitzharris, who allegedly drove the decoy car for the Invincibles), Bloom admits to, as he muses over Fitzharris' involvement in the episode, having 'a certain kind of admiration for a man who had actually brandished a knife, cold steel, with the courage of his political convictions', James Joyce, *Ulysses* (Paris, 1922; repr. London, 2000), 744.   **56** O'Connor was not the first nor last writer to use 'the informer' as a prominent theme in Irish literature. Sean O'Casey's *Juno and the paycock* (1924), Liam O'Flaherty's *The informer* (1925), George Shields' *The rugged path* (1940), Tom Murphy's stage-adaptation of O'Flaherty's novel, *The informer* (1981) and Seamus Deane's *Reading in the dark* (1996), for example, all explore Irish people's attitudes towards those that 'inform'. John Ford also adapted O'Flaherty's novel to film, *The informer* (1935).

brating off-stage. Their toasts to Parnell and the Irish Republic are listened to by three old women – Shuvaun (Cady's mother), Biddy and Sorry – and the maid, Nellie. Ned makes a speech proclaiming their steadfast faith in Parnell and the future liberation of their country. Kate, Cady's sister, shuts the door on them at this point and, reminiscent of Joyce's Dante, virulently denounces Parnell as the 'damned adulterer'. Kate's betrothed died in the 1867 Fenian rebellion and she is still bitter. Joan, Cady's daughter, appears and the audience learns that both Ned and an English officer, Lieutenant Fortescue, are her suitors. When Ned discovers that Jer also wants to marry Joan he loyally decides to postpone his proposal for six months, as both Ned and Jer are convinced that Home Rule is within their grasp and this takes priority. In contrast to Ned and Jer, Fortescue is actively pursuing Joan. Her father is only interested in making a prosperous 'match' and pays scant attention to her. They learn the party has split, 'split like Moses' Rock', and the Act finishes with Kate crying over the split.

Act 2 is set in the summer of 1891, Ned is still supporting Parnell and believing that the people will too. Jer and his brother, Father Henry, are supporting the Church's anti-Parnellite stance, Cady is playing both sides and Joan is becoming disillusioned and starting to have real doubts about the country. Cork, to her mind, is changing from a lovely, beautiful place into something 'mean, ugly, sordid'; she wants to go to Parnell's campaign meetings but both Cady and Ned refuse to take her. Ned and Jer disagree bitterly about the political situation and both then propose to Joan, she refuses them. When Jer reveals that Fortescue was also named as a co-respondent in a divorce case, she agrees to marry Jer. Cady then declares his loyalty to the anti-Parnellites and the Act finishes with Kate crying again. Act 3 is set in October 1891, the day after Parnell's funeral and the day before Joan's wedding to Jer. Cady is once more only concerned with backing 'the right horse', he provides patriarchal advice to Joan about her wifely duties and considers running in the elections for 'the sake of Ireland'. Ned is deeply regretful of losing Joan, his 'one great chance', and Joan has become bitter and angry with the Irish men in her life:

> JER: I didn't ask for the split.
> JOAN: Of course you asked for it. You and Ned and all the others. All the pretence is broken down at last, and you can indulge all the meanness of your mean little souls, spitting in your neighbour's fence, stealing his trade, plotting and intriguing against him, and all in the name of Ireland and religion.[57]

---

57 O'Connor & Hunt in Ruth Sherry (ed. and intro.), *Moses' rock* (Washington, 1983), 100–1.

By the end of the final act, the split produces a more positive affect on characters such as Kate and Jackson. The continual crying is cathartic for Kate and releases deep-seated negative emotions. She softens in her attitude towards everything. As Joan is so unhappy about marrying Jer, Kate urges Joan to meet with Fortescue who has called to see her one last time before his regiment leaves for India; Joan elopes with the English officer. Jackson, the emotionally reserved intellectual type, whose keen insight is capable of predicting future political developments, also begins to open up and reveals a long-hidden love for Joan (he chases after Joan but he has left it too late).[58] Cady, upon learning of Joan's flight, is only concerned about the effect on himself, Jer is furious and the play ends with Kate emotionally declaring that 'this town is no place for the young. All that is young and beautiful is leaving Ireland now, like seagulls flying into the dark. It's a poor divided country we'll be from this night on'.[59]

O'Connor's second attempt at dramatizing Irish history produces a better play. Rather than depicting the historical event, he focuses less on the actual facts and instead imagines how it might have affected an Irish middle-class Catholic family. This results in the second play having more creative dialogue, better characterization, tighter scene arrangement and a more imaginative plot. The main instances of the historical crisis – the Catholic church's reaction, the party splitting, the by-election campaign meetings and Parnell's funeral – take place off-stage and the on-stage action is more of a reaction to these events. Like *Cathleen ni Houlihan*, Ireland is once more personified as a woman, this time through the figure of Joan. Allegorical readings of her three suitors suggest themselves. Ned is the idealistic pro-Parnellite faction, Jer adopts the church's anti-Parnellite stance and Fortescue represents the British Empire. The minor female characters, apart from Shuvaun, also serve as little more than stock figurations of these divisions. (While she is a minor character, Shuvaun signifies O'Connor's recurrent attempts in the 1930–40s to symbolically represent the surviving fragmented remains of a traumatized past, the Great Famine in this instance, and the dying out of traditional Gaelic culture.) In the play, the destruction of Ned and Jer's friendship, their fighting and ensuing rivalry for Joan results in neither side winning her hand, instead Joan leaves with the English officer for colonized India. Ireland has been firmly re-attached to its colonial status. Like one of O'Connor's prominent short-story themes, the play also questions the personal

---

58 The only manuscript of the play that has survived stops at this point. Hugh Hunt reconstructed the ending of the play for Sherry's edition. **59** Sherry, *Moses' rock*, 110.

cost of political involvement. Ned neglected everything, including his domestic happiness, in the pursuit of his political idealism and is left at the end with only regrets; Kate allowed the personal consequences of political action to ensnare her in bitterness and, despite her redemption over twenty years later, is left at the end as a rather lonely woman; Parnell lost his life. Yet O'Connor is careful in the play to avoid condemning Parnell's actions or Irish nationalism. The rather sympathetic portrait of Ned, Kate's late praise of the Fenian movement, Joan's desire to attend Parnell's monster meetings, her disinterest in marrying Jer and ultimate disregard for Fortescue being named as co-respondent in a divorce case, would seem to indicate O'Connor's own conclusions on the historical event. Shuvaun's recitation of part of 'A lament for Art O'Leary' as Kate cries indicates O'Connor situating the downfall of Parnell as an unjustifiable tragic episode in Irish history. Jer and Cady's depiction as self-interested middle-class opportunists, and their expedient obedience to the church's position, reveals instead O'Connor's indictment of those who rejected Parnell. The play stages his retrospective regret at the political repercussions and also highlights his thoughts on similarly recurring trends in the 1930s. Passive obedience towards Catholic church dictates, a spectator-ship role among Irish intellectuals in politics and society, and those who use political events as a pawn in their own personal power battles, are similarly indicted. Interestingly, the play was revived in the Abbey in 1994 and it was positively reviewed in terms of its apt resonances to the issues of the 1990s.[60]

Critical reaction to the staging of the play in 1938 was generally favourable. The *Irish Press* review praised the acting and character portrayal, and declared that 'the ground around Parnell's feet is scraped inquiringly, as in "The Invincibles," less they be of clay … there is bitterness in the play. But there is also entertainment'.[61] David Sears pronounced it 'sound and wise … searching in its analysis of national and personal emotions … comprehensive in its imaginative span'.[62] In contrast to these opinions, a review of the 1983 publication described it as a 'middle-class Cork City soap opera'. The reviewer also queried the relevance of the Irish party split to 'Moses cleaving of the rock whence water and salvation flow' and dismissed it as a 'hazy symbol'.[63] A possible explication of O'Connor's title is, as mentioned earlier, connected to a Joycean influence at work. Literary Parnellism was well established by the time O'Connor wrote the play. The literary connection between Moses and Parnell was also established, and a paralleling

---

60 See *Sunday Tribune* (17 Apr. 1994), *Irish Times* (21 Apr. 1994), *Irish Independent* (21 Apr. 1994). **61** *Irish Press* (1 Mar. 1938). **62** *Irish Independent* (1 Mar. 1938). **63** Christopher Griffin, 'The betrayal of Parnell', *Irish Literary Supplement*, 3 (Fall 1984), 40.

between the Jews and the Irish in *Ulysses* is well known. In the bible, in the Old Testament's 'Book of Numbers', as Moses was about to strike the rock, he said, 'Listen, you rebels, shall we bring water for you out of this rock?' (20:10). 'The Lord', angered by Moses' words as he did not give due recognition to his Holy work, does not allow Moses to lead the people into the promised land (20:12). It was in this context that Joyce paralleled Moses with Parnell in *Ulysses*. In 'Aeolus', J.J. Molloy points out that Moses died before getting to the land of promise, similar to Parnell's failure to lead the Irish to Home Rule and his subsequent death, and also similar to Bloom's status as a wanderer and failure to be socially accepted in Dublin, or as an Irish citizen in the 'Cyclops' chapter. Parnell is reincarnated in Bloom even more concretely in 'Eumaeus'. In the 'Cyclops' chapter, the Citizen calls Bloom a new apostle to the gentiles as well as the new Messiah for Ireland, thus linking Bloom to both Moses and Parnell. (O'Connor wanted to explore nationalist sensitivities in his trilogy and it would appear that Joyce's Citizen imparted the material; the Citizen, while linking Moses with Parnell, also mentions the Invincibles and makes reference to 'the men of sixtyseven' – O'Connor's subject matter for his next play, *Time's pocket*). Other minor details in these *Ulysses* chapters – the incorrect historical year of the Phoenix Park murders (O'Connor also takes creative liberties with historical dates),[64] a brass and reed band playing, the singing of 'A nation once again', Professor MacHugh's reference to the death of the imagination, Bloom's brand of Parnellism, the vulgar name-calling of Kitty O'Shea, and Bloom's depiction of political quarrels as largely a question of money, greed and jealously – all reappear in different ways in *Moses' rock*. Despite the several condemnations of Joyce in O'Connor's literary criticism, the analogous crossover of ideas would seem to reinforce the impression that *Ulysses* was a fruitful source of inspiration for the inexperienced dramatist.

O'Connor's last play for the planned historical trilogy, as well as his final Abbey play, was *Time's pocket*. Hunt had left the theatre by this stage so O'Connor went ahead with it by himself. Staged on 26 December 1938, it turned out to be the play that attracted the most public attention for him. While O'Connor had described *Moses' rock* in his letters as a 'sequel' to *The invincibles*, chronologically his trilogy does not follow any linear historical narrative as *Time's pocket* returns to 1867, to the time of the failed 'physical-force' Fenian uprising. Apart from the Citizen's referral to it in 'Cyclops', another possible reason for O'Connor's return to the 1867 rebellion might be because the Fenian movement

---

64 See Sherry, *Moses' rock*, 28, 91 (fn. 53).

contributed in the 1870s to a social and political shift away from deference to the state and its institutions and towards a more assertive and
confident nationalism ... it was this that enabled the political assertion of
the home rule and land war years of the 1880s ...[65]

Moreover, as Seamus Deane has pointed out, the debates of the post-independence period had their origins in the 1870s due to the

> long-standing effects of the late nineteenth-century 'Devotional
> Revolution' among the Catholic beneficiaries of the Land War [precipi-
> tated by the First Vatican Council's identification of 'modernism' as the
> enemy], whose descendants also became the chief beneficiaries of the
> Irish revolution ... By the 1920s, nationalism had begun to yield [almost]
> entirely to this anti-modernist Catholicism.[66]

O'Connor's understanding of this would seem to be evident from the prominence
given to the church's position in the play. The Catholic church's hostility towards
the Fenian movement, and its influence in social and political affairs, is a theme
that O'Connor focuses on in the play; this also allowed him to use the historical
event as a comparative vehicle for his thoughts on the church in the 1930s. The
play's title itself indicates a place where nothing has changed, life has continued in
the same patterned, timeless way in this 'pocket' of the world. O'Connor's
thematic focus might also have been because of the deliberate efforts by the Fianna
Fáil government in the mid-late 30s to shift the party away from more extreme
republican positions, as it strongly and legally distanced itself from the IRA. This
might well have inspired O'Connor to try and provocatively stage what was
considered a tragic physical-force republican episode in Irish history.

Two copies of the unpublished play have survived but both copies are missing
most of the eighteen-page first act.[67] The NLI copy claims an Act 6 but these four
pages available appear to belong to the first act, and this is confirmed by the MML
copy. What one can deduce from the surviving pages of Act 1 is that the action

65 James H. Murphy, *Ireland: a social, cultural and literary history, 1791–1891* (Dublin, 2003), 113.
66 Seamus Deane, *A short history of Irish literature* (London, 1986), 210–11. **67** O'Connor, *Time's pocket*, Abbey Theatre Papers, National Library of Ireland, MS 1426 (hereafter referred to as the NLI copy). The second copy is held in Mugar Memorial Library, Boston University, The Frank O'Connor Collection, 990, Box 5, Folder 5 (hereafter referred to as the MML copy).

appears to be set in Abbey's house (an old Irish-speaking woman similar to Shuvaun in *Moses' rock*) in an urban city setting, the Fenians are organizing an armed rebellion, Sullivan (who is planning to marry Nance, Abbey's daughter) is against the rebellion because the priests are, the local priest is more concerned with building an even bigger chapel than the one already in the town, Nance is a Fenian sympathizer and her brother, Patrick, is more interested in making money than in politics. Conlon, a wandering old poet, has been searching for forty years for a missing but very important Irish language book, and some Irish soldiers in a British regiment are also in the house, including Daly, Fahy and Dargan. The available text for Act 1 is enough to indicate leading character development and some of the direction of the plot in the rest of the play. In Act 2, frustration with the delays for the Fenian uprising are voiced, the church's criticisms are strongly revealed, and Dargan, as one of the leaders of the Fenians, is arrested. Set in Victoria Barracks, Abbey, Nance and Conlon have come to plead for Dargan's life in Act 3. Sullivan is viciously smug towards them and obsequious towards the general and his wife. As she pleads for Dargan's life, Nance confesses to being pregnant and Dargan is the father. Sullivan is furious but the general wife's suggests he still marries her and she will 'put in a word' for Dargan so Nance agrees to the marriage for Dargan's sake. Disillusionment is strongly expressed by Conlon and he is outraged at what has happened to the young couple. Transportation for life is Dargan's sentence and Conlon vows to watch over Nance (mainly because of his guilty feelings for unwittingly revealing Dargan's whereabouts before his arrest).

In Act 4, ten years later, old and haggard Nance is working in her kitchen and Conlon returns after wandering for two months, disappointed at the standard of spoken Irish he encountered on his travels and having learnt that the prisoners have gained early release. An old, sickly-looking man appears – Dargan has returned for Nance and meets his son – and the suffering both Nance and Dargan endured for the ten years is revealed; Sullivan enters and his name-calling convinces Nance to leave with Dargan as both her and Conlon's 'purgatory' is over. Conlon returns to his poor hungry people in the hills, 'with great tongues of Irish to understand my books' (NLI, 62), where he will live out his dying days. A year later, in Act 5, the family are living in a bright, cheerful house, and mother and child are much happier in appearance and behaviour. Dargan's nightly nightmares are started to recede but his mental health has deteriorated. Some of the harrowing treatment he received as a prisoner is relayed to his son. After having ignored Nance's existence for the previous ten years, Patrick arrives and wants the unmarried couple to break up because it is affecting his social standing. The climax of the play is Nance and Father Costello's fiercely bitter argument over Nance and Dargan's co-habitation. Costello uses very threatening, forceful language but Nance is not cowed and valiantly defends the man she loves. When Costello realizes the condition of Dargan's mental health, the NLI copy ends with his giving an apology to the couple. The MML copy is a half-page longer. In this ending, Nance refuses to be affected by the priest's warnings of what will now happen to her – spiritually, socially and economically. She can deal with life because of Dargan's love, she states, and asks the priest to leave so she can return to her true husband.

Time's pocket is a tragic romance set against the background of politics. Hunt's absence from the transferal of O'Connor's plot and characters into a useable script is evident. The play contains such an over-abundance of characters that their depictions are attenuated and they simply serve as representatives of various political and social clichéd machinations. While it is difficult to judge a play that has over half of the first act missing, Nance and Dargan's love story is not fully believable and yet their story is compelling. It is for Nance and Dargan that the audience is asked to feel the most approbation, the young couple that is torn apart by forces outside their control, a tragic love story that has no satisfyingly happy ending. The materialistic Patrick, the Catholic church, British imperialism, its prison system and its informers, are portrayed in an extremely unflattering light. A more sensitive treatment is given to Abbey and Conlon. Similar to his unstaged *Rodney's glory*, O'Connor is once more using this type of character to represent the collision between ancient Gaelic tradition and modern commercialism, as well as rebuke society's growing disrespect for the artist.

O'Connor is also careful to insert details that align with the actual facts of the 1867 rebellion. This includes the Irish Republican Brotherhood's emphasis on physical force nationalism as opposed to constitutional methods, the church's antagonism towards the secret oath-bound society, the poor socio-economic background of a majority of the Fenians, the influence of French socialist thought on the Fenians' ideological thinking, the infiltration of the Fenians into British regiments, the betrayal of this and the authorities' arrest of some of the men before the rising ever took place, the delays on setting a date for it, the harsh conditions of the prisons, and the early release of many prominent Fenians from prison.[68] The historical details are casually interspersed throughout the drama but, like *Moses' rock*, O'Connor imaginatively dramatizes the effect of this on the young Fenian

---

68 See Robert Kee, *The bold Fenian men: the green flag, volumn two* (London, 1972; repr. 1977), 3–51.

couple. Again, O'Connor is exploring the personal consequences of physical-force political involvement and the price that one could pay – a loss of one's personal happiness, deep emotional suffering, a loss of one's sanity or life – as well as the price the families have to pay too. Yet, it is not the Fenian movement that is impeached by O'Connor. The ongoing threat to indigenous traditional culture, the economic hardship that is endured by the Irish poor, mistreatment of Irish women by the 'swaddies', arrogant displays of imperial might, and the pain of forced emigration are also interpolated throughout the play as reasons for the planned uprising. Imperialism, the Catholic church, and the propertied classes are judged on their treatment of 'ordinary' people and are found guilty of maltreatment and a narrow-minded sexual morality (the 'showdown' over adultery was perhaps no coincidence considering O'Connor was by now opening living with Bowen). It is the latter two groups that are portrayed as unappreciative and hence unworthy of any heroic sacrifice made on their behalf, and O'Connor provocatively stages the priest apologizing near the end of the play to the co-habiting couple.

The play was not well-received. Andrew Malone denounced the first act, thought the play focused too much on the 'bold Fenian men' and the real drama of the play, Nance and Dargan's suffering, was completely lost. The critic put the play's failure down to O'Connor's 'amateurish' efforts.[69] David Sears found it 'a rather dull, ambling play', reserved the majority of his criticism for the construction, plot and character development but was more positive about the final two acts: 'his theme is unusual, tragic, cruel, and inevitable, and he handles it in masterly fashion'.[70] The most interesting reactions appeared in the New Year. O'Connor rather arrogantly defended the play and issued a statement to the *Irish Independent*, declaring that:

> the critics think only of 'construction' and 'action' and 'development' and 'psychology' – all of which have about as much to do with the theatre as the man in the moon … we had had two civil wars, and a whole generation of embittered men and women … and the Abbey had never even become aware of their existence. Now the Abbey is aware of them … there is something about a critic's job which makes him blind to the things that are happening in the world about him.[71]

---

69 *Irish Times* (27 Dec. 1938). **70** *Irish Independent* (27 Dec. 1938). **71** *Irish Independent* (6 Jan. 1939). The reference to the second civil war perhaps could be explained by O'Connor describing the

Sears rose to the bait and responded the next day in the same newspaper to O'Connor's 'pernicious nonsense … it is very disheartening to find crass igno- rance enthroned in the very citadel of Irish drama'. To which O'Faoláin weighted in with a lengthy letter in O'Connor's defense: 'Mr O'Connor's play was reviewed with unusual acidity. The clichés with which the main reviews … were packed exasperated many of us. Mr O'Connor assailed these cliches [*sic*] – the usual armoury of the text-book critic … Mr O'Connor is right … I recommend Mr Sears to take his little text-book … and gently deposit it in the Home for the Blind'.[72] A letter from an 'onlooker' on 12 January mocked the O'Connor and O'Faoláin 'scratch-my-back-and-I'll-scratch-yours brigade'. Further readers' letters appeared during the following days (14, 16, 18 January). The argument also moved to the *Irish Times* with many readers expressing their opinions on the squabble.[73] Of these letters, the most humorous exchange took place between O'Connor, O'Faoláin and Flann O'Brien. The unknown O'Brien satirized the other two writers' depiction of themselves as artistic superiors to the critics, and they replied to this 'personal abuse' by questioning the identity of O'Brien. O'Brien responded by writing in letters from 'Frank O'Connor', which O'Connor himself had to bring to the editor's attention on 16 January. The letters that followed were mostly readers' reactions of delight. Little was achieved by O'Connor in this episode, apart from sparking a very minor debate on the role of the critic versus the artist in Irish society; but importantly for O'Brien, who would soon become the *Irish Times* 'Myles na gCopaleen' columnist, it brought him to the attention of the *Irish Times*' editor. After this reaction to his play, O'Connor submitted one more play, *The statue's daughter*, to the Abbey board in 1940 for their consideration but it was bizarrely rejected on the grounds that it would offend Terence MacSwiney's family[74] (the play concerns a small-town committee that want to erect a statue in memory of a local War of Independence hero. A rumour spreads that he had a daughter born outside wedlock and the townspeople are throw into turmoil). The Abbey's rejection of the play was simply symptomatic of O'Connor's relationship with the theatre's directors at this stage.

Parnell split as a civil war (*Moses' rock*, 80).   **72** *Irish Independent* (10 Jan. 1939).   **73** See *Irish Times* (11, 13, 14, 16, 18, 19, 21, 30 Jan., 1 Feb.).   **74** Matthews, *Voices*, 412, fn. 12.

O'CONNOR'S DEPARTURE FROM THE ABBEY

Throughout the 1930s the boardroom was continually entangled in a fractious state of dealing with ongoing resignations, hirings and firings. However, during this period the Abbey began to have new plays to produce and money in the bank. Shortly before the opening of O'Connor's *In the train* in 1937, Yeats told O'Connor that, while he had opposed many of his decisions, he knew they were necessary and offered him the position of managing director which O'Connor accepted (F.R. Higgins' departure for America with the Abbey tour had made this offer possible). The following two years would find O'Connor embroiled in numerous disputes with the other directors over issues such as the style of acting that the Abbey should represent, Hunt's production and directing of Yeats' dramatic works, and the Abbey Festival in 1938. Alongside all of these disputes was an ongoing power battle within the greenroom. By 2 May 1939, O'Connor had resigned, pushed out by the rest of the directors. It was not the first time he had offered his resignation but this time it was unanimously accepted. His relationship with the Abbey board had deteriorated to the point where he had fallen out with every other member and his relationship with the Abbey ended on a bitter note. O'Connor had started to gradually withdraw from the boardroom meetings and intrigues since 1938 as his health was quite poor and he wanted more writing time. However, the dominant factor in his decision to resign was his complete frustration and annoyance with the other board members. Robinson and O'Connor had never succeeded in patching up their differences and unbeknownst to O'Connor, his position with the other board members had always been precarious. Their disgruntlement stemmed from O'Connor having such a free hand in the theatre. O'Connor's desire for a more critical and open approach to contemporary social and political issues was in direct conflict with the rest of the board members more prudent response and predisposition to comply with the nation's increasing conservatism. His ongoing love affair had also increased the board's animosity towards him. Yeats returning the position of managing director to Higgins when he returned from America also irretrievably weakened O'Connor's position of influence (Yeats' close friendship with Higgins and O'Connor's gradual withdrawal from board meetings might have been behind this decision). The board simply tolerated him up to the time of Yeats' death. Yeats' death on 28 January 1939 was a time of deep grief for O'Connor as, despite his quarrels with Yeats over Abbey policies, he had had the greatest of literary respect for Yeats and had looked upon him as a father figure. It also meant that O'Connor no longer had the support of a formidable ally on the board. It set the stage for their imminent removal of O'Connor from the board, by removing his responsibilities, gradually declining to invite him to important theatre social functions, and setting in motion a change in the Articles of Association which would empower them to dismiss a director.

When the only responsibility left to O'Connor was removed (editing the *Arrow's* commemorative issue to Yeats), he knew it was time to go and he sent in his letter of resignation on 2 May 1939. His numerous letters to Seán O'Faoláin and Denis Johnston in the subsequent months reveal O'Connor's hurt and anger over his departure from the Abbey. What did ensue was a brief battle by O'Connor over such issues as Abbey shares, access to Company Articles, a threat of legal proceedings and indirect accusations of embezzlement at some of the other directors. O'Connor engaged Denis Johnston in a detailed account of this fight in his letters, who dissuaded him from proceeding with the legal battle.[75] He left the Abbey with a sense of loss and failure, he had not achieved his dream for Ireland's national theatre and none of his theatrical theories had been realized. O'Connor might have resigned from the board on a bitter and angry note but he did not harbour a revengeful attitude for long. Less than two years later, he would walk out in protest at the unflattering caricature of Robinson in Louis D'Alton's play, *The money doesn't matter* (10 March 1941). When F.R. Higgins died on 8 January of that year, O'Connor was genuinely upset when he heard the news: 'Higgins [*sic*] death came as a bit of a shock after the news of Joyce's death: he was an enemy but an enemy whose steps I knew so well that he might as well have been a friend, and it's a little bit of oneself that died'.[76] On a more positive note, his departure from the Abbey ignited his desire to develop an alternative Irish dramatic society. While this did not come into being, his letters and meeting with Seán O'Faoláin and Denis Johnston on the matter helped spark the resurrection of the Dublin Drama League in the Gate Theatre (O'Connor's last play, *The statue's daughter*, was the opening play on 8 December 1941). The letters and meeting also culminated in the growth of an idea for the beginning of a new periodical to challenge social and political notions of Ireland; this would became known as the relatively remarkable literary periodical, *The Bell.*

---

75 O'Connor, Letters to Denis Johnston, Trinity College, Dublin, MSS 10066/287/2285–90.
76 O'Connor, Letter to Evelyn Bowen (16 Jan. 1941), HODSC. In a tribute to him, O'Connor gave a reading from a selection of Higgins' poetry on BBC Radio on 1 March.

Memories

HARRIET O'DONOVAN SHEEHY

To begin I'd like to clarify something which may seem strange. This book is a compilation of essays about an Irish writer named Frank O'Connor. I am going to write about my life with a man to whom I was married for thirteen years, whose name was Michael O'Donovan. I've never been able to call him Frank. For me Frank was the writer, but I was married to Michael. I also want to apologize for the fact that there is a lot about me in this discourse. I've never found a way to write about him except as my husband – as he affected my life and as I saw him. So you may learn too much about Harriet and not enough about Michael.

HOW WE MET

In 1952 I was twenty-nine. I was working in Baltimore, Maryland, and, as a mature student, taking courses at Johns Hopkins University. I was sort of engaged to be married; sort of because I wasn't sure Alan was the man I wanted to spend the rest of my life with, though he was very handsome, a decorated World War II bomber pilot, and highly intelligent. However, he was also super-serious and guilt-ridden about the bombs he had dropped on German cities. Because of this he had converted to Catholicism and as an Anglican I sometimes found his scrupulosity difficult to deal with. He was getting tired of my shilly-shallying so we agreed to spend the summer apart in the hope that this would result in a definite decision – marriage or good-bye. I decided to take some courses at Harvard Summer School and to stay with a friend who had an apartment in Boston. In my usual fashion I was dithering between courses on Henry James and Southern writers. I was also vaguely interested in something called Anglo-Irish literature, which was being taught by a writer of whom I had never heard … Frank O'Connor. However, before school began, I picked up a copy of *Mademoiselle* magazine which contained a story by Frank O'Connor. 'The saint' is not a particularly well-known story.[1] It's the account of a small boy's disillusionment with the lack of power (as he

---

1 Frank O'Connor, 'The Saint', *A set of variations* (New York, 1969).

sees it) of the Virgin Mary. I found it delightful, but also surprising. It was making gentle fun of overzealous piety. Was this an attitude I could take? Maybe if I took this course I'd have a better idea abut whether or not to marry Alan. In retrospect, this seems the oddest possible reason for taking one academic course rather than another. I'll never know whether it was luck or destiny, but it was certainly the best decision I ever made. Anglo-Irish literature it was.

I'll always remember the first time I saw Michael. He was not a particularly handsome man, but there was something about his presence which caught and held your attention. Summer in Boston is very hot, and someone had warned him that his usual Irish tweeds would be distinctly uncomfortable. So he had on a seer-sucker suit, but it was set off by a thick (almost hairy) tweed tie. He had two pairs of glasses which he was forever either losing or changing, often incorrectly, and his voice is simply impossible to describe. In its cadences and timbre it was unlike any voice I have ever heard, then or since. He started the class by giving a brief history of Ireland (which was all news to me) and then began to talk about ancient stories called the Sagas. There were forty or so students in the class and, from word one, we were putty in his hands. Michael was a superb natural teacher. We loved the class and were touched rather than censorious about the fact that his seersucker suit got more and more rumpled and limp (nobody had told him you had to have two so you could get one cleaned). Halfway through the course there was a mini-exam. Only the students who were taking the course for credit had to sit the exam and, since many of them were only auditing it, the classroom was half empty. My usual seat was several rows back but directly in front of O'Connor's desk. That day there was nobody in front of me. The questions were complicated and there was one in particular which puzzled me. I remember frowning and then, as I was wont to do, starting to scratch my head with my pencil. Suddenly I felt compelled to look up and there was Mr O'Connor staring straight at me with a very amused expression on his face. Naturally, I blushed, dropped the pencil and quickly bent my head over my exam book. He told me later that when he saw me scratching my head with a pencil he thought 'I'd like to know that one', but the chances were against our even having a chat. In fact, I had already made a fool of myself by saying, not knowing he was within earshot, 'I don't care what Mr O'Connor says, I think Deirdre [of the Sorrows] was a bitch.' Actually I was in awe of him, and shy about joining the graduate students who often followed him to a café for coffee after class. However, a few weeks later, some of the class decided to have a party for him and, since I had a car, they asked me to fetch him. I was nervous but couldn't resist the opportunity of being alone with him. At least if I made a fool of myself again he'd be the only person to know, and I had a hunch that he would be kind. I was right. He was astonishingly easy to talk to and I found myself relaxed and confident, so I was thrilled when he said: 'Don't give anyone a lift home. Let's go have a cup of coffee after the party, and you can tell me about yourself.' Who can resist being found potentially interesting? We went to Hazens, a casual student café, and I've no idea what we talked about (aside from my future) but we got there at 10 and when I remembered to look at my watch it was midnight. I took him back to his rooms and drove home in a daze. I was hooked. I felt, sentimental as it may sound, as though I had finally met the one person I had been looking for all my life.

Soon after that evening I asked why his wife wasn't with him and he told me that they were in the process of getting a divorce. I was relieved because by then I knew that, improbable as it seemed, I wanted to spend the rest of my life with him. His divorce was not final until early in 1953 and by that time I had already suggested that he might like to marry me. In truth I didn't believe it would ever happen (Michael returned home in '52 and '53 after the summer schools finished), and had resigned myself to occasional letters. Those duly appeared, but the one that changed my life came in mid-October 1953. The envelope was so light I was afraid to open it. But when I did I found what may be the briefest proposal on record. Three lines: 'H. I finally feel free to ask you to marry me. I can't promise an easy future, but if you are willing to take a chance with me, I will be very happy. Love M.' We were married on 5 December 1953 in a registry office in England. There were five of us there: Michael's son Myles, Bill Naughton[2] and his wife Erna, and Michael and myself. It was not exactly what my parents had had in mind for their only child; but, bless them, when I said this was the first man I had ever been sure I wanted to marry, they sent me off, alone, with their blessings. They didn't even get to meet my husband until they visited us in the spring.

At that time Michael was living in a small, draughty but beautiful Elizabethan house in a tiny village called Nash. I had no idea what living with a writer, his teen-aged son, in a freezing house, when meat, sugar and butter were still rationed, would be like. I quickly realized that my glamorous dresses were useless, and spent most of the time in a pair of flannel pajamas, covered by trousers and a heavy

---

2 Author of *Alfie* and long-time friend of Michael's.

sweater. I also learned that, although he didn't go 'out' to work, my husband had a very strict working routine. When he was in his study and the door was shut, he was working and was not to be disturbed until 11 o'clock, when I took a cup of coffee to him. I could always tell if the work was going well, because he would be in what he called his 'poor Chekhov' mood, delighted and in no humor to chat about what her is writing. But if it was going badly he would ask me to stay and talk with him and sometimes even read the sticky bit. His favorite description of writer's block was what Æ had said to him: ' Oh, I know Michael, you feel like the poor old hen who says: 'Oh God God God, no more eggs'. There was so much to learn, so much to be amused by and appreciative of, living with Michael O'Donovan and Frank O'Connor. One such example is that both the man and the writer were fanatical collectors of pens and soft pencils and if they borrowed one, never gave it back. Once, in imitation, I borrowed one of his and he immediately wrote a poem against me. I've never forgotten it: 'Hallie Rich stole a pen. Never gave it back again. Punish her, O Lord, Amen.' Life was austere, we were often cold, sometimes hungry (due to rationing) but supremely happy.

HARD TIMES IN IRELAND

A friend recently remarked that if Michael and I had been married in the 70s or 80s I would have been described as a 'trophy wife' (a young one, marrying the professor). However, whatever else I was, I was certainly no trophy. I doubt anyone was ever less prepared for what it was going to be like to be married to a divorced Irish writer, particularly one who had a history of fighting the government, the Catholic church, the Censorship board, the directors of the Abbey Theatre, the board of Works, to name a few. Like many men of his generation he had fought on the 'wrong side' in the Civil War, been interned in Gormanstown, and excommunicated by the church. His books were banned and at one point he had had to write for the *Sunday Independent* under the pretend name of Ben Mayo. However, now that he had a certain amount of financial security from what is known as a 'first reading agreement' with the *New Yorker*, he was not about to retire from the fray or to assume that people would be delighted to meet his new wife. After all, at this time the Catholic church was enormously influential and quite a few people felt that Michael had done something unforgivable by getting divorced and remarrying. Bearing that in mind, if there is one word to describe our life in Dublin when we spent our first year there in 1958, I think it would be 'edgy'.

We lived near Baggot Street in one of the 'Mespil Flats', which was considered very modern in those days. There were two sources of heat, an open fire and a storage heater which was hot at night but got colder and colder as the day wore on. Michael and our five-month-old baby Hallie Óg were fine with the living arrangements, but I found it hard to adjust. However, Michael also seemed to be on edge, wary. I noticed immediately that some people crossed the street when they saw him coming. Michael's old friends, Nancy McCarthy, Dermot Foley and the Montgomerys among others, were wonderful and did their best to explain how things worked and to cheer me up. But I was puzzled by so much. Little things, like why there were no plugs on the electric appliances I bought, or why there was no diaper service (having exhausted the Yellow Pages I called the American Embassy to ask how to find it. The consul laughed and said that, as his wife had discovered, it didn't exist). Also, why there was no black pepper, why the shops closed for a week around Christmas, why nobody warned me that you had to cook spiced beef. Of course these were minor annoyances and usually Michael and I could laugh about them. But there were more serious problems. That winter there was an important Arts Council literary meeting to which our friend, Pierre Emmanuel (French poet whom Michael had met at Harvard), had been invited as speaker. He came to stay near us and when he discovered that Michael hadn't even been invited as a guest, he was astonished. His wife took me aside and said: 'Harriet, this is no good. You cannot live in this place. You say to Michael: enough, now we go home [she meant to the US] where people know that Frank O'Connor is an important writer.' When I told Michael this he said: 'I know that it is hard for you, but I am damned if I am going to let them drive me out of my own country. If you can stand it, we are staying, at least until next summer.'

So stay we did. Looking back I realize that I often inadvertently made things harder for Michael. I was incredibly insensitive to the Irish situation. I remember saying something like: 'I am sick of you people complaining about the puritanism of the Church. Why don't we do something about it?', or 'I just can't understand why Ireland was neutral during World War Two. It was perfectly clear that England was in trouble and needed to use the Irish ports.'

When my mother and father came to visit us that year we took them to see some of Michael's favourite places – Clonmacnoise, Cashel and Kilkenny. They were highly amused by a scene which took place at lunch in Kilkenny. It was Friday and when we asked for the menu the waitress said: 'Ah, there is lovely fish today'. The three of us loved fish so we said fine, but Michael hated it and said: 'Isn't there anything else?' Then looking around the dining room he saw a man eating ham. 'What about ham?' he asked. 'Ah no sir, you wouldn't want that. It is Friday and that gentleman is a Protestant.' Michael was not as amused as we were and muttered under his breath about being sick of having people mind his business for him.

But that is how things were. People were ready, even happy, to judge your behaviour and to correct it. In a way you were part of everyone's family. This had its advantages as well as its disadvantages, something I learned when my Dad sent me baby food from the US. Tired of the limited selection here I'd asked for a case and specified half of it should be beef and vegetables. Imagine my surprise when I got a notice from the department of Agriculture saying I had to have a licence to import meat. I asked Michael why but he didn't know, he guessed it was to protect the cattle from contamination when I threw the empty jars out. This drove me into a frenzy. I was going to feed my precious daughter something which would kill a cow? I grabbed up pen and paper to write a scathing letter to the minister for Agriculture. Michael wisely decided this was a good moment to go meet David Greene[3] at Davy Byrne's pub to work on the translation of an Irish poem which was giving them trouble. When he came back, there was a smug smile on his face. 'I've solved the problem of the baby food', he said. 'David has a friend in the department of Agriculture, who said he would give you a licence if you promised to say nothing about it to anybody.' I was outraged. I started on a diatribe about honesty and principles and the evils of influence and God knows what other abstract matters. He shrugged and then said, very gently, something I've never forgotten. 'Well, my love, you have to decide what you really want. Is it your grievance, or is it the baby food?' I hardly need to tell you that the baby food arrived two days later, and I had learned a very important lesson about how things worked in Ireland.

We stayed in Ireland until the spring of 1959 and by then everything was improving. RTÉ accepted Michael's suggestion that he write radio plays based on several of his stories; in February they broadcasted *Fighting men*, which he wrote and produced. We became friends with the writer Mary Lavin (who lived nearby) and she and Dan Binchy (the great Celtic scholar) used to come for tea. Michael was working on his autobiography and the first chapter had appeared in the *New Yorker* in December. But his American editors and his literary agent were anxious for him to come back to the US where they could more easily discuss offers and

3 Professor of Irish, Trinity College Dublin. Co-edited with Michael *A golden treasure of Irish poetry, A.D. 600–1200* (London, 1967).

promote his work, so in September we returned to New York and rented an apartment in Brooklyn Heights. Needless to say, I was delighted.

We had a wonderful apartment with big windows looking out across New York Harbour at Wall Street, and a tiny balcony with a view of the Statue of Liberty. We lived there until January 1961 when we went to California, where Michael taught a writing as well as a literature course at Stanford University. The three of us (our daughter, Hallie Óg, was now two and a half) loved being in California, but Michael's writing class was tough. It was challenging and took up a lot of his time and energy (among his students were some who already had published work to their credit, including Ken Kesey and Larry McMurtry).[4] He was really working too hard and towards the end of term had a minor stroke. We went back to New York somewhat chastened and before long I began to hear that plaintive note in Michael's voice which meant he was missing Ireland. In *My father's son* he wrote:

> when I applied for a job as municipal librarian in Dublin, I still had the notion that I should do it only as a temporary expedient until a similar job turned up in Cork. Nothing could cure me of the notion that Cork needed me and that I needed Cork. Nothing but death can, I fear, ever cure me of it.[5]

Cork always featured very strongly in Michael's creative imagination. However, once, when I was fed up with Dublin, I suggested we might go live in Cork. His reply was to cast his eyes up to heaven and say: 'Are you totally mad, woman?' Despite his aversion to actually living in Cork, nothing ever did cure him of the notion that he needed Ireland and Ireland needed him and so, in September 1961, we moved back to Dublin where we lived until he died in 1966. Forty years after Michael's death, I am still living in Ireland.

RECOGNITION

I think perhaps the words to describe this section should be 'bemused contentment'. A reporter once asked Michael what prizes he had won and he laughed and said not any, but then stopped and remarked, 'I did win a prize for an essay on

---

4 Kesey is the author of *One flew over the cuckoo's nest*, Larry McMurtry wrote *Terms of endearment* and *Lonesome dove*.   5 O'Connor, *My father's son* (London, 1968), 58.

Turgenev which I wrote in Gormanstown [a prison camp during the Irish Civil War], but it was money and the sponsors of the competition went bust ... so I never got the seven pounds I'd won.' It seems strange now, to think that he had never been asked to lecture at an Irish university or received any sort of formal recognition in Ireland. But this changed radically in 1962. He was awarded an honorary doctorate degree, a D.Litt by Trinity College in July of that year. He hardly knew what to make of it. A man who had never seen the inside of a college as a student, he was in awe of the rituals and ceremonies inherent in academia. Honor Tracy wonderfully captures his feeling on the day:

> The association with Trinity meant a great deal to him. I well remember the scene when he got his doctorate *honoris causa* there. Apparelled in hired formal dress and academic robes ... he looked strangely unlike his bohemian self. As he went by he gave me a broad wink and a sardonic grin, which didn't fool me for a moment. This was one of the good days of his life.[6]

I am amazed when I reflect on all he accomplished in the years between 1962 and his death in March 1966. A letter from his literary agent reads: 'wonderful news that you have finished the book on the short story [*The lonely voice*] and are at work again on stories and the second volume of the autobiography'.[7] She was accurate, but this was not all he was doing. At the same time he was writing reviews and essays for the *Irish Times*, the *Sunday Independent*, and the *New York Times*. It was in October 1963 that he also began to give a series of weekly lectures, plus a writing class, at Trinity College.[8] But the truth is that once again he was working too hard and too steadily and it began to take a toll on his never-robust health. In March of 1963 he was diagnosed with ulcers and told to stop smoking and to stop drinking so much coffee, advice to which he paid scant attention despite my perpetual nagging. Then in April he had a severe gallbladder attack which was followed by a sort of perpetual malaise, culminating in an operation in February 1965. But in spite of this ill-health, he was happy. Happy to be back in Ireland, happy to be living in a flat overlooking a little park and only steps from the Grand Canal, happy to take our daughter for walks to town, to listen to her

6 Honor Tracy, 'King of the castle' in Maurice Sheehy (ed.), *Michael/Frank: studies on Frank O'Connor* (Dublin, 1969), 4.   **7** Letter to Frank O'Connor (Sept. 1962), Harriet O'Donovan Sheehy's private collection of O'Connor papers.   **8** The lectures were published posthumously as *The backward look: a survey of Irish literature* (London, 1967).

chatter and then report it back to me. He loved discussing, and even arguing with
Dan Binchy or David Greene about the meaning of some phrase in an old Irish
poem, or talking about poetry with Brendan Kennelly or discussing stories with
Mary Lavin. Our lives were very full.

Each year we spent at least ten days in France, usually in an area where we
could visit romanesque churches. Michael had an abiding interest in and knowledge about architecture. He wrote many articles for the *Sunday Independent*
bemoaning the neglect of early Irish ecclesiastical monuments, and could spend
hours in happy contemplation of a carved tympanum or the layout of a Cistercian
abbey. My job on these trips was to remember to bring the guide books and to
drive the car. Michael had tried driving when he was the head librarian in Cork's
public library, but having run the library van into a ditch while he was wrestling
with the shape of a story, he decided that his talents lay elsewhere. As well as architecture, the other attractions of France for Michael were eating French food and
seeing Donal Brennan. Donal was in charge of the Paris office of Aer Lingus and
Michael and I always made a point of having at least one meal with him. Donal
and Michael knew each other well and I have always been amused by something
Donal wrote after Michael died, something that is also an accurate insight:

> He was pleased, too, that the Commissaire of Police at Le Bourget Airport
> had read his stories and his harmless vanity was obviously flattered when
> the Comissairre called him 'Maître' and personally escorted him and his
> wife through the state controls at the airport.[9]

This was true. Michael wrote of his mother's 'innocent vanity' which resulted in
her tearing her photograph out of her passport because, as she said, 'it made me
look like a poisoner'. Michael had that same vanity, always about small things. I
gave him a silver Indian bolo which he wore constantly. A lady once stopped him
on the street and asked him if it was a very special holy medal. I fear he answered in
the affirmative. He was vain about clothes, being particularly fond of his hand-
tailored peacock blue Avoca tweed jacket. But he wasn't vain about his reputation
as a writer, or as teacher and, in fact, was much more likely to worry about his lack
of talent or his non-academic attitude to teaching.

Michael burned himself out and died too young, but I feel that he died
content. Content that, at last, his fellow countrymen understood, if only partially,

---

9 Donal Brennan, 'Reminiscences from France', *Michael/Frank*, 119.

why he had been such a fighter, and understood that it was love for Ireland which made him critical of the mediocre and shoddy. He always said that he wrote for the lonely person down the country who read a story and said to himself: 'Yes, he understands, he knows what it is like', or who read an article in the *Independent* and thought: 'Yes, that is what I want, we can be or do better'. I think he finally was able to say to himself, 'Well, after all, my life's work has made a tiny difference … what I've been able to do has mattered.'

I'd like to give him the last word. This is what he wrote in *An only child* when, as a young man, he had given a speech, which as he said was all 'vague words and vaguer impressions that with me passed for thought'. But, he discovered for himself:

> All that did matter was the act of faith, the hope that somehow, somewhere I would be able to prove that I was neither mad nor a good-for-nothing; because now I realized that whatever it might cost me, there was no turning back. When as kids we came to an orchard wall that seemed too high to climb, we took off our caps and tossed them over the wall, and then we had no choice but to follow them.
>
> I had tossed my cap over the wall of life, and I knew I must follow it, wherever it had fallen.[10]

10 Frank O'Connor, *An only child* (New York, 1961; repr. Belfast, 1993), 180.

A landscape of betrayal: Denis Johnston's *Guests of the nation* (1935)

EMILIE PINE

In the first decades of independence Ireland went 'cinema-mad'.[1] In the 1930s, the leading film genre was the domestic comedy, with American and British films dominating the box-office. Cinema was enormously popular throughout the country with thirty-six cinemas in the greater Dublin area, nineteen in Cork, Limerick and Waterford, and one hundred and ninety, comprising over one hundred thousand seats, in the Irish Free State altogether.[2] J.T. Beere, in an analysis of cinema-going in this decade, estimated that between 1934 and 1935 there were approximately eleven million admissions to Irish cinemas. However, as Liam O'Leary – film critic for *Ireland Today* and the *Irish Press* – frequently lamented, cinema output was relatively homogenous and low in quality with many international and foreign language films never receiving releases in Ireland. Positive developments included the formation of the Irish Film Society in 1936. This struggled against high import duties on 35mm film but nevertheless filled a space in the market for more intellectual foreign films as well as supporting indigenous film, for example, reviving Denis Johnston's film of *Guests of the nation* (1935) in 1938.

Inspired by the developments in film style and technology and aided by a period of political stability, the 1930s saw the growth of an indigenous Irish film industry. These films explored issues ranging from urban development to life on the Blasket Islands, and two films also dramatized events from the War of Independence. *The dawn* (1936), made by Tom Cooper, a Kerry garage-owner and ex-Volunteer, is Ireland's first native sound-film and represents the War of Independence as a glorious moment in Irish history that should be remembered for the strong bonds that it forged within Irish communities. In contrast, Denis Johnston's film adaptation of Frank O'Connor's short story 'Guests of the nation' is a critique of the origins of the Irish nation and an exploration of the betrayals caused by the war. While Johnston's *Guests of the nation* has received passing crit-

1 Lord Longford, quoted by Seán Ó Meadhra, *Ireland Today* (Mar. 1937), 70–1.   2 T.J. Beere, 'Cinema statistics in Saorstát Eireann', *Journal of the Statistical and Social Society of Ireland*, xv (1935–6), 83–110 at 85.

ical attention, it has tended to be dismissed on the basis of its technical flaws. Ruth Barton comments that it is the 'sole film of the period to question the prevailing orthodoxies of heroic nationalism' but that it is 'certainly the most amateurish of the independence films'.[3] Yet, *Guests of the nation* deserves to be revisited and recognized for its illuminating contribution to our understanding of O'Connor's story. In addition, as the only film that Johnston made, while 'amateurish' it is also significant for its construction of landscape throughout the film and the role that landscape plays in connection to constructions of the Irish past.

Denis Johnston, the son of a High Court judge and a barrister himself, is most often associated with drama or television.[4] In 1928 he submitted his first play, *Shadowdance*, to the Abbey Theatre, only to have it rejected. Johnston re-titled the play *The old lady says no!* as an ironic comment on his impression that it was Lady Gregory who objected to the play.[5] Despite this initial rejection, the play was accepted by the Gate Theatre and it was staged to great success and critical acclaim in 1929. Two years later Johnston's second submission to the Abbey met with approval. Yet *The moon in the yellow river* (1931), though more in line with the Abbey's realistic, domestic style, combines this with violence and cynicism and this led to public controversy over its first performance run.[6] *The moon in the yellow river* is a disillusioned look back at the War of Independence and its aftermath. As *Guests of the nation* a few years later would show, Johnston's vision of the fight for independence is coloured by his disillusionment at the perceived intellectual failure of the Free State and its inability to foster intellectual talent or individualist values.

'Guests of the nation' is the title story of Frank O'Connor's first collection of short stories.[7] O'Connor and Johnston would later work together at the Abbey Theatre – O'Connor was a member of the board of directors from 1935 to 1939 and Johnston one of its leading playwrights. Indeed, Johnston paid tribute to the 'impact' that O'Connor had had on his life.[8] It is clear that O'Connor and

---

3 Ruth Barton, *Irish national cinema* (London, 2004), 46.   **4** Johnston wrote for both the Abbey Theatre and the Gate Theatre, reported for the BBC during the Second World War and became director of programmes for the new television service.   **5** For a discussion of the play –and its title – see Nicholas Grene, *The politics of Irish drama* (Cambridge, 1999), 150–7.   **6** The *Irish Times* review reports that 'prolonged hissing ... mingled in the dominant applause when the curtain fell. Looking at the Ireland of the days subsequent to 1922, [Johnston] has found little cause for satisfaction.' *Irish Times* (28 April 1931), 4. Joseph Holloway records that Johnston 'should not be let write such lying things about Ireland and Catholicism', in Robert Hogan and Michael J. O'Neil (eds), *Joseph Holloway's Irish theatre*, 1 (Dixon, CA, 1968–70), 76.   **7** Frank O'Connor, *Guests of the nation* (London, 1931).   **8** Johnston writes that 'I would very much like to praise people like Frank

Johnston share a similar outlook from their criticism of what they perceived as authoritarianism in the Free State.[9] O'Connor had been involved in the War of Independence, though he never saw active duty and was only seventeen when the truce was announced in June 1921. From his time in prison camp, O'Connor's attitude to nationalism changed and he became disillusioned about the effect of war on the ordinary man. In his autobiographical work *An only child* O'Connor writes of his time during the Civil War in the Gormanstown prison camp and the attitude to the martyrdom of victims during the War of Independence, 'I was sick to death of the worship of martyrdom, that the only martyr I had come close to ... hadn't wanted to die any more than I did; that he had merely been trapped by his own ignorance and simplicity into a position from which he could not escape.'[10] In this episode, O'Connor's cynicism concerning Free Staters is keenly felt – despite his attack on the republican prisoners for their 'worship of martyrdom', O'Connor also lays the blame for the death at the hands of those now in power: 'It's as well for you fellows that you didn't see that lad's face when the Free Staters had finished with it.'[11] For many, the Free State proved to be a disappointment; as Nicholas Grene writes, 'the long promised Utopia of national liberation provoked comparison with the reality achieved in an actual Free State with all its limitations'.[12] In addition to disenchantment with the war and the travesty that was made of the deaths of the young and innocent, in the '30s O'Connor was also concerned with the stultification of Irish culture in the wake of Irish independence. This disappointment was acutely felt by artists in the Free State and both O'Connor and Johnston were opposed to the increasingly censorial and isolated climate of the Free State in the '30s.[13]

O'Connor's story deals uncompromisingly with the harsh reality of being an IRA volunteer during the war. Two IRA men, Bonaparte and Noble, are assigned

O'Connor ... because of their impact on [me] ... at different periods of my life', in Rory Johnston (ed.), *Orders and desecrations: the life of the playwright Denis Johnston* (Dublin, 1992), 176.   **9** Johnston also deals with this issue in *The moon in the yellow river* in which one character argues that 'the birth of a nation is no immaculate conception' and the play represents the killing of dissident republicans by the Free State army, *The moon in the yellow river* (London, 1931; repr. Gerrards Cross, 1983), 164. **10** O'Connor, *An only child and my father's son: an autobiography*, intro. Declan Kiberd (London, 2005), 177.   **11** O'Connor, *An only child*, 176–7.   **12** Grene, *The politics of Irish drama*, 267. **13** As Terence Brown argues, the atmosphere of moral vigilantism in Ireland from the late 1920s and into the 1930s was found by some to be 'odiously heavy-handed in a democracy beginning to feel and anxious to express a developing self-assurance', *Ireland: a social and cultural history, 1922–1985* (London, 1985), 141. Although Alvin Jackson argues that social and cultural policies in this period 'did not so much impose as reflect a shared value system', *Ireland 1798–1998: politics and war* (Oxford, 1999), 297.

to guard two British prisoners, Belcher and Hawkins. Bonaparte and Noble befriend the two Englishmen but, as a reprisal for British executions of Irish men, they are ordered to execute their prisoners. The story focuses on how the guards are distressed by the course of events and how, eventually, they must face their task. Bonaparte's closing words on the execution scene are a chilling reminder of the dehumanising effects of war: 'I was somehow very small and very lost and lonely like a child astray in the snow. And anything that happened to me afterwards, I never felt the same about again.'[14] Johnston takes O'Connor's story and amplifies it, so that we question not only the tactics of warfare but also the role of landscape as an image that symbolizes and justifies nationalism. The perspective of the film is thus, to an even greater extent than O'Connor's story, shaped by the disappointment felt at post-revolutionary Ireland in the twenties and thirties.

Johnston adapted O'Connor's story, with help on the script from Mary Manning, in the early months of 1933, and the film was made over the course of the summers of 1933 and 1934. The production was entirely amateur, using actors Johnston knew from the Gate and the Abbey theatres, as well as friends. Barry Fitzgerald, Denis O'Dea, Shelah Richards, Cyril Cusack and Hilton Edwards all make appearances, as does Frank O'Connor himself, playing a volunteer in one of the early scenes of the film. The film was shot in various outdoor locations around County Wicklow, such as the Scalp and Ticknock, while the cottage interior scenes were filmed on a set built in Johnston's parents' backgarden in Lansdowne Road in Dublin city. The scenes set in Kilmainham Gaol were filmed on location at the Gaol and in the Gate Theatre. It was this last location at which the premiere of the film was held in January 1935, playing to 'a packed auditorium of gate-crashers'.[15] The film was well received by the audience and reviewers, perhaps indicating a responsiveness to O'Connor and Johnston's revisionist attitude to the War of Independence. However, the film, unfortunately, was made on 16mm film and therefore not suitable for commercial distribution, limiting the film's initial audience.

The film's format was just one of the issues Johnston encountered. Amateur filmmaking is beset with problems and, as Johnston records, 'all of these difficulties we discovered for ourselves ... in those few months we must have lived through the history of the film industry'.[16] So, for example, the crew returned in 1934 to Ticknock, only to find that in the intervening months a 'new lane had been

14 O'Connor, *Guests*, 18. **15** Johnston records that the screening was intended only for cast and crew, *Orders and desecrations*, 94. **16** Ibid.

driven through a field' and a number of trees had been cut down. This necessitated 'some very tricky angles' to ensure a sense of continuity in the film.[17] Lighting proved to be another difficulty. The set for the cottage interior was roofless so that the crew could film without artificial lighting, resulting in strange shadows on the walls of the cottage caused by the changes in the sunlight. A more dramatic problem occurred in the shortage of film stock, thereby making it impossible to have long tracking shots and forcing the crew to come up with a creative solution. The outcome is one fast-paced editing sequence, which cuts between the country cottage and Bonaparte cycling to Dublin. The rapid editing suits the mood of the film at this point and what may have begun as a problem for the filmmakers has resulted in an assured feature of the finished film. Whether this is just a happy accident or not is debatable. Irish directors, despite the limited types of films that found distribution in Ireland, were very aware of film style and Johnston (and his cameramen Harold Douglas and John Manning) were aware of the style of Russian filmmaker Sergei Eisenstein, one of the pioneers of the montage style and director of *Battleship Potemkin* (1925).[18] The rapid editing of this sequence may thus be equally due to Eisenstein's influence as it was due to shortage of film stock.

Though Johnston writes off much of the making of the film as one great 'adventure', on closer investigation there is more design to it than claimed by the director. Johnston describes the adaptation of O'Connor's story in a casual manner, claiming that 'having no producers to tell us how to spoil it, we stuck to the storyline faithfully.'[19] Yet the film is not a straightforward adaptation; the setting is moved from Cork to Dublin for practical reasons, many scenes are added and the execution scene, the climax of the story, is changed in the film. Moreover, in unpublished notes for a lecture on the making of the film, Johnston states the importance of planning each shot and using editing as a technique to generate meaning. He makes particular note of the way that editing controls interpretation and that this is always noticed by the viewer, at least subconsciously.[20] Johnston's specific reference to editing techniques alerts us to the important role it plays in *Guests of the nation*; it also directs one to examine more closely the deliberate meanings generated by these techniques, as this essay will discuss, particularly in the instances where the film diverges from the story.

---

17 Ibid.   **18** Johnston records that the 'camera positions showed much of the influence of Flaherty and Eisenstein', *Orders and desecrations*, 94. Robert Flaherty directed the 1934 film *Man of Aran* and was a friend of Johnston's and the inspiration for his play *Storm song* (1934).   **19** Johnston, *Orders and desecrations*, 93.   **20** Denis Johnston collection, Trinity College Dublin, MS 10066/26.

LANDSCAPE AND NATURE

Guests of the nation is characterized by an overarching emphasis on natural imagery and landscape. The IRA are shown comfortably navigating the hills and country-side, whereas the Black and Tans are depicted as dependent on the road. Johnston adds a prologue to the story at the beginning of the film as he depicts the IRA flying column holding up an RIC barracks and taking the two soldiers, Belcher and Hawkins, prisoner. This prologue is key to the film's emphasis on Bonaparte and Noble as part of an organized resistance, whereas O'Connor's story concentrates on the intimacy of Bonaparte's relationship with the prisoners and his counterpart, Noble. In response to the film's IRA raid, the Black and Tans, alerted to the presence of the column, attempt to capture them but the noise from the army trucks warns the IRA of their presence. The IRA scatter to the hills and, from their safety, attack the trucks. The two IRA men who remain on the road to fire on the trucks are the only ones captured and the road is thus coded as British territory, while the IRA are linked with the wilderness of the hills as their natural habitat. The road is a symbol of modernity; it is thus the terrain of the British armoured trucks. In contrast the wild landscape symbolizes the anti- or pre-modernity of Ireland, and a different kind of freedom, which exists beyond the colonial zones of the city and the road and which is impenetrable to the British. Remaining on the road when the Black and Tan trucks are advancing is thus lethal to the two IRA men who 'belong' to the wild landscape. Though these scenes are absent in 'Guests of the nation', Johnston may have been influenced by O'Connor's short story 'September dawn' (1931) in which a small band of local Irish Irregulars use their knowledge of the hedges and ditches of the countryside to make their escape from the soldiers pursuing them.

   Though the landscape is of great importance in 'Guests', and as will be shown especially in the execution scene, in this story O'Connor depicts the British prisoners as having the closest affinity to the landscape: 'you could have planted that pair down anywhere from this to Claregalway and they'd have taken root there like a native week. I never in my short experience saw two men take to the country as they did'.[21] The film is careful to maintain this closeness between the British prisoners and the land but in the opening scenes it is the IRA who are aligned with the wild landscape. It is crucial to understand that the film does not endorse a romanticized vision of the IRA in the portrayal of landscape. However, at the outset the

---

21 O'Connor, *Guests*, 5.

IRA, and by extension Irish nationalism, are allied with the wilderness as opposed to roads and modernity. This alliance is strengthened throughout the film, in particular when Bonaparte and Noble are summoned to meet their commandant. They are first shown sleeping under some trees on a grassy hill. The tolling of the church bell, calling the community to Mass, wakes Bonaparte and though he shakes Noble awake they both lie back onto the turf, until finally they give in to the bell and get up. The motifs of religion and nature are thus linked. After church a woman meets the two men and gives them a message to meet their commandant. This meeting takes place in the hills and, following the meeting when they are assigned to guard Belcher and Hawkins, Bonaparte and Noble go to retrieve their weapons. The weapons are hidden and the shot shows Bonaparte pulling the guns out of a hiding place in the ground. This literalizes the link between the volunteers and the landscape and lends to the nationalist fight a sense of an organic relationship with the actual land of Ireland and with nature. Though this scene is absent from 'Guests of the nation', Johnston may again have borrowed an image from 'September dawn', in which the men conceal their guns in a secret hiding place in the ground.

This organicism is extended to the relationship that the four men develop. The prisoners are being held in a cottage owned by an old woman, the archetypal vision of the Irish peasant.[22] Initially the four men are differentiated from one another by their appearance. The first shot of the prisoners pans up their bodies from their feet, exhibiting them, in uniform, as different or alien. This shot is from the perspective of Bonaparte and Noble and thus the controlling gaze belongs to the Irish characters. Yet, the film overturns this by using humour to break down the barriers between the four. The relationships are further naturalized by the next scene as Johnston alternates between shots of a tree in blossom against a clear sky and men in the distance ploughing. Later in the film we see images of sheep being sheared, cementing the naturalness of the men's friendship and seeing it in the context of eternal, seasonal rhythms. In these shots Johnston literalizes O'Connor's phrase in the original story that 'you could have planted that pair down anywhere from this to Claregalway and they'd have taken root there like a native weed'.[23]

In contrast to this vision of pastoral harmony, the IRA prisoners in

---

22 The old woman can be read as a symbol of 'Mother Ireland' or Cathleen Ní Houlihan. In the story she is also representative of the persistence of paganism: "'nothing but sorrow and want can follow people who disturb the hidden powers." A queer old girl, all right.', O'Connor, *Guests*, 8.
23 O'Connor, *Guests*, 5.

Kilmainham Gaol in Dublin are held under harsh circumstances. Using the location shooting in Kilmainham Gaol itself, Johnston shows one prisoner gazing out of a barred window in a bare cell. When he is taken to see his captors he is marched along the prison corridor to stand before a panel of judges. The judges sit at a long table, underlit so that their faces appear ghostly and they cast huge ominous shadows on the wall behind. This was one of the few scenes shot in the Gate Theatre which Johnston says 'turned out to be much the least successful part of the picture' due to the artificial lighting.[24] However, the lighting conveys very successfully a sense of foreboding and authoritarianism and this severity is underlined when the film cuts back to a contrasting outdoor shot of Bonaparte, Noble, Belcher and Hawkins in the countryside watching horses cantering.[25] Again, both in terms of locations and characters, Johnston chooses to widen the context of O'Connor's story to include a representation – though brief – of the Irish prisoners. The film also uses this to add to the suspense of the film as Bonaparte cycles to Dublin to try to stop the executions.

The four men enjoying their pastoral bliss are not alone, however, but are watched by an IRA leader who then informs the guards that they may have to carry out the reprisal executions. The IRA leader is depicted as slightly sinister, shot in close-up from a low-angle. He is not associated with the four men nor is he aligned with nature, recalling O'Connor's depiction of him in the original story as coldly watching the prisoners and causing Bonaparte to realize 'that he had no great love for the two Englishmen'.[26] Though the film cuts between shots of sheep being sheared and the four men enjoying the countryside, the IRA leader is set apart as an outsider. As the film then cuts back to the panel of judges in Kilmainham, Johnston suggests that both the IRA leader and the British judges are external forces affecting the natural group which Bonaparte, Noble, Hawkins and Belcher comprise.

In O'Connor's short story the climax of the narrative is the execution. Hawkins pleads for his life, to the point of offering to defect to the IRA, arguing that he would not let allegiance to country stand in the way of friendship and the morally right action. In contrast, Belcher stoically receives his fate. In the story the

---

24 Johnston, *Orders and desecrations*, 94.   **25** These shots are possibly influenced by German expressionism on film, which is characterized by stark black and white and atmospheric lighting. **26** O'Connor, *Guests*, 8. Though it is important to note that at the beginning of the story O'Donovan seems to treat the prisoners differently, especially Hawkins, 'as if he was one of our own' (5). The later apprehension is thus part of the series of realizations that Bonaparte comes to in the story, about himself and others.

landscape also plays a role in the situation as they must dig the graves 'by the far end of the bog'; to get there they must walk along 'the edge of it in the darkness', both descriptions emphasising the isolation of the location for the execution.[27] This isolation is key to Bonaparte when it is only: 'the picture of them [the Irish guards] so still and silent in the bogland [that] brought it home to me that we were in earnest, and banished the last bit of hope I had'.[28] Building on this sense of desolation, O'Connor depicts the executions in a detailed and matter of fact way, thereby pointing up the horror of the situation: 'I saw Hawkins stagger at the knees and lie out flat ... We all stood very still, watching him settle out in the last agony.'[29] Yet Hawkins is not quite dead and they have to shoot him again. Belcher, when it comes his turn, is reasonable and accepting of his fate, again pointing up the conflict between humanity and war: 'The big man went over like a sack of meal, and this time there was no need for a second shot.'[30]

The film, however, is silent and instead of striving to replicate the grim realism of the story, Johnston extends the role that landscape plays, acting as a substitute at the point of the executions for the human drama explored in the story. The actual executions are not explicitly depicted, though it remains quite clear that the prisoners have been shot. The final scenes of the film show the men trudging through the bogland, and one shot focuses on an image of four pairs of feet walking through the bog, leaving their impressions upon its muddy surface. The following shots show a man digging a grave in the bogland while the men walk towards it. Belcher ties on a blindfold and Hawkins realizes what is about to happen. He drops to his knees and pleads with Noble. At this point the film cuts to the old woman in her cottage, blowing out two candles and kneeling down to pray.[31] There are then shots of a man filling in a grave and Bonaparte and Noble silhouetted against the sky as they walk down the mountain. Then the film cuts to two pairs of feet walking through the same piece of muddy bogland that had been focussed on a few shots before. This shot is held for a few seconds – emphasizing the discrepancy between the two pairs of feet now walking across it and the

---

27 O'Connor, *Guests*, 11–12. **28** Ibid., 13. **29** Ibid., 15. **30** Ibid., 17. **31** There is, in the old woman's actions, a sense of personal spirituality and by editing the blowing out of the candles into the execution scene, Johnston implies that the old woman is uncannily and symbiotically connected to the two prisoners. This scene is in the story though it occurs after the guards return. The film also responds to O'Connor's depiction of the old woman as associated with paganism, and her close relationship with the two men (O'Connor, *Guests*, 17, 8, 12). The old woman's disapproval of the executions is evident both in the story and film. Furthermore, this scene stands in contrast to the film's only other image of spirituality, the early scene where the insistent church bell ensures that Noble and Bonaparte go to Mass.

previous impressions made by the four men. Rather than show the execution, Johnston uses the extinguishing of the candles and this image of landscape, which represents the greater indentation on the land of their graves, to depict the deaths of the two men. Whereas previously the land had been a symbol of regeneration and life in the film it is now an image of death.

INTERPRETATION

The absence of the actual shooting of Belcher and Hawkins has tended to influence how the film is read, with Kevin Rockett referring to it as a 'playing down of the execution scene'.[32] In one way then, the film lacks the rawness and shock that O'Connor creates so well in the story. Belcher and Hawkins merely disappear into the landscape, somehow organically swallowed up by the bogland.[33] The film thus focuses on nature and avoids confronting the rights and wrongs of warfare. Just as the landscape earlier provided shelter for the IRA, the bogland now safely houses their dead. Johnston thus ultimately avoids confronting the rights and wrongs of the War of Independence and chooses to focus on nature as a symbolic site of contestation.

Yet both the friendship between the men and the unsympathetic portrait of the IRA leader would seem to directly critique the consequences of war. Certainly, contemporary commentary of the time did not view the disappearance of the men into the landscape as either a playing down of the executions nor as a flaw. The reviewer for the *Irish Independent* argued that 'Mr Johnston has raised it to the heights of tragedy' and that the execution scenes 'lose nothing of their intensity because they are deliberately laconic',[34] while the reviewer for the *Irish Press* noted the key part that the bogland plays in 'the final tragedy'.[35] Indeed, Frank O'Connor, interviewed by the *Irish Press*, commented that the film 'tells the story better than literature could ever draw it'.[36] By seeing visual representation as more effective than textual narrative O'Connor himself suggests that the richness of the image of landscape may express more than words ever could.

Another interpretation of the bogland scenes may come closer to the true message of both O'Connor's story and Johnston's film. From the beginning of

---

32 Kevin Rockett, '1930s fictions' in Rockett, Luke Gibbons, and John Hill, *Cinema and Ireland* (London, 1988), 61. **33** As Cheryl Herr writes, 'the body in Irish discourse always seems on the verge of reabsorption into the landscape', cited in Geraldine Meaney, 'Landscapes of desire', *Women: a cultural review*, 9:3 (Autumn, 1998), 248. **34** *Irish Independent* (21 Jan. 1935). **35** 'A story of war days', *Irish Press* (21 Jan. 1935). **36** *Irish Press* (21 Jan. 1935).

Guests of the nation the IRA are indeed associated with the wilderness as their natural territory. When the flying column march away from the burning barracks at the beginning of the film, they march along the road, guns over shoulder with an air of triumph; yet it is their guerrilla tactic of fleeing back to the hill and, indeed, merging with the landscape which enables them to survive. The Black and Tans in contrast are tied to their trucks, the noise of which prevents them from carrying out a successful ambush of the flying column. As mentioned earlier, the IRA is thus strongly associated with the landscape, whereas the British (and the IRA leadership) are associated with the city and modern methods of war.

However, the attempt to remain on the road by the two IRA men reveals the recognition that to become a free and modern state (as opposed to remaining in the essentialized idea of nation) the IRA would have to appropriate the space of authority, the road, currently held by the British. While from a practical perspective the route taken by the flying column is probably the shortest one to their destination, at a figurative level, their march along the road, following their decimation of the RIC barracks, represents the desire to attain and to reoccupy the space then held by the British colonizer. This, by extension, parallels the adoption, rather than dismantlement, of British forms of government by the Irish Free State once the War of Independence had been won.[37]

In contrast to the IRA's attempt to leave the landscape and appropriate the road, stand the four men who enjoy a strong relationship with the land. Furthermore, it is not just land which the four men are associated with, but a particular vision of land. While the IRA are, in their transition from wilderness to road, still partly associated with the landscape, it is not farmland but the wilderness and the unproductive bogland that they are connected to. Conversely, Bonaparte, Noble, Hawkins and Belcher are part of a natural, seasonal order through their connection to a productive landscape as the images of sheep being sheered and men ploughing imply. The absorption of Belcher and Hawkins' bodies into the bogland may be organic, but their previous harmony with nature implies that their deaths are, in fact, against the natural order – an alternate yet still powerful image to O'Connor's depiction of the executions.

---

37 Joseph Lee discusses the 'British influence' over the establishment of the Free State, concluding that it is, at best, a fraught question. Is Ireland influenced by Britain only when it imitates it and to what extent was the logic of establishing new forms of government merely that of a modern society? In large part the civil service and banking systems 'closely and consciously imitated the English model' (89) and there was significant British influence also over the Irish Free State constitution, J.J. Lee, *Ireland 1912–1985: politics and society* (Cambridge, 1989), 87–94; for a contemporary, although British, account see Nicholas Mansergh, *The Irish Free State* (London, 1934).

By using the two shots of footprints in the bog and the grave being dug and filled in to convey the deaths of the prisoners, deaths which the film's humanist overtone condemns, Johnston problematizes the use of landscape in nationalist imagery and suggests an alternative reading of the land. Rather than explaining away or lessening the impact of the execution, the bogland shots serve a dual function. Firstly, they imply the poverty of land as either an explanation or a rationale for murder. Secondly, they suggest that the landscape associated with hard-line nationalism is a barren waste. By substituting images of the bogland for the actual execution, Johnston suggests that landscape, as a national icon, has reached a crisis of meaning and raises the issue of whether the myth of the sanctity of land should still occupy such a valorized and central position in Irish identity.

Furthermore, as Kevin Rockett points out, the film gives 'little indication ... as to why the people were fighting, merely that they were pawns in a system outside their control'.[38] Both O'Connor and Johnston's refusal to give the two guards any motivation beyond 'duty' to kill the prisoners reveals the extent to which, from a post-revolutionary perspective, the nationalist cause may have damaged or ignored the needs of Irish people, in the fight for the larger cause of freedom. Coming a decade after the War of Independence, both film and story do not merely stand as a testament to the actual violence faced by ordinary men and women during the war, but Johnston and O'Connor also question whether the sacrifices made were a price worth paying. Though O'Connor refuses to indict the guards – including O'Donovan – for the executions, their wastefulness and negative impact are clear. The system of war that necessitates these executions is thus reprehensible. In the film there is a much stronger sense that the villains are the representatives of nationalist power – the IRA commanding officers who order and insist upon the executions and, by extension, the founders and founding principles of the Free State, what Johnston would later condemn as 'murder as a political argument'.[39]

Guests of the nation is thus highly critical, on several levels, of IRA procedure during the War of Independence and as such illustrates Johnston's cynical attitude to nationalism. Indeed, in reviewing Johnston's earlier play, *The moon in the yellow*

38 Rockett, *Cinema*, 61. **39** Johnston, *Orders and desecrations*, 77. This comment is made in relation to the 'murders' the Free State government carried out of its political prisoners after independence.

river, Seán O'Meadhra comments that though Johnston is 'amazingly brilliant' it is a pity that he has no sense of sympathy with the native Irish and speaks instead from an Ascendancy position, resulting in a 'distorted sense of values'.[40] Certainly, Johnston's refusal to admit any benefit to Ireland from nationalism can be viewed as a 'distorted' representation; nevertheless, his attitude to the IRA is indicative of the changing attitudes towards the IRA in 1930s Ireland, represented by Fianna Fáil's jettisoning of its connections to the organisation.

Despite the increasingly negative attitude to the IRA in the thirties, it is still surprising to note that Frank Aiken, the then minister for Defence, and his secretary, attended the premiere at the Gate. Aiken had strong ties to the IRA, indeed upon his election his first act as a government minister was to release twenty IRA prisoners from Mountjoy Gaol.[41] In fact, he not only attended the premiere of the film, but helped in its making by loaning Johnston all the weapons used for props in the film.[42] As a republican one would expect Aiken to have reacted against a film so openly critical of the IRA. His help and his presence, which was reported in both newspaper reviews, indicate the growing ambivalence of Fianna Fáil. During the mid- to late 1930s Fianna Fáil gradually positioned themselves further and further away from the IRA. Indeed, in 1934, just two years after his triumphant visit to Mountjoy, Aiken had founded the volunteer force, which was intended to 'siphon off some of the old IRA who wanted jobs' and the young men 'who might otherwise join Óglaigh na hÉireann'.[43] These ventures, designed to becalm the IRA and aid Fianna Fáil in securing the confidence and the vote of the nation, significantly moved the party away from its militant and radical republican roots. Aiken's role in the making of *Guests of the nation* thus illustrates the shifts in public and state opinion about the War of Independence and the problematic leftover presence of a terrorist army in a time of peace.[44] The idea of the

---

40 Seán Ó Meadhra, 'Poet and peasant', *Ireland Today* (July 1936), 64.   **41** J. Bowyer Bell, 'Introduction' in Uinseann MacEoin, *The IRA in the twilight years, 1923–1948* (Dublin, 1997), 4. **42** Johnston records in his diary the continuing shadowy presence of the IRA: 'Spectacular day in the Scalp, filming the Ambush sequence, with an Armoured Car and a lorry lent by the Army and which came from the Curragh. I was told afterwards we were nearly raided by the I.R.A. led by the Gilmore brothers while on the job – information on which had been given them before by our helpful Mary Manning – in order to seize some of our rifles.' Omnibus notebook (4 June 1933), Trinity College Dublin, MS 10066/181.   **43** Bell, *IRA*, 8.   **44** The resurgence of violence on the part of the IRA was partly because of the Blue Shirt movement, led by General Eoin O'Duffy. Crackdowns on the movements of the IRA by the government were largely attributed to the clashes between the IRA and the Blueshirts. The demise of the Blueshirts in the mid-1930s and internal splits within the IRA as to its leadership and direction aided de Valera's attempt to exclude the IRA from the future of the Free State. The divisions within the IRA meant that when in June 1936 the organisation was declared 'nation', which had held so many disparate groups together, was now, amid the realities of the Free State, being reframed. Johnston reflects upon this reframing in *Guests of the nation* by portraying the IRA in a period of transition from the wilderness to the road, mirroring both Fianna Fáil and the Free State's jettisoning of its terrorist roots.

Johnston's greatest indictment of the War of Independence and modern Ireland's failure to address the past is the image of the bogland grave. What is buried in this grave is natural compassion and anti-essentialism. The most positive aspect to the relationship between the four men is the way in which it collapses boundaries. While the men are first differentiated from one another by their appearance and dress sense, the subsequent comic scenes serve to break these differences down and unite the men in a common bond of camaraderie. Bonaparte and Noble become real characters when their compassion for Belcher and Hawkins leads them to try to break with the IRA order and try to stop the executions in Kilmainham. It is key for Johnston to add scenes such as this to display the humanity of the Bonaparte and Noble, something that O'Connor is immediately able to create through the tone and intimacy of first-person narration. The insistence of the IRA leadership that the reprisal shootings be carried out must be seen not only as their wish to retaliate over the executions of the IRA prisoners by the British but also as a recognition of the inherent danger of the relationship between the four men. A friendship between prisoners and guards must be broken as it threatens to destabilize the essentialisms or polarities which the war and nationalism itself are founded on. The graves of the Englishmen, figured in the footprints in the mud, are like wounds upon both the landscape and the Irish psyche, an image that is still resonant today.[45] Thus, rather than being a powerful cultural icon, the bogland is a clandestine cemetery. What *Guests of the nation* ultimately suggests is that these wounds still exist, that they have not been resolved. The deaths of Belcher and Hawkins prove what Johnston wrote in *The moon in the yellow river*, that 'the birth of a nation is no immaculate conception'. In *Guests of the nation* Johnston follows in O'Connor's footsteps in asserting that nationalism, while it fights for collective freedom, can all too often fail its citizens as individuals.

The ability of O'Connor's story and Johnston's film to address these issues while both challenging and entertaining readers and viewers is reason enough for

unlawful there was no sustained confrontation between the army and the IRA.   **45** The (British) Commission for the Location of Victims' Remains continues to search for the bodies of victims of IRA terrorism in Northern Ireland.

their critical success and endurance. Though Johnston's film has not received much detailed analysis it is recognized by Irish film historians as 'one of Ireland's most important screen ventures'.[46] While the film differs from the story in key ways, and, as a silent film, must sacrifice the intimacy and searing honesty which is so crucial to the story's integrity, the film does maintain the original sense of the defeat of humanity and the appeal to the audience's compassion. For both O'Connor and Johnston, 'Guests' was a first – first short-story collection, first film – and for both it was to be a highlight of their artistic careers.

---

46 Taken from the programme for the 2nd Annual Boston Irish Film Festival (2006), accessed at http://www.harvardfilmarchive.org/calendars/oomarapr/irish.htm. *Guests* has screened at a number of festivals in recent years – including the annual International Frank O'Connor Festival of the Short Story (Cork, 2002).

Frank O'Connor's autobiographical writings

RUTH SHERRY

Frank O'Connor's major autobiographical work, *An only child*, had a very long genesis. It appeared in book form in 1961 when he was in fact approaching the end of his life, his death occurring in 1966. The book consists of four sections, each of which was initially published separately in the *New Yorker* between 1958 and 1961. These sections have titles which are taken from familiar songs: 1 – 'Child, I know you're going to miss me', 2 – 'I know where I'm going', 3 – 'Go where glory waits thee' and 4 – 'After Aughrim's great disaster'.[1]

An only child gives an account of O'Connor's life from birth through to the age of 20. It presents his family and their backgrounds, and recounts his growing up with an alcoholic father and a much-beloved mother (ch. 1) in a poor district of Cork City (ch. 2). It reports his attempts at acquiring an education and at finding an occupation by which he can make a living (ch. 3). In the final chapter the book concludes with his account of his involvement as a republican in the Civil War, his resulting internment in a camp in County Meath, his release, and his return to Cork. On his return from internment, he reports, 'Mother suddenly burst into tears and said: "It made a man of you".'[2] It is at this point in his life that the book ends.

However, some elements found in this autobiographical volume had been treated much earlier. As early as 1934 O'Connor published an account of his imprisonment and internment in the Civil War under the title 'A Boy in Prison'.[3] This piece covers essentially the same ground as the final section of *An only child*, but differs in emphasis and is darker and more bitter in many details than the later version; it had not been republished and was probably virtually unknown to readers by the time *An only child* appeared. In addition, a radio talk bearing virtually the same title as the eventual book, 'Only child', was broadcast by BBC Scotland on 11 October 1950; it is largely made up of very brief pieces of material relating to O'Connor's childhood, material which appears in more developed form in the book *An only child* and/or in various short stories. Both of these

---

1 Frank O'Connor, *An only child* (London, 1961). 2 Ibid., 274. 3 Frank O'Connor, 'A boy in prison', *Life and letters*, 10:56 (Aug. 1943), 525–35.

obscure items were fortunately republished by Michael Steinman in *A Frank O'Connor reader*.[4]

In general one is initially interested in a writer's autobiography because one is already interested in the writer's other work; unlike those who believe that 'there is no writer', I think that one of the great attractions of literature is that it gives one the sense of becoming acquainted with a personality, that of the writer, even if partially and at a tangent. If you find the personality attractive or intriguing, on the evidence of what you have read, you want to know more, make closer acquaintance – hence the great flourishing of literary biographies in the past twenty years or so. The autobiography of a well-established writer will at best have a similar appeal. Inevitably, the autobiography of an author takes on some of the shape of the *kunstlerroman*. *An only child* provides a 'portrait of the artist', but only up to the point of maturity; when it closes, he – like Stephen Dedalus – has not yet achieved anything significant artistically. But we know that he will, and after reading the autobiography we also know something about the basis for his later accomplishments.

To a large degree *An only child* also corresponds to Richard N. Coe's description of a sub-genre of autobiography, one which he identifies and labels as 'the Childhood' in his book *When the grass was taller: autobiography and the experience of childhood*, a study which has a good deal to say that is illuminating for reading Frank O'Connor. Coe defines 'the Childhood' as

> An extended piece of writing, a consciously, deliberately executed literary artifact, usually in prose (and thus intimately related to the novel) ... in which the most substantial portion of the material is *indirectly* autobiographical, and whose structure reflects step by step the development of the writer's self; beginning often, but not invariably, with the first light of consciousness, and concluding quite specifically, with the attainment of a precise degree of maturity.[5]

What is striking is Coe's observation that in 'the Childhood' the most substantial portion of the material is 'indirectly autobiographical', for in *An only child* O'Connor devotes approximately as much space and attention to others as he does to himself. The lives and personalities of other people are presented, and the

4 Michael Steinman (ed.), *A Frank O'Connor reader* (Syracuse, NY, 1994).   5 Richard N. Coe, *When the grass was taller: autobiography and the experience of childhood* (New Haven and London, 1984), 8–9, emphasis supplied.

autobiographer himself virtually disappears for long passages. Not surprisingly, his parents come in for the greatest part of this attention; indeed, the very title invites one to look to the parent-child relationship for its main subject. O'Connor's relations with his father were at best uneasy and at worst openly hostile, while he adored his mother, and this conflict is one of the main themes of *An only child*.

Again, Coe's observations are useful: he claims that the autobiographical 'Childhood' is frequently marked by

> the indirect approach to childhood – the reconstruction of the writer's child-self, not through direct reminiscence, but by way of a previous generation … [This approach can be seen as] a heroic attempt to tackle one of the basic problems inherent in the genre: the total absence of confirmatory evidence in support of whatever arbitrary recollections the adult poet may retain of his former existence … [T]he authentic, factually verifiable biography of a father or a mother … offers a framework in which that self may be apprehended and, in a sense, understood, inasmuch as it may be felt to be predetermined: '*they* were like this, therefore *I* was like that'.[6]

Coe's account nevertheless takes one only part of the way in apprehending the autobiographer's approach in *An only child*. O'Connor certainly creates a vivid portrait of his father by means of an encapsulation of his domestic behaviour, with particular emphasis on his alcoholism and the threat it constituted to the family's security. There are also some brief descriptions of other members of his father's family – including the grandmother who memorably appears again in some of the short stories. But on the whole the presentation of the father appears to be derived, not, as Coe would have it, from some 'factually verifiable biography' but rather from the narrator's own observations and recollections – experiences which obviously retained a largely negative emotional charge long after the man's death.

In the course of the narration O'Connor also makes many observations, likewise derived from his own recollections and assessments, about his mother's characteristic behaviour, but in this case a substantial part of the narrative – a forty-six-page long section of the chapter titled 'Child, I know you're going to miss me' is in fact derived from something much closer to Coe's 'factually verifiable biography'. Minnie O'Donovan had been raised mostly in an orphanage and then

6 Coe, *When the grass was taller*, 32.

been put out to domestic service, and here and elsewhere O'Connor gives the impression that she often talked about these periods in her life, before her marriage. She is also reported as having frequently taken her young son to visit the convent in which she was brought up. At some stage O'Connor encouraged her to record her reminiscences of this part of her life and perhaps took over as a scribe when she felt unable to continue.

> I picked up … fragments of Mother's past life that have never ceased to haunt me … They were merely a few hints, but they were sufficient to sustain my interest through the years, and later I wrote down and got her to write down as many of the facts as she remembered – or cared to remember. I stopped doing this one day when she put down her pen with a look of horror and said: 'I can't write any more – it's too terrible!'[7]

He certainly caused these reminiscences to be published – anonymously – in the journal *The Bell* during the period when he was one of its editors. They appeared in two instalments, under the title 'Orphans', in the first two issues of that journal in 1940.[8] Like the other early autobiographical pieces mentioned, this account of his mother's life was never republished after its appearance in *The Bell* and it would have been virtually forgotten by the time *An only child* appeared more than twenty years later.

The origin of the material is, however, immediately recognizable to anyone who comes across it and who has read *An only child*. But although there are a number of word-for-word reiterations from 'Orphans' in the autobiography, the style and scope of the two accounts is so notably different that one does not doubt that 'Orphans' represents an authentic attempt to convey Minnie O'Donovan's account in her own language.

> There were four of us, myself, the eldest; Maggie, Tim and Nora. I was my father's favourite and sometimes he used to take me to work with him and leave me in the playground of the nuns' school. He was an athlete, and one day when he was at work he took a bet that he wouldn't lift a heavy tierce. He won the bet but his spine was injured, and he had to be taken to hospital … I set off across the city by myself. I found the hospital

7 O'Connor, *An only child*, 44.   **8** Part 1: [Anonymous], 'Orphans', *The Bell*, 1:1 (Oct. 1940), 33–41; Part Two: 1:2 (Nov. 1940), 69–75. This piece is not to be confused with short story by the same title, 'Orphans', first published in 1956.

and my father sitting upstairs in the men's ward. When I was leaving he came downstairs with me. He stood on the steps and asked if I knew my way home again. Suddenly he stooped, picked me up in his arms and went home with me. He died there a little while after.[9]

O'Connor retells this episode:

> She had been the oldest of four children whose parents lived in a tiny cabin at the top of Blarney Lane beyond the point where I grew up ... My grandfather was a labourer in Arnott's brewery ... Mother was his pet and sometimes when he went to work he carried her with him in his arms, left her in the playground of the convent to amuse herself, and then came back later to carry her home again. He was a powerful man, a bowls player and athlete, and one day, for a bet, he began lifting heavy casks and injured his back ... One day [Minnie] left the children behind and ran all the way down Sunday's Well and Wyse's Hill and across the old wooden bridge where St Vincent's Bridge now stands to the hospital. She found him, fully dressed, sitting on his bed in the men's ward upstairs, with a group of men about him who played with her and gave her sweets ... [H]e ... asked if she knew her way home. She said that she did, but he realized that she was confused, caught her up in his arms and made off with her for home. Mother told that part of the story in a rather tentative way, and I suspect that, with a child's belief in magic, she had always felt that her visit had cured him and could not face the possibility that it might have been the cause of his death. Anyhow, I doubt if it was. I think he knew he was dying and wanted to die at home.[10]

O'Connor's own text is marked by far greater fluidity, notably in the length and variety of the sentence structures, as well as by the tendency to include detail which permits the reader to imagine the scene (the men playing with the child and offering her sweets, for example). Also significant is the addition of speculation about motives and interpretation of his grandfather's actions ('he realized that she was confused'). The contrasts in the two tellings of essentially the same story obliquely testify to the authenticity of the mother's account, the authenticity which Coe claims is sought by the author of a 'Childhood'.

9 *The Bell* (Oct. 1940), 33.   **10** O'Connor, *An only child*, 43–4.

While the first chapter of *An only child*, 'Child, I know you're going to miss me', provides descriptions and histories of the author's parents, the second and briefest chapter, 'I know where I'm going', consists entirely of delicious portraits of three women neighbours – that is, the second chapter is scarcely about the autobiographer himself at all, although we do not completely lose sight of him. There is also a presentation of Daniel Corkery to be found in *An only child*, and many other vividly realized figures are introduced more briefly. The presentation of all these 'characters' helps to create the social milieu in which O'Connor's growing-up occurred; it makes specific for the reader what would otherwise be a generalized 'growing up in the slums of Cork'. The individuation also asserts the full human value of life in that setting.

While other characters – within or outside the family – may provide a deflection of interest from the narrator, they also can present an implied standard of value against which to measure him. When O'Connor is actually writing about himself – which, as previously noted, he does for rather less than half the total extent of *An only child* – the tone of the narrative is very often ironic and self-deprecating. Throughout much of the narrative, serious and sympathetic assessment tends to be reserved for others, most notably for the author's mother, but also, for example, for a boy who goes mad after his mother dies while he is in internment camp. In contrast, the narrator's own activities and responses are frequently treated as evidence of his limitations, shortcomings, ignorance and immaturity – even though some of the narrator's qualities can implicitly be projected as assets for the adult artist he is to become (his fascination with languages, reading, and the theatre, for example; his dreaminess, which can be seen as a capacity for imaginative detachment from the present moment; and his 'being a sissy' which implies living under an alternative set of values).

> I adored education from afar, and strove to be worthy of it, as I later adored beautiful girls and strove to be worthy of them, and with similar results. I played cricket with a raggy ball and an old board hacked into shape for a bat before a wicket chalked on some dead wall. I kept in training by shadow-boxing before the mirror in the kitchen, and practiced the deadly straight left with which the hero knocked out the bully of the school. I even adopted the public-school code for my own and did not tell lies, or inform on other boys, or yell when I was beaten. It wasn't easy, because the other fellows did tell lies, and told on one another in the most shameless way, and when they were beaten, yelled that their wrists were

broken and even boasted later of their own cleverness, and when I behaved in the simple, manly way recommended in the school stories, they said I was mad or that I was 'shaping' (the Cork word for swanking), and even the teachers seemed to regard it as an impertinence.[11]

Very occasionally the reader is permitted a direct response to some of the horrors of being the child of an impoverished family with an alcoholic father, as for example:

> Whenever he brandished the razor at mother, I went into hysterics, and a couple of times I threw myself on him, beating him with my fists. That drove her into hysterics, too, because she knew that at times like that he would as soon have slashed me as her. Later, in adolescence, I developed pseudo-epileptic fits that were merely an externalization of this recurring nightmare, and though I knew they were not real, and was ashamed of myself for indulging in them at all, I could not resist them when once I had yielded to the first nervous spasm.[12]

Yet even here there is an element of self-evaluation, carried by words 'ashamed', 'indulging' and 'yielded'. It is partly this refusal to engage in self-pity which separates *An only child* from works of the *Angela's ashes* school and lifts it above them.

To the extent that *An only child* conducts such an assessment of the younger self, it falls within the tradition of spiritual and moral self-examination which, historically speaking, is a strong strain in the genre of autobiography, starting with St Augustine's *Confessions*. But in the case of *An only child* this self-examination is often rather muted, consisting less in direct self-analysis than in implicit contrast with both finer souls (his mother and his saintly neighbour Minnie Connolly in particular) and less fine souls (his father and bullying school teachers, for example).

If one now looks back at O'Connor's many stories of childhood through the glass provided by *An only child*, a few observations suggest themselves. One is that, as with autobiography, the narrator is an older version of the child protagonist, at least in the later versions of the stories of childhood.[13] These stories tend to be characterized by the same tone of irony and self-deprecation in relation to the

---

11 O'Connor, *An only child*, 119–20. **12** Ibid., 35. **13** For a discussion of the various versions of 'First confession' and 'The genius', see Michael Steinman, *Frank O'Connor at work* (Syracuse, NY, 1990).

protagonist that we can see in O'Connor's treatment of himself in *An only child*. Some stories, such as 'The man of the world' and 'The face of evil', conduct fairly severe assessments of the young character's actions and interpretations. As adults, we probably feel entitled to conduct such assessments in relation to younger ourselves, but would be reluctant to make the same judgments about a child with whom we do not identify. Especially retrospectively, after one has read *An only child*, it may be this often ironic, self-assessing tone which makes the stories of childhood seem to be autobiographical.

For in fact, although the germs of plot and incident for many of O'Connor's childhood stories are recounted in *An only child*, it is by no means the case that the origins of all the childhood stories can be found there. Furthermore, even when one can recognize a kernel of a story in *An only child*, only a few of these stories correspond in detail in their ostensibly fictional and ostensibly autobiographical forms (one which does is 'Old fellows'). In 'My Oedipus complex', for example, the relevant elements are the father's absence at war and his return, disrupting the cosy household of mother and son. But the family constellation in the story does not correspond with that in O'Connor's own family: no little brother 'Sonny' arrived and there was no rapprochement between the son and the father. To put it another way, in order to make the father/son relationship work out happily, in order to make the oedipal relationship the subject of a comedy rather than a tragedy, the story had to be fictionalized. It was only years later that the more tragic version was told, in *An only child*.

Eight of the stories of childhood, including 'My Oedipus complex', have a central character named Larry Delaney, who also appears as an older character in four other stories.[14] But other names and family constellations are also used: for example, the little boy in the later versions of 'First confession' is called Jackie and he has a sister. But although Jackie is not identical with Larry, and Larry is not altogether identical with the young Michael O'Donovan, Jackie's grandmother, with her bare feet, her shawl and her porter, is recognizably Michael O'Donovan's grandmother as presented in *An only child*, and a very similar character appears in other stories: 'The long road to Ummera' and 'The patriarch'.

A feature which does carry through from story to story, even where family details and names are blurred or missing, is setting. Somehow, even if the family constellations are shifting, everything seems to take place in more or less the same

---

14 These stories have conveniently been collected by Patrick Cotter in *Larry Delaney: lonesome genius* (Cork, 1996).

house, certainly in the same part of town. The life of the 'square', the neighbours in and out of each others' houses and well aware of the intimate details of each others' lives, the geography of Cork, the views from the lanes and rooftops – these seem essentially identical in the stories and in the autobiography.

An only child concludes at a point in which the protagonist has attained, in Richard N. Coe's phrase, 'a precise degree of maturity', while it also conforms to Roy Pascal's description of the function of autobiography:

> The autobiography is the means to review one's life, to organize it in the imagination, and thus to bring the past experience and the present self into balance. The object is not so much to tell the truth about oneself as to come to terms with oneself.[15]

With *An only child*, it is easy to identify retrospectively the impulses that ultimately led O'Connor to be, pre-eminently, a writer of realistic short stories, rather than – as he had initially envisioned – a poet. Indeed, the final section of *An only child* outlines a general shift of philosophical perspective from the romantic and idealising to the practical and factual; in the structure of the narrative, this constitutes the final stage in the process of 'growing up'. It involves definitively replacing the unreliable world of the imagination with 'reality', replacing the ideal or the abstract with the concrete and the everyday, just as earlier developments required replacing English boys' school stories with models more congruent with life in Cork (also the topic of the story 'The idealist'). In the internment camp, O'Connor learns to reject republicanism because he finds it in conflict with common sense, natural impulses and the ordinary demands of life; ironically, the conclusion of the process is summarized in the quotation from the highly romantic Goethe: 'Grey, my dear friend, is all your theory, and green the golden tree of life'.

Although *An only child* locates this crucial change of perspective and values in the internment camp experience, O'Connor had by no means abandoned writing poetry at this stage (in 1923). Nevertheless it was at about this time that he began to produce fiction. Gradually throughout the 1920s and 1930s he left behind the writing original poetry and instead focussed a major portion of his attention on short stories. When *An only child* was finally written, it showed the same elements that had come to mark most of the stories: the instinct for character portrayal, the

15 Roy Pascal, *Design and truth in autobiography* (Cambridge, MA, 1960), 59.

focus on ordinary domestic life and emotions as he had known them. The sense of place and the grasp of conflict, internal or familial, are similar in both genres.

If one considers O'Connor's career chronologically, the circumstances and characters of his early years obviously provided some of the material which he reshaped into short stories. But in both psychological and creative terms it seems as if this material had to be worked through in fictional form – where it could, if necessary, be modified – before it could, in turn, eventually be faced directly and given an openly autobiographical expression. From this perspective, the stories seem to lead up to the understood life (the autobiography), rather than deriving from it.

Roy Pascal has also observed: 'many modern autobiographers become pre-occupied with their lives as representative of their generation'.[16] In *An only child* we are repeatedly invited to place the individual life into its contexts. One might see three rings: 1 – Michael O'Donovan and his family, 2 – working class Cork and 3 – Ireland.

One of the several themes in *An only child* involves parallels between the auto-biographer's own growth, education and maturing, on the one hand, and developments in the Irish nation, growing in stages toward independence in the first part of the twentieth century, on the other. Creating this parallel may imply that the autobiographer's self is typical for his time and place. As O'Connor describes his childhood, he does not in fact seem typical, but rather anomalous, notably unlike the other boys in his school and neighbourhood. His life begins in poverty and deprivation, but he ultimately escapes from this condition through a form of education. Correspondingly, perhaps, the subject nation matures; from being poor and apparently inadequate, it achieves its independence, although not without a struggle, and goes on to 'take its place'. This 'plot' and 'theme' line is particularly prominent in the second half, or the last two major sections, of the book: 'Go where glory waits thee' and 'After Aughrim's great disaster', both song titles which place O'Connor's life in a larger historical context.

For O'Connor personally, education is not provided by schools and colleges, which fail him. He is educated largely by way of nationalism itself: for example, he is moved to learn Irish by the Easter Rising; he reads, studies languages and listens to music under the informal tutelage of Daniel Corkery, a die-hard 'Irish Irelander'; and he finds life in an internment camp – where there are lessons in a

16 Pascal, *Design and truth*, 171.

wide variety of fields available – to be 'the nearest thing I could have found to life on a college campus, the only one I was really fitted for'.[17]

The last section of *An only child* can easily be seen as a miniature 'jail journal' – such 'journals' often involve a contemplation of, or a polishing of, one's political convictions, perhaps one's philosophical and religious convictions as well. In *An only child* the narrator's political convictions are not strengthened. Rather, as a result of his experiences in the internment camp he abandoned his – as he later saw it – rather adolescent adherence to republicanism. The experience of imprisonment and internment led rather to his questioning and ultimately rejecting not only republicanism but dogmatic political positions in general; it is an aspect of rejecting idealism and accepting fact. By the end of *An only child*, the autobiographer has assumed a more confirmed and comfortable individualism which permits questioning and, if necessary, rejecting and contesting accepted beliefs. And there this work of autobiography concludes, although readers familiar with O'Connor's entire career can see the relevance of such a transformation.

In the last years of his life, probably prompted partly by the great critical and popular success of *An only child*, O'Connor made some moves toward producing a second volume, which would in fact deal with his adult life and his career as an ultimately successful writer, but he died before the work was completed. Compiling and editing of existing drafts was undertaken by the scholar Maurice Sheehy on behalf of Harriet O'Donovan, and the result was published in 1968 under the title *My father's son* – a title which might not have been O'Connor's own ultimate choice, but which certainly continued the focus on family relations as central.[18]

My father's son has passages, and a few characters, that are as memorable as anything in *An only child*. While one certainly would not want to be without it, the work as a whole is less satisfying than *An only child*, perhaps inevitably, as it has not achieved the overall shaping that marks *An only child*. *My father's son* is also understandably but frustratingly reticent about aspects of O'Connor's private life without, however, being completely silent on the subject. This volume also gives some detail about his difficult relations with the Abbey Theatre, but not enough to give the reader a sense of the full story. On the plus side, probably taking a note from *An only child*, the editor chose to include long and often fascinating descriptions of several leading figures in Irish literary and artistic life, notably Yeats and Æ about whom O'Connor wrote on many other occasions. Others memorably

17 O'Connor, *An only child*, 259–60. **18** Frank O'Connor, *My father's son* (London, 1968).

presented include the Tailor and Ansty, as well as personal friends like Nancy McCarthy and Tim Traynor. A characteristic feature is the unique mixture of reverence and irreverence with which major figures – notably Yeats, but also a number of others – are viewed. If *My father's son* has a consistent thread apart from that of a search for surrogate fathers, it is that of occupying a different ground for battle, now a battle against the forces of mediocrity and moral repression. While *My father's son* includes material which has relevance for O'Connor's later fiction and drama, it does not often give the impression that his own personal experiences are reworked fictionally in his later years.

Returning to the initial idea that we strive to become better acquainted with a writer whose work we respond to, I would suggest that *My father's son* leaves us feeling we want more. There really is not much more to be had, at this stage, in the form of unpublished autobiographical writings, but there does exist a vein of material which thus far has been relatively little used: O'Connor's letters, which certainly shed more light on both the life and the personality. There are hundreds, probably thousands, of letters, and they are largely an unexplored gold mine, as will be apparent to anyone who has read the published exchange of letters between O'Connor and William Maxwell.[19] Some of O'Connor's letters are held in Trinity College, and a number are in other public collections. As a letter writer O'Connor manifests the same wit, the same eloquence, and, indeed, the same capacity for self-deprecation and irony, that we see in the autobiographical works. In these works the next generation of scholars could find a new body of material for the illumination of O'Connor's life and mind.

---

19 Michael Steinman (ed.), *The happiness of getting it down right: letters of Frank O'Connor and William Maxwell* (New York, 1996).

'A phase of history' in the house: Frank O'Connor's 'Lonely rock'

MICHAEL STEINMAN

Although no one quite knows the context, most readers of Frank O'Connor are aware of W.B. Yeats' remark that O'Connor was doing for Ireland what Chekhov did for Russia. I suspect that Yeats liked the sound of that oracular pronouncement more than he concerned himself with its precise meaning, but I believe that we should read O'Connor with the same reverent attention we offer Chekhov. This may seem hyperbolical praise for a writer so often condescended to as simple, but only superficial readers dare to take his work at face value.

Although he urged his students to begin their stories by reducing them to four-line themes, O'Connor's stories defy such reductions. His plots appear plain only when they are detached from the actual texts; his characters refuse to conform to our expectations; his denouements make us feel that our expectations have quietly turned on us, as if a striped kitten suddenly became a tiger cub. And his stories are often mirrors in which we might see ourselves. Readers who value the appearance of modernity above all have said his work is 'dated', which is an unfortunate assessment of art when its creator has not been dead long enough to be classic, nor recent enough to be contemporary. Yes, his stories do not deal with what we read about in the morning's paper; the cultural landscape belongs to the preceding century; when his characters go to bed we are not invited to join their activities. Yet, when properly understood, his work seems timeless, his moral concerns equally so. To think otherwise is equivalent to rejecting Austen because Elizabeth and Mr Darcy do not have automobiles. Some readers have also seen his fiction as 'sentimental', but that is perhaps because his belief in the redeeming powers of love seems unfashionable. And for those who have accused him of writing stories which end in unrealistically happy ways, perhaps they have not read as many stories as they might (consider 'The cheat', 'Bridal night', 'The weeping children'): even those stories where all problems appear to have been solved ('My Oedipus complex' for one) have bittersweet resolutions.

Other factors have limited O'Connor's literary reputation. Ironically, the mastery exhibited in his most reprinted stories has not encouraged readers, academics, and publishers to venture beyond 'Guests of the nation', 'My Oedipus complex' or 'First confession'. In academia, Joyce's work is so dominant as to make nearly everyone else seem minor, and no one thinks to put O'Connor's stories next to 'Counterparts' or 'After the race' to show that other Irish writers in the last century were not intimidated into silence. And the generation that subscribed to the *New Yorker* after the Second World War because of that magazine's extraordinary fiction is diminished or dead; their children and grandchildren have little interest in writing not self-consciously contemporary. The Tailor of Gougane Barra told O'Connor that his stories had too few 'marvels' in them, and I fear that O'Connor's fiction is often too subtle for postmodern readers craving fiction that resembles graphic novels (which his generation would have called comic books). Finally, his work does not announce itself as obscure and therefore worthy of study; unlike his bookshelf neighbour Flannery O'Connor, his stories are not gleefully grotesque, populated by tattooed husbands and one-legged women named Hulga.

But even when O'Connor's stories seem to be narrowly domestic, mocked by Francis Stuart as taking place around the kitchen table, they dramatize rapidly changing cultural and moral history against sharply defined political landscapes. A particularly neglected 1946 story, 'Lonely rock', – the majority of its characters are members of an Irish family reconfigured against their will into an 'entirely emancipated' London household – reassesses 'modern' social mores and behaviour. Although O'Connor seems to have nothing more to offer us than an extended family in wartime, he is examining conflicting beliefs about family, monogamy, sexuality, and religion. What happens when those beliefs, put in motion, collide? 'Lonely rock' also describes an episode of self-realization, as its narrator, once naive but emerging into partial awareness, rejects contemporary freedom as selfish in principle, cruel in practice. And the self-realization extends outward: 'Lonely rock' is an intensely moving parable about the irreversible consequences of *our* acts.

A story thus praised, one would think, would be invulnerable to misreading and misinterpretation, but that has not been the case. For one thing, superficial autobiographical connections have misdirected critics, including myself, into misidentifying characters. But in the fashion of other O'Connor stories, the text is dangerous for the unwary, almost inviting us to misread it at the outset, again speaking to an underlying moral purpose: only after we have realized our errors might we understand what it would be like to be nearly right next time.

'Lonely rock' first invites us to take it for granted by presenting a triangular arrangement of characters, an apparently familiar grouping that encourages a complacent reading. Meeting Husband, Wife, and the Husband's Mother under the same roof, we might foresee nothing more than drawing-room comedy about the man poised between them, who has to decide whether he will be Son, Husband, or both at the dinner table. Beneath the light tone, an astute reader might anticipate conflicts based in loyalty or power, one woman saying unhappily, 'You love her more than me,' or any of the three characters asking, 'Who's in charge here?' That Sylvia, the Wife, is an English schoolteacher, her Husband and Mother-in-Law from Cork is an added complication, but that in itself might only lead us to expect formulaic comedy about cultural differences enacted on the domestic front. Adding Mistress to the cast – and to the house – might make us expect naughty bedroom farce, with every door slamming. But our predictions and expected allegiances turn false, which is surely the point, when the character we are first invited to admire is unmasked as hollow, and the character everyone initially satirizes is seen as remarkable and remarkably alone at the end, staying faithful to fidelity.

The story begins with the casual voice of a man telling a small-scale series of anecdotes about something that seems not terribly important. The speaker, amiable and unusually self-effacing, doesn't identify himself or demand the spotlight but talks of someone he identifies as more worthy of chronicling: 'In England during the war I had a great friend called Jack Courtenay who was assistant manager in one of the local factories.' The war, of course, is the Second World War, and although none of the characters in this story see action while they are play-acting, the bombers fly overhead. Phil, the speaker, is so shadowy at first that we only find out his name – he is a man named for love – when Sylvia, Jack's wife, speaks about Jack to him. Phil tells us, with some embarrassment, that he is 'fresh from Ireland' and Jack thinks him a 'puritan'. Jack, who has left his Cork home at eighteen to recreate himself as English, happily chooses his cultural displacement, acknowledging his Irish heritage only in rebellion against it.

Phil's portrait of Jack is an admiring one, but that he is so little uneasy about what he admires makes readers uneasy. Although Phil says that he disapproves of Jack's behaviour, he portrays it as harmless, as if he wishes he could be as self-assured, equally handsome, athletic, and rakish: 'I have known [Jack] to invite someone he liked to his office to discuss an entirely imaginary report from the police, accusing the unfortunate man of bigamy and deserting a large family. He could carry on a joke like that for a long time without a shadow of a smile, and end up by promising his victim to try and persuade the police that it was all a case of mistaken identity.'[1] Indulgently, Phil presents this as 'a schoolboy mania for practical joking', that Jack can 'get away with', but it is difficult to see it as comic and

---

1 Frank O'Connor, 'Lonely rock', *More stories by Frank O'Connor* (New York, 1956), 370. Further citations are given in the text.

thus forgivable rather than cruel. And the abuse of power, a possible crime, bigamy, desertion, two homes and fathering illegitimate children, are serious matters that reverberate through the pages that follow. Nothing is too sacred for Jack to mock, no matter what its consequences, and Phil says nothing of the victim's feelings when Jack reveals, if he ever does, that it was all an exceedingly good joke.

After pointing out Jack's second reversion to self-absorbed childhood, 'a toothache or a cold in the head could drive him stark, staring mad', Phil equates this with Jack's 'other weakness', for 'girls'. Jack defines himself as a sexual outlaw and his wife encourages his activities. Sylvia has been trained by Jack to reject monogamy as passé – an unusual ethical position, one would think, for a school-teacher, wife, and mother of two boys, seven and nine. However, her rebellion is vicarious, enacted through her husband. Like Sylvia, Phil has agreed to collaborate in Jack's fiction that his adulteries are only 'flirtations' that 'never went too far', and he lingers over the details with some muted envy, although he confesses himself unable to emulate Jack. Readers alert to impending disasters may well sense that they are visiting a world governed by schoolboys oblivious to the possible repercussions of their escapades.

In the comedy of manners Jack and Sylvia stage over cocktails when their two (nearly invisible) children are put to bed, Jack is the Irresistible Leading Man, and she plays a Blasé Blonde modelled on Marlene Dietrich, flattered by Jack's sexual attractiveness to other women, proud of her modernity. Phil plays an Irish Provincial, his mouth open in fascinated astonishment, as behaviour unthinkable at home is championed in London as fashionable, appropriate to an 'entirely emancipated' household:

> 'Did you know that Jack's got a new girl, Phil?' [Sylvia] asked, while he beamed proudly on both of us. 'Such a relief after the last! Didn't he show you the last one's photo? Oh, my dear, the commonest looking piece.'
>
> 'Now, now, who's jealous?' Jack would say severely, wagging his finger at her.
>
> 'Really, Jack,' she would reply with bland insolence, 'I'd have to have a very poor opinion of myself to be jealous of that. Didn't you say she was something in Woolworth's?' (371)

Sylvia is an exceedingly complicated character, even given her rather tedious snob-bery. Yes, she is less the beauty commended by swains of *The two gentlemen of*

Verona than someone who has modelled her satiric, flirtatious persona on film goddesses. She is almost always seen with a cocktail in her hand, throwing one long leg over the arm of the chair. Later, we hear her sing 'Lili Marlene' from the kitchen, providing a wartime soundtrack, that song depicting separated lovers and broken relationships, although Sylvia regards the war, as she does most things, flippantly. She remains a mystery to Phil, a character partially opaque to us (I regret that we never see her in daylight, in the classroom). It is left to readers to decide if her sexual posturing, her cynical comedy, are evidence of her emulation of Jack's values or poses she tries to live up to. She is, after all, the schoolteacher taught, the London girl recreated and modernized by a Corkman.

While these three characters are moving in wobbly, elliptical orbits, we encounter Jack's widowed mother, Mrs Courtenay, whom Sylvia, generously, has invited to live with them. Mrs Courtenay is not involved in the nocturnal play-acting and would understand little of it if it were pointed out to her, but has been assigned a part: she is Granny, a simple-minded relic of the nineteenth century, another comic figure, someone less educable than Phil. That this characterization is both inaccurate and unkind matters not at all to Jack and Sylvia, who need to satirize her to validate their own identities. Mrs Courtenay is naturally proud of Cork, of Ireland, of her piety. If readers have made themselves comfortable in the world of Phil, Jack, and Sylvia, they are encouraged to view the old woman mockingly, especially when Sylvia is sarcastic about Mrs Courtenay's lifelong friend, 'Sister Mary Misery', and the old woman is said to be so backward that she knows nothing of the nuances of modern romance, which, tellingly, focus on venereal disease.

Perhaps because he is also from Cork, Phil, to his credit, recognizes her as 'a phase of history', upholding traditions of unconditional affection, religious belief, loyalty to home, family, and spouse (372). We also learn that Mrs Courtenay is 'an excellent housekeeper', which is more than a simple statement about her embracing an established woman's role instead of Sylvia's career. In this story, the stability she embodies goes beyond dusting and mopping. That house itself, the stage for these brittle comic sketches, is sharply divided: while Sylvia is at work and the little boys are at school, the house is Mrs Courtenay's, but it is hers only to clean, not to govern. While she is awake, Jack drinks only sherry; when she goes to bed, at the clearly old-fashioned hour of ten, he turns to whiskey and everyone puts the daytime world aside. At night, we gather, everything is permitted.

Mrs Courtenay is presented to us as 'a third adult in the house', in contrast to the childish play that precedes her. The world Jack inhabits views formality as obsolete, but O'Connor identifies Jack's mother as 'Mrs Courtenay' twenty-five times, titular homage to her stature and identity as wife, widow, and mother. Amidst the mockery, she is the central figure of the story's prelude, her description more detailed than any other characters. Only she understands home (her nostalgia for Cork is deep, for she is a displaced person searching for a role and a place, whether among the other women in the park or in her son's house), she loves nature (babies, she says, are 'very fond of trees'); she values family while everyone else is dismantling it. Most unfashionably, she talks to God – in a secular house where such behaviour is denied or derided. In the environment where a child's birth can be defined as 'rotten luck' and death can be invented to deceive others, only she recognizes tragedy; she knows there are things one must not do, even though nothing seems to be forbidden.

In the second section, Jack's 'philandering' (its very name an odd mirroring of the narrator's, or is it the reverse?) becomes active and tangible, its results viewed from a distance, retrospectively. The comedy of Jack, caught between conflicting loyalties to Mother and Wife, women representing his past and present lives, vanishes when he tells Phil that he is 'having trouble about Margaret', his latest conquest, who has chosen to play 'The Modern Young Woman Who Has Done It All for Love', and Phil responds:

> 'Serious?' I asked.
> 'Well, she's had a baby,' he said with a shrug.
> He expected me to be shocked, and I was, but not for his reasons. It was clear that he was badly shaken, did not know how his philandering could have gone so far or had such consequences, and was blaming the drink or something equally irrelevant.
> 'That's rotten luck,' I said.
> 'That's the worst of it,' he said. 'It's not luck.'
> 'Oh!' I said. I was beginning to realize vaguely the mess in which he had landed himself. 'You mean she—?'
> 'Yes,' he cut in. 'She wanted it. Now she wants to keep it, and her family won't let her, so she's left home.'
> 'Oh,' I said again. 'That is rotten.'
> 'It's not very pleasant,' he said. (374–5)

Jack's vocabulary shows him as reconstructing history to separate him from any responsibility for it. *Margaret* has had a baby; *she wanted it*. Where, one might ask, was the father? A remorseful Jack would be implausible, but he speaks of the unnamed child as a neutered inconvenience, and Phil (helpful as always) tries to find the second part to harmonize with the theme. When Sylvia talks of the event 'months later', she attempts the same verbal detachment, cocktail at the ready: 'Did you know Jack's got himself into a scrape with the brunette, Phil?' Margaret, she explains briefly, is alone and unemployed; the baby is sick. Phil, perhaps surprising himself as much as readers, feels that the only solution is for Jack to bring Margaret and Teddy to the house; he encourages Sylvia's kindness and bullies Jack into accepting it. Creating a world where reality can be manipulated to fit the chosen script, Sylvia invents a missing soldier as Margaret's absent husband to make Margaret respectable for her mother-in-law, a mockery of the wartime deaths that surround them: 'And at a time like this who's going to inquire …? We can kill him off in the most horrible manner' (376).

When Margaret and Teddy arrive, Mrs Courtenay immediately and instinctively cares for the baby. She goes to him when he cries in the night before Margaret can leave her armchair and put down her drink. Generations and expectations clash as Margaret, a modern woman, believes in 'a time-table, stipulating when he should be fed, lifted, and loved,' as opposed to the unregulated love of Mrs Courtenay, who 'read nothing but holy books', but Teddy thrives in her unfashionable care, and she is a better parent although powerless to claim Teddy as hers (379). Mrs Courtenay is obviously an actively 'practicing Catholic'; her devotion to Teddy is as logical to her as is her daily morning mass. Because she has knows, intuitively, that social roles are rooted in obligations to individuals, she still finds monogamy natural and tells Phil: 'how shocked she was by the character of the English, who seemed from the age of fifteen on to do nothing but fall in and out of love. Mrs Courtenay had heard of love; she was still very much in love with her own husband, who had been dead for years, but this was a serious matter and had nothing whatever in common with those addlepated affairs you read of in the newspapers' (373). Yet even while she is trying to replicate her lost world, based on fidelity, in an alien London, she cannot unite isolated individuals whose first priority is self-gratification.

The story's moral and dramatic crisis arises when she impulsively speaks the truth that Jack is Teddy's father. But her words are not a melodramatic unmasking of a secret, but the exuberant request of someone urging a parent to do what is natural: 'Ah, here's Daddy now!' she said triumphantly. 'Daddy will play with us'. (O'Connor's use of 'play' is notable. Hopeful, optimistic readers might envision Jack, at last seated on the floor with his child and his child's toys, but the verb has sharp teeth, for Jack has treated his emotional responsibilities casually). Jack, Sylvia, and Margaret respond awkwardly to what they believe is the old woman's blunder, although readers do not know how much Mrs Courtenay actually knows. Consciously or unconsciously, however, she is goading Jack to acknowledge his paternity in morally unambiguous terms: he must protect and accept Teddy as she has done. But Jack glibly chooses a child's egocentric position: 'Daddy will do nothing of the sort,' he says, 'Daddy wants somebody to play with him' (381). In confidence, he laments to Phil how 'awkward' it is to have both his wife and mistress in the house, and complains that Sylvia insisted he keep Margaret company (however the reader wishes to define it) while an air-raid alert is on. Phil, still the amiable male assistant in whom everyone confides, sympathetically agrees that Sylvia's behaviour is 'tactless' (382), although Jack has failed as father, husband, son, and paramour.

Quickly, Margaret finds a job and 'a home where Teddy would be looked after', a poor substitute for the house where he has been healed and loved, but she and her baby depart (383). Privately, Mrs Courtenay tells Phil that she knew at once that Jack was Teddy's father but said nothing: 'I suppose he thought I'd tell Sylvia, but of course I wouldn't dream of making mischief. And the two of them such great friends too – wisha, isn't life queer, Phil?' ... It was then the real poignancy of the situation struck me. I had seen it only as the tragedy of Jack and Sylvia and Margaret, but what was their loneliness to that of the old woman, to whom tragedy presented itself as in a foreign tongue?' (384–5). Even when she is obligated to watch her son desecrate all she has taught him, to have lost family in Margaret and Teddy and her last opportunity to care for another generation, she remains compassionate with no hint of self-congratulation. Initially, her commentary seems oblique, her philosophical position undeveloped, but her love and innocence offer profound alternatives to sexual encounters that end in abandonment. Only Phil recognizes her wisdom and acknowledges it by keeping her secret, acting out the idea that some things must be kept private. Although he has listened to everyone's confidences, he chooses a surprising discretion. When Sylvia, still alluring, turns to him for affection, he refuses to imitate Jack, either for his own pleasure or to help Sylvia get revenge. 'Lonely rock' ends with his words, 'I had shifted my allegiance.' Although Phil's epiphany is charged more by sympathy than moral illumination, it seems genuine, as he turns away from the 'modern' and makes a small, perhaps futile, gesture to champion the integration of body and soul. Even more telling than Phil's flat statement is his view of the inhabitants of the house once Margaret and Teddy are gone. Sylvia and Margaret, he thinks, 'were linked by something which excluded Jack. To each of them her moment of sacrifice had come, and each had risen to it, but nobody can live on that plane forever, and now there stretched before them the commonplace of life with no prospect that ever again it would call on them in the same way' (383).

At the end, because Jack has thought only of the moment and what it offers him, his future is empty. Because he has denied his obligations to others, he is alone, complaining and bewildered. Although he has had the most power, he has done the most damage, and his awareness never goes beyond his own hurt feelings. The papier-mâché marriage he and Sylvia have had has disintegrated, although they continue to enact its routines. But his fellow characters seem almost as incomplete. Margaret removes Teddy from his ideal grandparent, and readers must wonder about their future, with no rescuer at hand in a world less tolerant of single mothers. Sylvia, once Jack's best pupil, then his eager accomplice, continues morally unaware, and her magnanimous act has not transformed the lives of the characters in any permanent way, although one might argue that she has saved Teddy's life. Phil has intermittently acted on his feelings and gained a partial understanding, but he seems exhausted by the effort: his statement that he has shifted his allegiance is both passive and removed. In his case, perception does not carry with it the power to affect change.

Only Mrs Courtenay remains whole, yet she is neither young nor vigorous. And, as a transient guest in an alien world, aware of her mortality, she is powerless to change others. Her restraint seems noble, and she even chooses not to judge what she sees as wrong; she can only mourn its consequences. When she dies, no one will care for children and grandchildren with the same selflessness; the history she embodies dies with her. And the loss is much sadder because so few of the characters understand it. Ultimately, this is a story of communities discarded and attempted. Nineteenth-century Cork, shaped by traditional beliefs, is disdained as obsolete, but modern London seems filled with figures that have unthinkingly chosen illusory freedoms that entrap them. Read in the most simplistic way, this story might seem bare, stating two elementary principles: 1) any individual act has larger effects; 2) adultery reverberates in ways unimaginable in the heat of passion; but O'Connor's feelings for his characters make 'Lonely rock' grieving, powerful, and generous. Even Jack's selfishness is portrayed as destructive but not malicious.

The story's place in O'Connor's work is also clear, as it follows the arc familiar from 'Guests of the nation' and 'The man of the world,' among other fictions, where a character uncomfortable in a treacherous situation chooses not to acclimate himself to it, and the story tracks his increasing separation from what he sees as wrong, ending in some version of moral recognition. But that journey from ignorance to enlightenment is not Phil's alone. 'Lonely rock' is also about its readers, individuals transformed by the experience of reading. If we enter this text expecting a light, salacious story about the pleasures of 'open' marriage and the archaism of our grandmothers' values, our expectations reproach us at the end.

Because O'Connor recreated his stories and their titles so often, the details of his publishing history are revealing. No manuscripts or typescripts exist of his first version of the story, written in 1946, but apparently he called it 'The grand-mother', direct homage to its central figure. The title by which we know it is a link to his 1939 story, 'The bridal night', about the unrequited love that drives Denis Sullivan, a young country boy, to madness, and his elderly mother's grief that he will never be fulfilled as husband or parent. In the story, she thinks to herself, 'God help us, it was an old song of my father's that was going through my head, "Lonely rock is the one wife my children will know".'[2] That song, 'The lone rock,' is a lament attributed to Conor O'Leary for four young men drowned at sea; the title refers to Carraig Aonair. The reference asks us to consider that death is all around us, enacted in the air-raid alerts, the apocalyptic noise in the skies, signalling the possible end of a civilization. The song also comments on the way that Jack and Sylvia confront the war, almost in jest. In 'The bridal night', the song hints at unfulfilled yearning, solace denied, which suggests a connection to Teddy, rejected by Jack, a child who will be watched over by someone not his mother. But I think O'Connor's use of the song points again to Mrs Courtenay, who *is* indeed a lone rock: isolated, mourning yet unshaken in her beliefs.

In April 1953, O'Connor sent the story to Gus Lobrano, a fiction editor at the *New Yorker*, saying that it was among his 'half dozen best', an enthusiastic state-ment not typical of him. Lobrano, who sometimes missed the point of O'Connor's stories, praised it vaguely as 'a fine idea and, in general, nicely done', but 'a bit hurried, particularly in reference to Sylvia, after Margaret and the baby leave the house.' He would not accept it as it stood, and urged O'Connor to rethink it as he suggested, which O'Connor chose not to do.[3] I think little of Lobrano's decision to turn the story down, but his reaction is a paradoxical tribute to 'Lonely rock,' at once complete as written and a sketch for an unwritten novel, following the characters as if we needed to know what they would do to the end of their lives. O'Connor's agent offered it to *Harper's*, where it was published in 1954

2 Frank O'Connor, 'The bridal night', *Collected stories* (New York, 1982), 24.   **3** Michael Steinman (ed.), *The happiness of getting it down right: letters of Frank O'Connor and William Maxwell* (New York, 1996), 17–18.

as 'Ladies of the house,' a title which may not have been his choice, suggesting, perhaps, that someone else saw it as a light comedy or thought O'Connor's chosen title would mean nothing to American readers. Ultimately, O'Connor chose 'Lonely rock' as the closing story of his second American anthology, the 1956 *More stories*, his placement suggesting he thought it intensely and personally important. What story could follow it?

Ultimately, 'Lonely rock' is radical for its time in its praise of nineteenth-century ideals that O'Connor's literary contemporaries may have thought old-fashioned. It celebrates love, the emotional more than the carnal variety, for its own sake even when that love falls short or is insufficient balm, and commemorates personal devotion to religious ideals. It dramatizes how traditional forms, like marriage, built on mutual expectations, can be destroyed when someone chooses pure gratification, perceiving monogamous love, sexual fidelity, and parental responsibility as obstacles to pleasure. (And for those readers who identify O'Connor first with 'My Oedipus complex' and 'First confession,' I must point out that it is a story about sorrowing adults whose problems cannot be repaired, not little boys whose tragedies can be made to disappear by a kind adult.) O'Connor's famous image for the transformation essential to a short story was that 'an iron bar must be bent'. Here, the bar is terribly fragile and it snaps. The Courtenay house seems a microcosm of a struggle between ideologies, a demonstration of what becomes of principles when virtue has been cast off as tiresome. Ultimately, 'Lonely rock' is so avant-garde as to suggest that our parents' and grandparents' beliefs may not have been quite as wrong-headed as we always thought. And that is a kind of radicalism that O'Connor is not often given credit for.

In fairness, however, the very notion of radical conservatism may strike some readers as illogical, and I would be reluctant to use it as a way of characterizing his work in general. The Irish government of the 1940s certainly saw nothing conservative (read: 'commendable') in his Don Juan stories, and current readers may see nothing radical (read: 'commendable') in his stories celebrating wise ancestors, home, and love. It is plausible that 1946 readers might have seen Phil's new understanding of Mrs Courtenay as the only correct action, one that he (and Jack) should have been doing all along; perhaps future readers will wonder why Jack, Sylvia, and Margaret do not embark on a ménage of the kind we read of in certain personals advertisements. Yet those hypothetical reactions may be valid only as imagined snapshots of a particular moral climate of that time and place.

I propose that O'Connor's work will be read and re-read precisely because it

forces us to question those terms and definitions. Although acts and their consequences may be perceived in a relativistic way, so that what once seemed radical
now seems conservative, his essential championing of moral absolutes remains
constant. However, the situations that characters find themselves in and create are
so complicated as to make the search for those moral absolutes a difficult one. It is
easy to read 'Guests of the nation' and say (from a comfortable position) that its
point is that war is evil and one should not kill one's friends, but the story is deeper
and sadder than that. 'Lonely rock' champions love and monogamy, but suggests
that adherence to such ideals is not always the first reaction of flawed characters.
O'Connor's characters are always being asked or compelled to question their allegiances, with not always predictable results. Readers at times wish to reach into a
story and upbraid a character, or, at the very least, say, 'Why are you doing that?
Should you do that?' That is the mark of a fiction so lifelike that it will not stay on
the page – and although academics may gently tell their inexperienced students
that arguing with literary characters is a particularly futile pastime, I think it is
only the highest art that provokes in readers the absolute need to do so.

Coloured balloons: Frank O'Connor on Irish modernism

CAROL TAAFFE

In his introduction to a 1964 American edition of *A portrait of the artist as a young man*, O'Connor confessed that on first reading the book at the age of seventeen, Joyce had influenced him more than any other Irish writer. This unqualified admiration was short-lived, though in 1930 he was still sufficiently enthusiastic about Joyce's work to give high praise to *Work in progress* in the *Irish Statesman* – and this at a time when Joyce's reception in Ireland was almost resoundingly negative.[1] But O'Connor's introduction to *A portrait*, written towards the end of his own career, traces a gradual and inevitable disenchantment with what he now considered the 'associative mania' of *Finnegans wake*. For him, the readable portions of *Ulysses* had also dwindled year by year, 'till I was left with only twenty-five per cent of the book and had to admit that Joyce not only had no sense of organic design but – what was much worse – no vision of human life that had developed beyond the age of twenty-one'.[2] The self-styled humanist man of letters was now calling foul on the 'logomachic wordsmith'.[3] For O'Connor, the accumulating mass of academic criticism on Joyce was itself an indictment of his literary methods:

> Why should a work of art have to be subjected to analysis? And where is the Joyce whom Stanislaus knew and who cared deeply about the things Stanislaus and myself and so many others cared about and who never grew up?[4]

Whether this 'lost' Joyce was obliterated by later academic scholarship or by the cursive complexities of *Finnegans wake*, the insistence on a lost opportunity is suggestive. As O'Connor saw him, the masterful but hollow rhetorician who concocted *A portrait* was preceded by the 'poor, angry and idealistic' moralist who wrote *Stephen hero*: 'and to him the material had mattered intensely'.[5] It was this

1 Frank O'Connor, 'Joyce – the third period', *Irish Statesman* (12 Apr. 1930), 114–16. **2** Frank O'Connor, 'Introduction' to James Joyce, *A portrait of the artist as a young man* (New York, 1964), xvii. **3** Anthony Cronin, *No laughing matter: the life and times of Flann O'Brien* (London, 1989), 52. **4** O'Connor, 'Introduction', *A portrait*, xix–xx. **5** Ibid., xvii–xviii.

Joyce with whom the 17-year-old had identified, a writer who communicated with 'rage, anguish, pity, awkwardness' his experience of Irish life. The implication was that each writer's art was rooted in the kind of invigorating moral outrage that only Ireland could provoke, but evidently one of them had since gone astray along the way. His criticism of Joyce's later work certainly seems partly inspired by a hangover of revivalist ideas about the instrumental role of culture and art in the life of the nation. But equally revealing of O'Connor's priorities as a writer and critic – and how these reflected the values of a culture he so frequently criticized – is his irritation that a Joycean aesthetic deemed by *popular* consensus to be remote and inaccessible could hardly fulfill such a role.

Slightly perverse though it might seem that he would use his introduction to *A portrait* to express his ultimate disillusionment with Joyce, the context of his critical statement is telling. O'Connor, now a familiar figure to American readers from his stories in the *New Yorker*, was introducing a popular edition of a modern classic and in doing so, speaking as (slightly aggrieved) reader to reader. In some sense, he was deliberately patching up the lines of communication which had been equally deliberately ruptured by modernism, discounting the stylistic innovations in Joyce's work as products of the 'rhetorician's dream' in order to excavate an underlying universal, humanist element. The message was a comforting one; Joyce's prose might be read as a species of crossword puzzle, satisfying in its own way to the detective instinct, but it was the moral, and not the intellectual, instinct that was more valuable in literature (and it is not incidental that it was also more comprehensible to the reader). His initial response to Joyce was accurately represented as little more than an adolescent infatuation, since by the late 1930s he had already became a peculiarly rebarbative critic of Joyce's work. The antagonism was hardly unusual among Irish prose writers of his generation, most of whom stolidly ignored literary developments on the continent. The few who did engage with modernism, such as Flann O'Brien, managed at best a finely-honed ambivalence towards it. But what can be seen in O'Connor's criticism of Joyce over the following decades is a rather more contrived conflict of cultural values, an opposition, in his own terms, between the intellectual and the instinctive writer. This self-styled opposition between the two writers is itself emblematic of what O'Connor's biographer, James Matthews, has described as a 'partition' in literary Dublin: 'the alignment into rival camps pitting the Flann O'Briens and Francis Stuarts against the Frank O'Connors and Seán O'Faoláins'.[6] It was a version of

6 James Matthews, *Voices: a life of Frank O'Connor* (Dublin, 1983), 353.

literary history already being crafted by O'Connor in the 1940s and whatever it owed to personal politics, it was one he reiterated throughout his critical writing. The historical narrative he developed over the years, culminating in the lectures posthumously collected in *The backward look*, found little place for Irish modernism. Though this last work devotes two chapters to Joyce, they betray O'Connor's critical predicament – on the one hand, acknowledging Joyce's international status by presenting him as a counterpart (or counterweight) to Yeats, while providing a rather back-handed assessment of *Ulysses* as his 'manic'[7] technical masterpiece, valuable primarily for 'its description of the poetry of everyday life in Dublin in the first decade of this century'.[8]

Ironically, O'Connor and Flann O'Brien were more similar in their critical response to Joyce than might be assumed from their vastly dissimilar fiction, both being as preoccupied with his reputed egotism and arrogance as were most of their contemporaries in Ireland. O'Brien's sardonic impatience with the Joyce who 'asked of his readers nothing but that they should devote their lives to reading his works', a method of spending a lifetime sure to endow them with 'a unique psychic apparatus',[9] chimes with O'Connor's more empathetic address to the readers he was introducing to Joyce through the Time Reading Programme. In any case, in the looking-glass world of wartime Dublin, there was no easy division between an internationalist, modernist band of Irish writers and those, like O'Connor, whose work was more obviously indebted to the cultural ethos of post-revival, post-independence Ireland. By the mid-1940s it was O'Brien, the peculiarly domesticated modernist, who was wholly dependent on an Irish readership, his only literary outlet now being his *Cruiskeen Lawn* column in the *Irish Times*. O'Connor, on the other hand, was in the opposite position; with censorship limiting the domestic market for his books, his fractious relationship with contemporary Ireland (and its blacklisters) led to periods of self-imposed exile in London working for the BBC. Like O'Faoláin, who published abroad throughout the war years but whose fiction was censored at home, O'Connor was cast into the role of mediator between an insular, neutral Ireland and an international readership. His post-war *Irish Miles* was typical of many books which provided tourist trips of independent Ireland as a slightly exotic theocratic state, but it was

7 Frank O'Connor, *The backward look* (London, 1967), 204. 8 Ibid., 209. 9 Myles na gCopaleen [Flann O'Brien], 'Cruiskeen Lawn', *Irish Times* (20 Dec. 1957). Similarly, the varied contributors whom O'Brien gathered for the special Joyce issue of *Envoy* which he edited in April 1951 – including Denis Johnston, 'Andrew Cass' [John Garvin], Niall Montgomery, and Patrick Kavanagh – produced a rather ambivalent portrait of Joyce as a brilliant crank.

Horizon's Irish issue of January 1942 (devised, according to Cyril Connolly, to balance the neutral state's hostile press in Britain) which firmly fixed O'Connor and O'Faoláin as the central interpreters of the Irish literary scene to this broader public. In doing so, both took the opportunity to set out their own stall in the literary marketplace. Where O'Faoláin's contribution assessed the mixed legacy of Yeats for the new generation, O'Connor's ill-fated essay on 'The future of Irish literature' was a forceful statement of his thesis that de Valera's 'Holy Ireland' (caught in the stranglehold of censorship and with 'a fanatical and corrupt middle-class')[10] needed a literature that critically engaged with Irish life. While his polemic attracted predictable criticism in Ireland, it also irritated some contemporaries who – while being similarly disillusioned with the state culture – nevertheless detected a whiff of self-promotion in the piece:

> We are told (so help me) that Irish literature began with Yeats and Synge and Lady Gregory. That's a quare one for you. As to the future of the thing, we have four pages on Mr Seán O'Faoláin (good man, Seán) and a half a page on Mr Patrick Kavanagh. From the phrase 'when O'Faoláin and I began to write…' one deduces that Mr O'Connor is there too. This will help anybody writing an M.A. thesis. We now know where Irish literature began and the names of the three gentlemen responsible for sustaining it. Fair enough.[11]

It was characteristic of Myles na gCopaleen to be exasperated at being excluded from any important affair, much less the future of Irish literature, but his exclusion was tellingly echoed in the omission of writers such as Francis Stuart, Samuel Beckett, and Denis Devlin. Otherwise the most notable absence is Liam O'Flaherty, but O'Connor manages passing references to Kate O'Brien, Elizabeth Bowen, Yeats, Synge, Æ, Lady Gregory, Padraic Colum and Gerald O'Donovan. While Joyce turns up briefly, it is as the author of *A portrait*, the novel which 'every Irish writer who isn't a rogue or an imbecile is doomed to write when the empti-

---

10 Frank O'Connor, 'The future of Irish literature', *Horizon*, 5:25 (Jan. 1942), 62. 11 Myles na gCopaleen, 'Cruiskeen Lawn', *Irish Times* (2 Mar. 1942). Roibéard Ó Faracháin wrote in more vitriolic terms that provoked an angry response from O'Connor: 'One is successively angry, weary, indulgent, and perhaps, finally just bored, by Mr O'Connor's tantrums, eccentric literary judgments, and pathetic championship of great writers who are their own best champions. It is refreshing to find that Mr O'Connor believes we need satire. We do, indeed. And one could name one gorgeous subject.' *Irish Times* (21 Feb. 1942).

ness and horror of Irish life begins to dawn on him'.[12] O'Connor's partial appropriation of Joyce, as a Catholic dominated by his Irish material (as the Anglo-Irish revivalists were not),[13] ironically only serves to reinforce a sense that the modernist strain was being stealthily written out of contemporary Irish literature. Admittedly, O'Connor was not soberly surveying the literary field but setting an agenda for Irish writing; where he looked abroad for inspiration, it was pointedly to the political consciousness of British writers in the 1930s rather than to the modernist revolutions of the previous decades.[14] But the easy confidence inherent in the phrase, 'when O'Faoláin and I began to write', is telling. While it might be understandable that in the political heat of the 1930s this disillusioned, post-revolutionary generation threw out 'the modernist baby with the Romantic bathwater of the Literary Revival',[15] the curiosity is that it was an act so uncontroversial that it could be wholly unacknowledged.

Certainly, modernism hardly penetrated the arts in Ireland until 1943's Exhibition of Living Art, discounting a minor flurry of short-lived modernist journals like *Klaxon* and *Tomorrow* in the early 1920s. But with *Ulysses* quickly hailed as a masterpiece, and the ever more notorious *Work in progress* appearing piecemeal over the 1920s and 1930s, Joyce's position for the next generation of Irish prose writers was already promising to be overbearing. By 1937, Niall Sheridan was complaining in a review of Irish fiction that the dominance of Joyce was now so complete that Dublin itself was beginning to look like 'an inferior plagiarism from *Ulysses*'.[16] But Joyce was also becoming an important piece of cultural currency for younger writers; Samuel Beckett's stark sketch of the Irish literary scene in his 1934 review of 'Recent Irish poetry', which notoriously divided contemporary poets between 'antiquarians and others',[17] ossified Gaels and modernist innovators, had plainly drawn a new set of battlelines. The student narrator of *At swim-two-birds*, which was published at the end of the 1930s, had only to refer briefly to the contents of his limited bookshelf, ranging from the works of 'Mr Joyce to the widely read books of Mr A. Huxley'[18] to signal his credentials as a cynical sophisticate at odds with the culture of the Irish Free State. Wherever 'Mr A. Huxley' was

---

12 O'Connor, 'The future of Irish literature', 61. **13** See ibid., 58–9. **14** 'It is the way Spender, Day Lewis and Auden took in England, and it has always been a regret of mine that there was no corresponding movement in Ireland where the need for it was so much greater.' Ibid., 62. **15** Terence Brown, 'Ireland, modernism and the 1930s' in Patricia Coughlan and Alex Davis (eds), *Modernism and Ireland* (Cork, 1995), 38. **16** Niall Sheridan, 'The Joyce country', *Ireland Today*, 2:11 (Nov. 1937), 88. **17** Samuel Beckett, 'Recent Irish poetry', *Disjecta* (London, 1983), 70. **18** Flann O'Brien, *At swim-two-birds* (London, 2000), 11.

widely read it was not in Ireland, where his books were swiftly banned under the 1929 Censorship Act. From this perspective, the internationalism, ingenuity and relentless experimentation associated with modernism provided a natural antidote to the provincial and conservative culture of which O'Connor was so critical. Yet, as noted earlier, his own initial appropriation of Joyce was on significantly different terms. And despite Joyce's potential as a figurehead for opposition, by the time *Finnegans wake* was published in 1939, he appears to have solidified for O'Connor (and O'Faoláin) into a monomaniacal parody of himself. Already by the late 1930s, O'Connor was arguing that though *A portrait* created a protagonist whose 'despair is the despair of Ireland', it was nevertheless 'an extreme and fantastic book'[19] replete with an ugly hostility towards Ireland, and one to grow out of. His 1943 profile of Joyce in *The Bell* reduces him to a derivative artisan prone to literary affectation. It is hard to reconcile O'Connor's confession here to be a 'hero-worshipper'[20] of Joyce with his 'strong sense' of Joyce's artistic failure. Joyce's curious, not profound, elaborate, not subtle, cast of mind betrayed him in the second portion of *Ulysses*:

> as though the self-conscious literary artist were being doubled by a drunken Dublin medico whose superstition makes him avoid the mortar lines on the pavement and whose intellectual level is Gilbert and Sullivan. Joyce's virtuosity seems to me to belong to a second rate brain.[21]

O'Connor's much earlier, and short-lived, enthusiasm for the writer reflected Joyce's initial reception in Ireland as a representative of a disenfranchised Catholic middle class and as a realist whose fiction served as a rebuke to the grandeur of the Yeatsian aesthetic.[22] Both perspectives were obviously more difficult to maintain in the face of his later work. Padraic Colum could flag *A portrait* in 1918 as a 'profoundly Catholic book',[23] the first of its kind to allow Europe and America a glimpse of Irish Catholic life, but by 1943, for O'Connor the lure of authenticity had given way to an impatience with Joyce's pathological posturing. Stephen

---

19 Frank O'Connor, 'A broadcast that was cancelled: Lawrence and Joyce', *Irish Times* (21 July 1937).
20 Frank O'Connor, 'James Joyce – a post-mortem', *The Bell*, 5:5 (Feb. 1943), 370.   **21** Ibid., 371.
22 On this peculiarly Irish accommodation of Joyce see Joseph Brooker, *Joyce's critics* (Madison, WI, 2004).   **23** Padraic Colum, 'James Joyce', *Pearson's Magazine* (May 1918), repr. in Robert H. Deming (ed.), *James Joyce: the critical heritage: vol. 1, 1907–27* (London, 1997), 165. This reading can be seen as late as Thomas MacGreevy's 'The Catholic element in *Work in progress*' in Samuel Beckett et al., *Our exagmination round his factification for incamination of work in progress* (New York, 1929; repr. 1972), 117–27.

Dedalus was not, as Joseph Hone hailed him in 1923, 'a type of young Irishman of the towns ... now a dominating figure in the public life of Ireland',[24] but – in O'Connor's words – the '*composed* character of the shabby-genteel artist',[25] reminiscent of nothing but his creator, and his creator's vanities.

The culmination of this line of thinking can be seen in O'Connor's 1944 BBC broadcast on Joyce, which exposed the roots of his aversion to Joyce's work. By this time, it was not only the hectic orchestrator of *Finnegans wake*, but the more accessible Joyce of *Dubliners* whom O'Connor considered to be an entirely 'self-centred' writer. For all the 'wonderful things' to be found in the former work, it was 'the culminating point of Irish literary egotism. Beyond it, there is the asylum; behind, a long, long way behind, is the reality to which our younger writers must sooner or later retrace their steps'.[26] O'Connor's image of modernism as a form of literary derangement, an outgrowth of Joyce's overweening arrogance and above all, the antithesis of his own realist aesthetic neatly shuts down the alternative reading which attracted some of Joyce's earliest Irish critics. Ironically, in 1929 it was Joyce to whom O'Connor was tracing his steps, paying his pilgrimage to the writer in Paris as did Samuel Beckett, Denis Devlin, Thomas MacGreevy and Flann O'Brien (albeit via a complimentary copy of *At swim-two-birds*). This rite of passage becomes more explicable if it is considered that in 1923, Ernest Boyd could flourish Joyce as a torch-bearer for a new post-revival mood, greeting *Ulysses* – one of his supposedly manic texts – as 'simultaneously a masterpiece of realism, of documentation, and a most original dissection of the Irish mind ... [Dedalus and Bloom] serve as the medium between the reader and the *vie unanime* of a whole community'.[27] A similar image of the individual character as a medium to a whole community would turn up in O'Connor's critical writing, but the difficulty in tracing any lineage of Irish realism from Joyce to O'Faoláin and O'Connor is the latter's almost visceral rejection of his work. While, in *The backward look*, he echoed Boyd in depicting Yeats and Joyce as thesis and antithesis, 'the idealist and the realist, the countryman and the townsman, the dead past and the unborn future',[28] he often implicitly placed himself on the Yeatsian side of that division. Apart from his personal relationship with Yeats as a young man, he had publicly secured the imprimatur of the older writer with his directorship of the Abbey

24 Joseph Hone, 'A letter from Ireland', *London Mercury*, v (Jan. 1923), repr. in *James Joyce: the critical heritage*, 298. **25** Frank O'Connor, 'James Joyce – a post-mortem', 368. My italics. **26** BBC Radio (18 May 1944), published as 'Egotism in Irish literature. Frank O'Connor on James Joyce', *The Listener* (1 June 1944), 609. **27** Ernest Boyd, *Ireland's literary renaissance* (rev. ed. 1923) in *James Joyce: the critical heritage*, 304. **28** O'Connor, *The backward look*, 162.

theatre in the late 1930s, and it was a connection which he sustained in his criticism and memoirs.[29] Tellingly, the image of Joyce which emerges throughout his occasional literary journalism – the rarefied magician, the obsessive intellectual 'with a second-rate brain' – is a figure who notably lacks the superior instincts of the unscholarly Yeats, as O'Connor saw him.

In casting himself as a similarly instinctive writer, he could certainly imply that Joyce did not naturally speak for his own constituency, the 'young Irishman of the towns'. The very different literary identity which O'Connor was concerned to develop is illustrated in his 1945 guide, *Towards an appreciation of literature*. Aimed at the inexperienced reader, this opens (like his later introduction to *A portrait*) with an anecdote about his own reading experience as a young man. O'Connor again puts himself in the place of his projected readers, recalling a haphazard process of self-education through the public library as well as the more unusual fortune of falling under the tutelage of Daniel Corkery (unnamed), A.E. and Seán O'Faoláin. Not only does he identify with the reader instinctively groping his or her way through modern literature, his version of a literary education is deliberately humanist rather than scholarly, emphasising above all its powers of communication:

> I came to literature as I fancy a great many people come to it, because they need companionship, and a wider and more civilized form of life than they can find in the world about them …[30]

O'Connor's comforting idea of a literary community (with an added hint of self-improvement) bears out his statement that the nineteenth-century realist novel, which provided his literary education, 'coloured and limited'[31] his views of literature. While he admits that '*Ulysses* opened up a new world'[32] to his generation, his assessment of the modernist novelists – naming Joyce, Proust and D.H. Lawrence as the most influential – is predictably double-edged. His final image in the book is of a modern literature uncertain what to do with the 'Little Man' crowded into the great modern secular cities, oscillating between the introspection of the writer who recoils from the urban mass (a Stephen Dedalus), or reacts to them with 'distasteful objectivity' (producing a Leopold Bloom). This introspection, which he identifies in the turn towards autobiography in the modern novel, seems only a

29 'O'Faoláin, myself, and I suspect Clarke and Kavanagh are merely the strayed revellers of the Irish literary revival …', ibid., 229. **30** Frank O'Connor, *Towards an appreciation of literature* (Dublin, 1945), 7. **31** Ibid., 13. **32** Ibid., 54.

more polite version of the egotism he earlier criticized in Joyce. But in this case, his analysis ends with a rumination on the fate of this disdained 'Little Man', a cipher who can be drilled into order by communism, or 'killed off in very large numbers as required – Kulaks, Communists, Japanese – the atomic bomb is a notable addition to the list of valuable scientific discoveries and will shortly make it impossible for the Little Man to live in cities at all.'[33] The associative link O'Connor makes between modernism and totalitarianism, two products of this historical moment, is allowed to drift off inconclusively. Nevertheless, it posits a dangerously distorted relationship between the modernist writer and the community, and one notably at odds with the empathy which his own autobiographical comments strive to establish with the reader.

The indiscriminate crowd haunting many modernist works found a peculiarly Irish incarnation in Corkery's image of the Irish writer 'sprung from the people'[34] who was emotionally and intellectually in tune with the thousands at a hurling match in Thurles. (Fittingly, it was mass spectator sport, a nineteenth-century import from a more urbanized Britain, which provided Corkery with his image of the massed Irish crowd, otherwise a fairly rare entity in depopulated rural Ireland.) O'Connor's attempted identification with the reader is closer to Corkery's image of the writer in tune with the people than it is to his own caricature of the modernist writer. Though O'Connor's lyric on the consolations of literature posits an imagined community that offers an escape from reality, 'a more civilized form of life' than that commonly available, the stress on empathy chimes more readily with Corkery's desire for a collective identity than it does with the picture of the solipsistic modernist writer haughtily removed from the 'Little Man'. In his terms, this modern literature is devoid of humanity, a point underlined by the startling imagery of annihilation which recurs in the conclusion to his 1956 study of the modern novel, *The mirror in the roadway*. In *Ulysses* (and later *Finnegans wake*), O'Connor complains, Joyce 'reduces man himself to a metaphor': 'Like the atom bomb, this can result only in the liquidation of humanity, and humanity has no choice but to re-trace its steps and learn the business of living all over again'.[35] The explosive imagery was far from new – it certainly would have met with the approval of Wyndham Lewis thirty years earlier – but while O'Connor invests it with the hindsight of the post-war world, he would have been on safer ground addressing it to the editor of *Blast* (and infatuated biographer of Hitler) than to Joyce's work.

33 Ibid., 57.   **34** Daniel Corkery, *Synge and Anglo-Irish literature* (Cork, 1966), 15.   **35** Frank O'Connor, *The mirror in the roadway* (New York, 1956), 312.

But such extreme responses to modernist literature were notoriously wide-spread and, for a great part, invited and provoked by modernist authors themselves. Perhaps the greater curiosity is that O'Connor drew such a stark opposition between the lonely modernist writer and the masses and nevertheless, in striving for empathy between the writer and the reader, implicitly (if unwittingly) aligned himself more closely with Corkery's model of the writer intuitively at one with 'the people'. (Though even Corkery's image has something of the lonely, individualistic O'Connor touch, describing his 'crowd' as an assembly of individual souls.) With the figure of the loner and the outsider resonating throughout his short stories – and being central to his critical writing on the form – O'Connor had more in common with the disaffected Stephen Dedalus than he cared to admit. While his earlier depiction of Joycean modernism as a kind of literary psychosis was anticipated in 1929 by Seán O'Faoláin's acerbic response to *Anna Livia Plurabelle*, O'Faoláin placed Joyce in a venerable tradition of distracted Irish visionaries which might have had a place for the idealistic Michael O'Donovan:

> is he not of the clan of Brendan who sailed for Ui Bhreasail, Bran who sailed for the Land of Heart's Desire, Ossian searching for the Land of the Ever Young ... Sweeney who lived in the tops of the trees that he might be like a bird, Cuirthir who would go in passion beyond Hell or Paradise, dreamers of the unattainable all.[36]

As a blacklisted critic in 1940s Ireland, a writer whose fiction was often denied a domestic readership, and an author working in the wake of modernism who nevertheless prized above all the lines of personal communication between writer and reader, O'Connor was perhaps another dreamer of the unattainable. His imagined community offering 'a more civilized form of life' forms a slightly desolate contrast to the 'lonely voice' of his short stories and particularly to his own uncertain reception in mid-century Ireland. Alongside O'Faoláin, he provided a vocal opposition to the conservative culture of de Valera's Ireland, with his criticism of contemporary Irish society being perhaps the more familiar aspect of his 1942 article on 'The future of Irish literature'. Nevertheless, the roots of his antipathy to modernist writers, who by default occupied a similarly oppositional position in post-independence Ireland, underline his own intellectual sympathies with that culture.

---

36 Seán O'Faoláin, 'Anna Livia Plurabelle', *Irish Statesman* (5 Jan. 1929), 354.

This is most clearly (and bizarrely) illustrated in the fact that however different the two writers, critical remarks made on O'Connor's work by his Irish contemporaries tend to echo his own complaints about Joyce. Whatever their true offences against literature, the response to each from their disaffected peers seems to draw on a common pool of Irish literary taboos. Flann O'Brien, for one, uncharitably diagnosed more egotism than realism in O'Connor's 1947 architectural travel book, *Irish miles* (or *Irish smiles*, as he dubbed it). O'Connor's pen portraits of the characters he passed along Irish roads, as he 'cycled about the country in shorts accompanied by ladies with French names', met with a withering response: 'It's one way of seeing the country, I suppose, though it seems to have more merit as an all-out plan *for being seen*. There's quite a point there, mind you. If you want to see really clearly, you must yourself be invisible, otherwise you are altering the sum of what you want to see by the addition of yourself.'[37] But O'Brien was not only perturbed by the paltry illusions, or delusions, of the realist writer who captured himself in every frame. More pointed was his response to O'Connor's attempts to 'draw out' the country people he met in conversation. These were another incarnation of 'the Little Man', the submerged population groups of *The lonely voice* that provided the foundation of O'Connor's short stories – those whom he felt Joyce's *Dubliners* had deprived of 'autonomy' by mediating their voices through the writer's irony.[38] O'Brien unwittingly reversed O'Connor's criticism of Joyce and, as he had in *At swim-two-birds*, hands autonomy back to the characters captured by the visiting writer cum anthropologist:

> I think the specimens have analytic powers at least as good as Mr O'Connor's but functioning much more efficiently, since the specimens are at home in their own kitchen, dressed soberly according to their station, quite at ease and with judgment unimpaired by superciliousness. *What was said after Mr O'Connor left?* ... Having read the book, why cannot the reader read the Other Book?[39]

Debunking the illusion of the realist aesthetic was wholly characteristic of O'Brien, who was constitutionally incapable of ignoring the nuts and bolts of fiction. But along with more personal jibes at the Corkman's avowed homesickness for the Strand, the supercilious literary caricature he creates ironically anticipates the modernist strawman of O'Connor's later criticism.

37 Flann O'Brien, *Further cuttings from Cruiskeen Lawn* (London, 1976), 106–7. **38** Frank O'Connor, *The lonely voice* (London, 1963), 121–3. **39** O'Brien, *Further cuttings*, 107–8.

O'Brien was not alone; Patrick Kavanagh's 1947 profile of O'Connor in *The Bell* takes a similar line, though more broadly muddling personal and literary criticism. While his article more explicitly shows the homegrown suspicion of the Cork boy made good – Kavanagh being particularly concerned that O'Connor may be peddling stories of the good-humoured Irish to readers of the *Daily Mirror* – there is a similar preoccupation with the distance between O'Connor, 'our most exciting writer', and his chosen material. The distance may be perceived as a social one, the mark of his early influence by Anglo-Irish literary revivalists (and specifically Yeats), but it is one Kavanagh thinly disguises as a matter of aesthetics:

> Yeats created a pose of swift indifference to the common earth, and the same isolation in the thin air of 'literature' is to be found in O'Connor. To read him now was never to imagine that he had once lived in a poor street in Cork or worked at a draughty railway station … It would not be entirely true to say that O'Connor had entirely detached himself from his background, but he dimmed it into a literary mist.[40]

There are many issues at stake in Kavanagh's reading of O'Connor's work, which he pictures as coloured balloons taking off into the rarefied world of literature, having lost touch with 'the soil of common experience'.[41] However, one of its more unlikely products is this image of O'Connor's fiction as being swathed in 'a literary mist'. As with O'Connor's reading of Joyce, it is as if 'literature' itself is the antagonist here (though since this generation wrote in an age of indiscriminate literary censorship, the notion of 'literary fiction' was already primed to be a handily offensive term). Since O'Connor set up his own work as the antidote to Joyce's – which he presented as the prime example of literature run riot, having lost all touch with the humanity he wished to capture in his own stories – his criticism had ironically come full circle. This did not prevent him, in later years, from neatly re-appropriating Kavanagh's ammunition:

> In reading Joyce, one is reading Literature – Literature with a capital L. The tide rises about the little figures islanded here and there in a waste of

---

40 Patrick Kavanagh, 'Coloured balloons – a study of Frank O'Connor', *The Bell*, 15:3 (Dec. 1947), 12. The echo of his early poetic manifesto, 'Peasant', is pointed. He was the representative of a people without a literary tradition, '… of a race that will persist/when all the scintillating tribes of reason/ Are folded in a literary mist.' *Dublin Magazine* (Jan.–Mar. 1936), 3.   **41** Ibid., 13.

waters, and gradually they disappear till nothing is left but the blank expanse of Literature, mirroring the blank face of the sky.[42]

The image of isolation inherent in the 'islanded' figures overcome and elided by a tidal wave of 'Literature' is wholly characteristic of O'Connor. But in the version of Irish literary history he crafted over the years in his literary journalism, university lectures and published works, it is Joyce (and other Irish modernists) who are the figures excluded from the final picture. The partial recognition he gives to Joyce's work depends on eliminating those aspects of it that broke the taboos of Ireland's post-revival literary culture, the taboos of what Daniel Corkery might have considered a 'normal' literature.[43] Where good literature was assumed to be in touch with 'the healthy clay',[44] the unhealthily deranged modernism of *Ulysses* and *Finnegans wake* ensured that Joyce did not belong. But neither did O'Connor, at least according to the censors who sporadically excluded his work from the readers (and the society) his stories addressed. Concluding his *Bell* article with a final argumentative flourish, Kavanagh perversely managed to pair O'Connor off with Joyce. Both were fine technicians, he wrote, the kind of writers who won great contemporary fame but would not last. In very different ways, both were also victim to the judgments of their day.

---

42 O'Connor, *The mirror in the roadway*, 308. The terms in which Kavanagh criticizes O'Connor's short stories also anticipates his remarks on Joyce's attitude towards the characters of *Dubliners*: '... I find an implied sneer, an insincerity ... A great poet never sneers. He may show people sneering but he does not take part in it as the author of this seems to take part', in 'Coloured balloons – a study of Frank O'Connor', 20. On Joyce, see *The lonely voice*, 123.   **43** 'The writers in a normal country are one with what they write of. The life of every other people they gaze upon from without, but the life of their own people they cannot get outside of. That is why they belong.' *Synge and Anglo-Irish literature*, 13.   **44** Kavanagh, 'Coloured balloons – a study of Frank O'Connor', 11.

The interpretation of tradition

ALAN TITLEY

In the introduction to his survey of Irish literature, *The backward look*, Frank O'Connor asks, 'Is there such a thing as an Irish literature, or is it merely two unrelated subjects linked together by a geographical accident?'[1] This question has been central to studies of literature in Ireland for more than a hundred years and has been answered, as could be expected, in at least two different ways. On the one hand scholars of the Irish language or of what is sometimes quaintly called 'the Gaelic tradition' have tended to ignore writing in English; while those involved in what used to be known as 'the Anglo-Irish tradition' generally treat writing in Irish as a kind of background which validates but doesn't disturb their own point of view. Thus standard works such as Douglas Hyde's *A literary history of Ireland* or Robin Flower's *The Irish tradition* and Seamus Deane's *A short history of Irish literature* or Maurice Harmon's *Modern Irish literature, 1800–1967* seem to be dealing with entirely different universes. It doth seem that 'Irish' in these interminable debates can mean anything the author chooses it to mean within a clearly defined ideological position.

Although Frank O'Connor was never one to shirk a good row or hide his heart up his sleeve, it appears that his wrestling with this problem of one or two Irish literatures was genuine. He was ideally equipped to deal with the dilemma. Not only did he speak English and modern Irish, but he also was a considerable scholar of old Irish, which he learned out of his passion for the country's literature and civilization. This love is evident in all that he wrote about it, but most especially in his many translations of Irish poetry from the earliest times down unto the nineteenth century. Unlike most other writers on this topic, O'Connor concluded that he was dealing with one subject and that this merited a unified approach. Very few people have followed him down this road, although recent work by Declan Kiberd on modern Irish literature[2] and Robert Welch's *Oxford companion to Irish literature* straddle both traditions with generosity and honour.

To treat of literature in the Irish language from its beginning and to do so

---

1 Frank O'Connor, *The backward look* (London, 1967), 1. 2 See in particular Declan Kiberd, *Inventing Ireland: the literature of the modern nation* (London, 1995) and *Idir dhá chultúr* (Dublin, 1993).

outside the academy of accepted scholars might have been a foolhardy thing to do. Scholars can be a notoriously prickly bunch, guarding their borders with as much zeal as any armed functionary; and scholars of old Irish in particular can be notoriously aggressive in defending their *tuath* with adzes and spears against encroaching blow-ins. O'Connor, although sufficiently knowledgeable and tough-skinned to beat off any attack, had the good fortune to be supported in some of his ventures by one of the high kings of Irish scholarship, professor David Greene.[3] He may also have been seen to be at a disadvantage in approaching the critical enterprise as a mere writer, but mere writers, as we know, get inside the skin of craft and of wonder in ways that nobody else can.

Writers of English in Ireland have oft been required to stake out their position with regard both to the vast bulk of writing in Irish which preceded them and to the not inconsiderable stream which flows parallel to them. They can ignore it as many do, exploit it as Yeats did, parody it as Synge did, weave through it as Joyce did, have good fun with it as Myles na gCopaleen did, or worry over it as Thomas Kinsella does. There can also be the relationship of ambiguity which Frank O'Connor had. On the one hand he stated that literature in the Irish language 'may be said to have died' with Brian Merriman in 1805;[4] on the other, he wrote stories in it himself and translated poetry composed well after the death of Merriman.[5] Whatever he thought about his relationship to writing in Irish during his own time – and most of his life he simply kept his mouth shut about it – he saw it as a necessary duty to translate as much as possible of the earlier literature in order to make it known both at home and abroad. His books *The wild bird's nest*, *Lords and commons*, *The fountain of magic* and *The midnight court*, later variously selected to make *Kings, lords, & commons* (1961), are among the very best translations of Irish poetry that we have. This is in itself curious because O'Connor did not have any success or much interest in original poetry himself.

It is doubly curious because any translator of poetry must have a lively and sympathetic understanding of the society and of the people who produced it. I

---

3 David Greene and Frank O'Connor, *A golden treasury of Irish poetry, A.D. 600–1200* (London, 1967). He also says in his introduction to *The backward look* that in his discussions on Irish literature with professor Greene 'I have long ceased to remember whose ideas I have put forward, his or my own'. **4** Frank O'Connor, *Kings, lords, & commons* (London, 1961), xiii. **5** *Kings, lords, & commons*, 131 and 132–5. Also Frank O'Connor, *The fountain of magic* (London, 1939), 64, 67, 68, 72. For one of his short stories in Irish see 'Darcy i dTír na nÓg' in Tomás de Bhaldraithe, *Nuascéalaíocht* (Dublin, 1952), 24–32. Some of his radio essays or reminiscences which are very similar to his short stories appear in *Aeriris* (Dublin, 1976), edited by Proinsias Mac Aonghusa, under the titles 'Fiche bliain d'óige', 'Nodlaig as baile', 'Leabhar a theastaigh uaim', and 'Oíche shamhraidh'.

cannot argue that O'Connor didn't have this, but he had a decidedly quirky and sometimes even batty judgment of writers and works of literature which is both his glory and his weakness. He can be at turns brilliantly insightful, searingly imaginative, and then just plain wrong. But we are always aware of an intense and personal engagement with the literature. He shows no tiresome detachment, no two-handed objectivity, and when he gets bored he just tells us straight on up. The result is to draw us into the debate, and when we disagree with him, as I do again and again with equal vehemence, we feel that he would thoroughly enjoy a robust altercation about the nature of Irish literature and the possibilities of translation.

In *The backward look*, for example, he has a wonderful way with sweeping generalisations. 'The Irish had the choice between imagination and intellect', he declares, 'and they chose imagination' (5). Matthew Arnold and Lord Macauley and purveyors of the myth of the helpless, hapless Celt would agree. 'Unlike Daniel Corkery, who wrote a very lyrical and wrongheaded book on it, I can see nothing to admire in Irish eighteenth-century poetry' (*backward look*, 114). This is an awful lot of poetry, and poets, and matters, and genres not to admire. Of twelfth-century Irish literature he says, 'It has no real prose, and consequently no intellectual content' (*backward look*, 86). This will be grating music to the ears of our thousands of poets. Ranging over more than a thousand years, he refers to 'the Irish type of mind, which is largely the mind of primitive man everywhere' (*backward look*, 11). This could be construed as being an insult to the Irish or more seriously to those primitive men wheresoever they might dwell.

As against such opinions, his critical comments which depend on taste and judgment are often brave and incisive. He does argue that 'scholars who are also men of letters should trust their instincts' (*backward look*, 33), and we suspect he might be referring to himself. His opinion of the *Táin* or 'Cattle raid of Cooley' as 'a simply appalling text' and a 'rambling tedious account' of a long-forgotten war strike chords in honest readers (*backward look*, 33). He captures the mood of what most aristocratic poets must have felt when poetry deteriorated from syllabic to accentual in the seventeenth century: 'Every peasant poet was hammering it out with hobnailed boots like an ignorant audience listening to a Mozart minuet. It is no wonder if it offended O'Hussey's delicate ear; it often offends mine' (*backward look*, 107). We know that O'Connor despised the poetry of vassals and churls composed in the misery of their hutments. And his assertion that the golden era of early Irish literature 'ended with what I may call the Cistercian invasion, which in intellectual matters was direr than the Norman Invasion' may seem like the sweep of another totalizing impulse, but it does have pith and substance (*backward look*, 256).

These whanging declarations make us wake up and take note. The exaggerating posture usually contains a big truth. His humorous description of the early Irish noun having twenty-five different cases with beautiful scholarly names such as the 'neglective, desidative, fundative, privative, comitative, ascensive, augmentative, ingressive, depositive, parentative, progenitive, circumdative, and trespassive' (*backward look*, 19–20) has its echoes in the professor who wondered how anybody could speak Old Irish at all since its verbal system was so complicated. O'Connor set himself the task of interpreting this tradition (which he often claimed to find 'weird' and 'strange') to a modern audience through his own translations.

There is no need again to revisit the difficulties or even the impossibilities of translation. The translator must choose either sounds or sense or meter or rhyme or a combination of them, or must interpret or crib or rewrite or whatever, but everything altogether can not be done. No matter what you do, finally and in sum, a translation is not the original poem. It may be a shadow, or an echo, or a ghost, or an excretion, or alike to a discursive description of live music, or a flat photograph of a once-pulsing multidimensional image, but the real thing it ain't. For any decent writer words are physical, tactile, sensual things and the living stuff cannot be scraped away or washed off. The translator of Lorca's *Poet in New York*, Ben Belitt, argues that

> words, in whatever language, have a history which is not Esperanto or Sanskrit, or 'the history of mankind,' but the cultural consequence of their activity in the linguistic experience of the group – that words must be shouted into, like wells, rather than joined in a series like pipe-lengths; and finally, that for the poet, the momentum of words is as important and mysterious a trust as their matter, and that their momentum – their brio, their capacity to reveal the spirit at work within the letter – is rooted irrationally in the densities and ambiguities of the individual language.[6]

A translator will usually have the humility to acknowledge that cooking the original poetic goose leaves most of the sauce ungarnered and simply go for whatever is possible.

O'Connor's best translations from the early period of Irish literature are of those brief sententious poems occasionally written on the margins of manuscripts

---

6 Ben Benlitt, Introduction, *Poet in New York/Un poeta en Nueva York* (New York, 1955), n.p.

by either bored or frightened monks. In the Ireland of the ninth century the monasteries feared the barbarian Vikings who terrorized western Europe as well as their own patch. One scribe wrote in O'Connor's version:

> Since tonight the wind is high,
> The sea's white mane a fury
> I need not fear the hordes of Hell
> Coursing the Irish Channel.
>> (*Kings, lords, & commons*, 45)

Brendan Kennelly's translation reads:

> There's a wicked wind tonight
> Wild upheaval in the sea;
> No fear now that the Viking hordes
> Will terrify me.[7]

It is very difficult to compare both of these verses and entirely unnecessary to do so. They are epigrams that depend for their effect on our knowledge of what they are about and on their quick brevity. There is the added simplicity that the original does not carry any echoes that we can now grasp. Even though we can discern modern Irish lurking within the old, there is no way we can extract its feel or touch its tenor. The emotional impact of Old Irish is very largely a closed book. We can make a good guess at imitating its sound system but it reverberates nowhere; nothing sticks to it. Translators of the earlier poetry have generally gone for these brief marginal pieces because they circumvent the cultural battle of dealing with longer legal or encomiastic or quasi-official verse which did have echoes and did have all manner of cultural baggage and dingleberries hanging out of it. Even though very few people ever read these marginal poems for a thousand years between the ninth and the nineteenth century – perhaps nobody at all in most cases – they appeal to a modern sensibility which smells the pristine and the fresh from the birth of the Irish world off them, a dewy voice from the dawn of civilization. This is still hard to resist and the religious verse in their midst gives succour to tired twentieth-century Catholics in search of a coffee-table Celtic spirituality.

A different cultural problem faced O'Connor in his wrestlings with the later

---

7 Brendan Kennelly, *Love of Ireland: poems from the Irish* (Cork and Dublin, 1989), 17.

middle ages. The poetry of courtly love was common to Ireland, Britain, France and elsewhere in Western Europe. Although he was sceptical of 'vague suggestions of influence from Provençal and Norman-French' (*backward look*, 97), it is generally accepted now that if the jongleurs themselves didn't bring their wares ashore then somebody certainly did jongle them into Ireland. The difficulty here is not one of making the strange accessible but rather a technical turn of getting complicated Irish verse into English. In a note on his own translations from the same period Robin Flower comments that

> some apology is perhaps necessary for the substitution of simpler English lyrical measures for the intricate and subtly interwoven harmonies of alliteration and internal rhyme in the Irish. But the attempt to borrow those qualities of verse could only end in a mechanic exercise, which might be a metrical commentary, but could not be poetry. And to translate poetry by less than poetry is a sin beyond absolution.'[8]

One feels that O'Connor would entirely concur. He solves the metrical problems by simply ignoring them, apart from giving his poems the shape and cut of what the originals looked like on the page. And yet in many cases, the point of these poems was their metrical ingenuity. Our age would accuse them of being all technique and no feeling, whereas the truth might be that the feeling resided in the perfection of the technique. It appears to be poetry of the starched collar, but within it bulges a powerful and sinewy neck. If we compare O'Connor's 'Hugh Maguire' to James Clarence Mangan's 'Ode to the Maguire'[9], both of which are a translation of Eochaidh Ó hEoghusa's poem to his chief and patron composed in 1601 while he was on a campaign against the troops of the strengthening English conquistadores, we can see that O'Connor at least keeps the cut of the original. He hints at tautness and makes the requisite nods towards the coiled and smouldering passion of Ó hEoghusa. Mangan on the other hand is wild and diffuse and cumulative and exclamatory and turns the author into a Jacobean mad dog.

A translation can do only what a translation can do. If it is the vector of something, even anything, of the original we can be a mite happy. If O'Connor had a knack it was to get at the spirit of the thing and let that spirit sing if it could. In translating most Irish poetry from the late middle-ages until the present century the translator simply has to dump any notion of getting the meter right. There is

---

8 Robin Flower, *Poems and translations* (London, 1931; repr. Dublin, 1994), 109.

not much point in being a life-support system for a piece of scaffolding. A good translator must soften hard facts and a good reader must take these boobs to be self-evident. O'Connor cottoned on to this early on and chose poetry which answered his own nature and sensibility. He was distinctly uncomfortable with the literary poetry from the mid-seventeenth century on, perceiving in it too many lumpen elements with neither the craft nor sullen art of the Bardic era, or the artless facility of the folk song. Consequently, we only get the very best of Ó Rathaille from him, one solitary poem by the great word-musician Eoghan Rua Ó Súilleabháin, and nothing at all by the who of whos of Irish poetry in the late seventeenth century, Dáibhí Ó Bruadair. Scrubbed from the record also, to name but seven more luminaries among dozens well translated by others, were Pádraigín Haicéad, Seán Clárach Mac Domhnaill, Séamas Mac Cuarta, Donnchadh Rua Mac Con Mara, Mícheál Óg Ó Longáin, Cathal Buí Mac Giolla Gunna, and Peadar Ó Doirnín. This seems all the stranger when we note his love of Anthony Raftery, a person whose works he describes as being 'as close as genuine poetry has ever come to doggerel' (*Kings, lords, & commons* 132). O'Connor, however, being the independent spirit he was, did not suffer from a literary-academic complex and hoisted from the tradition just precisely what he liked and nothing else.

He did like the two greatest poems of the last decades of the eighteenth century, and his versions of them are his finest and most important as a translator. 'Caoineadh Airt Uí Laoghaire' (*A lament for Art O'Leary*) and 'Cúirt an mheán oíche' (*The midnight court*) were composed within seven years of each other but are about as different as the proverbial chalk from the legendary cheese. *A lament for Art O'Leary* is a traditional keen or funeral poem composed in an extempore fashion in honour of the dead person. In this case, it was sung or chanted by Eileen O'Connell on the discovery of the body of her murdered husband, and perhaps added to by herself and by others for some time afterwards. Arthur O'Leary was an officer in the Austrian Army – the Irish having none of their own and certainly not wishing to enlist in the British one – and when on leave at home treated the authorities with much less than the obsequious respect which they thought was their due as a ruling caste. They did what all great powers do with the annoying little gadflies who nip at them. They shot him. There is some rich irony to be had in the fact that one of the great poems of the western world about death and blood-letting was occasioned by the agents of the British Vampire. The former

---

9 In Fiana Griffin, *Extracts from Irish literature* (Dublin, 1992), 24–5. O'Connor describes it as 'a torrent of nineteenth century romantic eloquence' in *The backward look*, 101.

professor of poetry at Oxford University, Peter Levi, called it 'the greatest poem written in these islands in the whole of the eighteenth century' and opined that 'Goethe, and Thomas Gray, and Wordsworth, and Matthew Arnold … might all have thought so'.[10] Whatever about the opinion, he errs a little when he refers to it being written. It was, of course, an oral artefact and survived beyond all those countless thousands of other laments because of the force of the poetry and the tragedy of the story.

Its orality presents its own problems to the translator. And not just the fact of its being spoken, or rather sung, or chanted, or wailed, but the fact of its being torn from its natural surroundings of death and performance. 'Natural' here is also difficult. The lament was generally composed and performed at the wake of the dead soul. These wakes were, more or less, a party for the departing person (and a celebration of life for those still around) accompanied by booze and whatever passed for debauchery at that time. The corpses themselves were often brought into the music or the card games or even the dance (which is probably the origin of the stiffness of Irish stepdancers). This pagan relic was, not surprisingly, in constant conflict with the church, which viewed death as a much more solemn occasion. The traditional lament was a composition without prayer or angels or devils or intimations of the other world. It was an explosion of remembered life in the presence of death. And while there were probably no fun and games at Art's wake, because of the unnatural nature of his murder, it had its origin and its being in this strange ritual as exotic to us now as the burning of Hindu widows or the tying together of Chinese female feet.

O'Connor could only translate the words ripped from their sockets. He gets the rhythm dead-on, so to speak. It is a rhythm based on a long breath and on a single thought. When the breath gives out and the thought finishes, the stanza, if that's what they are, dies. A kind of pantometer. There would have been some break in a longer piece like this, which speaks for itself:

> My love and my mate
> That I never thought dead
> Till your horse came to me
> With bridle trailing,
> All blood from forehead

10 Peter Levi, *The lamentation of the dead with 'The lament for Arthur O'Leary' by Eileen O'Connell translated by Eilís Dillon* (London, 1984), 18.

> To polished saddle
> Where you should be,
> Either sitting or standing;
> I gave one leap to the threshold,
> A second to the gate,
> A third upon its back.
> I clapped my hands
> And off at a gallop;
> I never lingered
> Till I found you lying
> By a little furze-bush
> Without pope or bishop
> Or priest or cleric
> One prayer to whisper
> But an old, old woman,
> And her cloak about you,
> And your blood in torrents –
> Art O'Leary –
> I did not wipe it off,
> I drank it from my palms.[11]

The original is as simple as that also, and as direct, and as uncompromising. It is difficult to foul up on the headlong rush of the poem and most translators have simply opened the gates and let it rip. The only infelicities take place with exclamations and endearments, which can be very culturally and linguistically specific. O'Connor, for example, translated Eileen's 'mo chara is mo lao thu!' as 'my love and my calf.' *Cara* is certainly more colloquially 'friend' than 'love' although it is analogous with other Indo-European languages that have the 'Car' bit linked with love; *lao* is certainly and literally a calf, but it hardly has romantic echoes for the normal twentieth-century English speaker who might not appreciate being compared with a young cow. Eilis Dillon gets round it differently by speaking of 'My friend and my treasure,' or 'My friend and my heart',[12] while Brendan Kennelly makes do with 'My lover' or 'My man', which may not be accurate but are at least sayable (*Love of Ireland*, 57–64). On the other hand, O'Connor can

11 *Kings, lords, and commons*, 111–12. This is a slightly different version from that published originally in *The fountain of magic* (London, 1939), 75–85.   12 See Levi, *The lamentation of the dead*, 23–35.

hardly be faulted for a line such as 'You gave me everything', which later became the first line of an early Beatles song and now jingles in the head accordingly.

The midnight court, which Frank O'Connor published in a separate volume,[13] has a much more sensibility-friendly look to it. It is a poem of more than a thousand lines of rhyming couplets in which the women of Ireland put their men on trial for being sexually timid, or just plain no good. It is funny, bawdy, explicit, dramatic and intelligent and in one declamation seems to destroy the stereotype of the repressed and puritanical peasant. That is to say, it is a poem which represents the direct opposite of the regnant assumptions of those ignorant of Irish culture. Apart from it being instantly attractive, and instantly accessible to people without any background in Irish society or history or literature, people are drawn to it because it is an endless source of ammunition for cultural and ideological battles. To the anti-clerical it is anti-clerical, to the libertarian it is libertarian, to the nativist native, to the Europhile Europhiliac, to the modernist modern, to the feminist it is pro-women or anti-women depending on which side of that particular Paglian-Dworkish camp they belong. This is partly because we know so little about the intentions of its author, Brian Merriman, and, intentional fallacies apart, so very little again about his life, origins, or literary circle. It was the kind of debate Frank O'Connor jumped into with his two feet flying and his two fists flailing.

His translation was published in 1945 and was promptly banned. This lengthy quote from his introduction gives a fair idea of the flavor of the ideas he was furthering and the battles he was fighting with this work:

> There is no tablet in Clare Street to mark where Bryan Merriman, the author of *The Midnight Court* died, nor is there ever likely to be, for Limerick has a reputation for piety. Merryman [*sic*] was born about the middle of the eighteenth century in a part of Ireland which must then have been as barbarous as any in Europe – it isn't exactly what one would call civilized today. He earned five or ten pounds a year by teaching school in a god-forsaken village caled Feakle in the hills above the Shannon, eked it out with a little farming, and somehow or other managed to read and translate a great deal of contemporary literature, English and French. Even with compulsory education, the English language, and public

---

13 Frank O'Connor, *The midnight court, a rhythmical bacchanalia from the Irish of Bryan Merryman, translated by Frank O'Connor* (London and Dublin, 1945).

libraries you would be hard set to find a young Clareman of Merryman's class today who knew as much of Lawrence and Gide as he knew of Savage, Swift, Goldsmith and, most of all, Rousseau. How he managed it in an Irish-speaking community is a mystery. He was obviously a man of powerful objective intelligence; his obituary describes him as a 'teacher of mathematics' which may explain something; and though his use of 'Ego Vos' for the marriage service suggests a Catholic upbringing, the religious background of *The Midnight Court* is protestant, which may explain more. He certainly had intellectual independence. In *The Midnight Court* he imitated contemporary English verse, and it is clear that he had resolved to cut adrift entirely from traditional Gaelic forms. His language – that is its principal glory – is also a complete break with literary Irish. It is the spoken Irish of Clare ... Intellectually Irish literature did not exist. What Merryman aimed at was something that had never been guessed at in Gaelic Ireland; a perfectly proportioned work of art on a contemporary subject, with every detail subordinated to the central theme. The poem is as classical as the Limerick Custom House; and fortunately, the Board of Works has not been able to get at it. (*Midnight court*, 1–2)

There is very little in that chunk above that is defensible on even mildly scholarly grounds. Even if we allow the entirely understandable barbs against Limerick and do not deconstruct the idea of a 'powerful objective intelligence' there is enough bullshivism in it to keep us busy for years to come. O'Connor's picture of an Irish-speaking world completely cut off from the rest of the universe is a picture of his own invention, and his assertion that Merriman imitated contemporary English verse has been easily demonstrated to be false. It can only have been because he was at constant war with the kind of Victorian Catholicism which held sway in Ireland that he imagined Merriman to be an 'intellectual Protestant', even though others might see that to be a contradiction in terms. There was always a kind of lapsed Irish Catholic having recovered from their scars who confused tepid Protestantism with a liberal point of view. Add to that O'Connor's (let us call it) hatred of de Valera, whom he saw as a severe, controlling, puritanical figure and whom he associated with devotion to the Irish language, and we can follow his train of thought that Merriman had to be influenced by English literature and by the philosophy of the Enlightenment. He went further and asserted that Merriman's ideas and spirit came directly to him from Robbie Burns; when it was pointed out to him that Merriman came first he simply declared: 'On his own statements the scholars believe he came before Burns, but the thing is impossible. He must derive from Burns!'[14] A classic case of if you don't like the evidence, deny it.

There is nothing in *The midnight court* that is not the common stock-in-trade of European mediaeval literatures. All of the themes of free-love, unmarried bachelors, horny priests, unfulfilled women, lusty young men, deceived cuckolds, healthy love-children and dicey marriages were as much part of literature in Irish as of literature in any other tongue. What made Merriman different is that he bound it all together in one large dramatic and poetic work of art which was driven by a bonking swashbuttoning style. If O'Connor's judgments were simply wrong he gained a kind of victory when his translation was banned. It gave him publicity which he would never have got otherwise and proved once again that too much moral fibre produces a lot of crap. Consequent on the Censorship Board's banning, O'Connor wrote to the *Irish Times* and his letter was published on 17 July 1946. Part of it read:

> Under the Censorship Act imposed on Irish writers by the Cosgrave government there was established a secret tribunal, empowered, without hearing evidence and without having to answer for its actions in law, to inflict some of the penalties of a court of law: to deprive an Irish writer of his good name, to seize his property and destroy his livelihood in so far as any writer earns a livelihood in this country. Thus, murderers, abortionists, bookies and publicans continued to retain the protection of the law, while literary men – some, like Mr Shaw, the glory of their country – were outlawed ... The Censorship Board banned my translation; they did not ban the original ... The implication of this was clear; that I had deliberately introduced material which was not to be found in any other edition, and that this material was sufficiently indecent to justify the banning of the whole work.[15]

---

14 *Kings, lords and commons*, xii. O'Connor sees revolutionary mores and boldness of spirit where others simply see good rustic fun. David Daiches (in his *Robert Burns and his world* (London, 1971) writes, 'But though Burns' sexual problems proved to be unique, he was far from unique in his country fornications. The simple fact is that such activity was one of the few pleasures available to the Scottish peasantry, and in spite of the thundering of the kirk ... it remained extremely common throughout Burns' lifetime', 29.   **15** Frank O'Connor, 'Justice – how are you?', Letter, *Irish Times* (17 July 1946).

If O'Connor wanted a debate on the specific question of his translation of
Cúirt an mheán oíche and on the more general one of censorship he certainly got it.
The correspondence continued through July and August of 1946 and is one of the
very few examples of a lengthy discussion of the merits of a work of Irish literature
carried out in the public domain of a newspaper. One reader from County Mayo
wondered what all the fuss was about:

> The more I read the correspondence on this subject, the more I admire
> the sturdy virtue of my grandmother. For everybody who knows that
> famous, but disastrous, poem knows that the original is far more hectic
> than Frank O'Connor's (more or less) bowdlerized translation. Yet that
> heroic woman (my grandmother) must have heard that poem recited
> scores of times at wakes and weddings (as I have) and with additions more
> lurid than any lines which have been printed. Yet somehow she managed
> to go to her grave with her character intact.[16]

More seriously and to the point the Censorship Board itself was drawn into the
fray and required to defend its actions. James Hogan was its chairman and had
little enough time for Merriman and probably less for O'Connor:

> His [i.e. O'Connor's] letter is a typically arrogant production. No one,
> apparently, unless he is a minor poet, or at least of Mr O'Connor's literati,
> can possibly rise to the level of one of Mr O'Connor's masterpieces … He
> would like them to regard him as the modern Irish literary equivalent of a
> Servetus or a Voltaire, a sublime victim to a wretched clique of obscuran-
> tists … it was not enough that Merriman's *Cúirt* is an immoral poem (to
> put it very mildly). It must also be made to sound a note of blasphemy.

He went on to accuse Merriman of 'searching for what he would like to find in the
way of scandalous and offensive meanings' but he really dug his canines into
O'Connor: 'I would also like to make it clear … that altogether apart from Mr
O'Connor's gross mistranslations, his *Midnight Court* is, in my opinion a book
which should not be allowed in public circulation … I do not think there is a
magistrate in Ireland who would allow this book to pass.'[17] This was not the kind

---

16 J.B.S. Co. Mayo, 'The midnight court', Letter, *Irish Times* (1 Aug. 1946).   **17** James Hogan,
'The midnight court', Letter, *Irish Times* (27 July 1946).

of letter designed to cool the atmosphere, and O'Connor replied that 'Whatever one may say of Merryman's poem, it is not immoral. Mr de Valera's favourite author, Machiavelli, is.'[18] Hogan returned serve with: 'Mr O'Connor was ill-advised to call his *Midnight Court* a translation. As an adaptation to his own humour and prejudice, his *Midnight Court* may have some merit here and there; as a translation it has none.'[19]

`This was one of the first references to the merit of the work *as a translation*. Much of the discussion had been predicated on the belief that a translation is a faithful rendering of an original, a kind of surrender and regrant which only changed the outer appearances. James Hogan drew the line between them. Then the editor of the original poem (who had produced an excellent scholarly edition in 1912 on which O'Connor's translation was based) entered the lists. In his letter he said that he had met O'Connor on College Green and they fell to discussing the *Court* and the correspondence in the papers. And then:

> On my asking why he had not made a close translation, which might be of use to some, his reply was: 'Were I to do that, I should only be trotting after Merriman.' So we may conclude that what he has produced is the result of a trot on his own account, and a most miserable result it is. I have no hesitation in declaring that it is a misrepresentation, a distortion of the sense, a false picture, and in one line in particular, theologically offensive … Altogether, it is enough to cause Merriman to turn in his grave.[20]

It was probably quite unusual to have the contents of a private conversation aired so publicly. O'Connor denied what had happened but added 'But I now perceive the value of my wife's remark that in a country like Ireland a man who values his reputation will use an elaborate filing system.'[21] The editor, Risteárd Ó Foghludha, was not at all happy to be accused of lying and reasserted his version of events. He said of O'Connor: 'He must be the victim of a most serious lapse of memory, but he might remember a particular question which he put to me, viz., 'When are you bringing out a new edition (of the original) so that I may crib?' These are his actual words: my memory is excellent.'[22]

Although this debate solved nothing it at least raised publicly, however

---

18 Frank O'Connor, 'The midnight court', Letter, *Irish Times* (3 Aug. 1946). **19** James Hogan, 'The midnight court', Letter, *Irish Times* (9 Aug. 1946). **20** Fiachra Éilgeach, 'The midnight court', Letter, *Irish Times* (9 Aug. 1946). **21** Frank O'Connor, 'The midnight court', Letter, *Irish Times* (10 Aug. 1946). **22** Fiachra Éilgeach, 'The midnight court', Letter, *Irish Times* (11 Aug. 1946).

tangentially, the important issues of the morality of literature and the nature of translation. And even if O'Connor's own evaluation of the nature of the poem is generally dotty he managed to access enough of the spirit of Merriman to make the finest of the (at least) ten full translations of the poem that have so far been done. The frabjous love of life, the Rabelaisian pisstake, the spirited admixture of the comic and the serious is not confined to any one culture or era. It is a universal cast of mind. Some have it, some don't. In the end it does not matter much what *The midnight court* is supposed to be about. Some Irish culturists have a vested interest in the primitive, the pagan, the folk, the poets in their darkened booths with stones upon their bellies pumping their brains; others wish to see the Irish world as utterly cosmopolitan, ultimately derivative, a part of the main. O'Connor veered between these depending on when he wrote and who was the enemy. His idea of Irish being a primary literature, meaning one 'that is in the main original' (which he put forward in *The backward look* [41]) has some credence for the earlier period. His assertion that 'the only significant element is English' in the Irish literature of the eighteenth century is pure tosh (*backward look*, 109).

What can never be denied is his passionate love for the thousand and a half years of literature in the Irish language. His translations lift the cloak of time and give the general reader an entrance into the Gaelic Irish tradition. Prescinding from all that stuff about stylistic equivalences, and how much a cultural conduit can carry, and what is or is not spirited away in translation, he presents the Gaelic world through time and form with an energy and courage that creates its own validity and truth. And he does this because behind every poet he translates we can clearly hear his own integral voice growling unmistakably away. Whatever gets lost in translation, Frank O'Connor certainly does not.

Index